0278780I

JSCSC Library

Date: -1 JAN 2005

Class Mark: 301.172.6 SHE

0333804384

CW01188767

Books Express
Specialist suppliers of Military History and Defence Studies
P.O. Box 10, Saffron Walden, Essex, CB11 4EW. U.K.
Tel: 01799 513726. Fax: 01799 513240
info@b

Hobson Library

428527

The Challenges of High Command

Cormorant Security Studies

General Editor: **Geoffrey Till**

Titles include:

Alex J. Bellamy
KOSOVO AND INTERNATIONAL SOCIETY

Andrew Dorman, Mike Smith and Matthew Uttley (*editors*)
THE CHANGING FACE OF MILITARY POWER
Joint Warfare in an Expeditionary Era

Deborah Sanders
SECURITY CO-OPERATION BETWEEN RUSSIA AND UKRAINE IN THE POST-SOVIET ERA

Gary Sheffield and Geoffrey Till (*editors*)
THE CHALLENGES OF HIGH COMMAND
The British Experience

The Challenges of High Command
The British Experience

Edited by

Gary Sheffield
Senior Lecturer
Defence Studies Department
King's College London
at the Joint Services Command and Staff College, Shrivenham

and

Geoffrey Till
Dean of Academic Studies
Defence Studies Department
King's College London
at the Joint Services Command and Staff College, Shrivenham

palgrave
macmillan

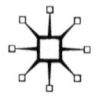

Editorial matter and selection © Gary Sheffield and Geoffrey Till 2003
Chapters 1 and 2 © Gary Sheffield 2003
Chapter 4 © Geoffrey Till 2003
Chapters 3, 5–12 © Palgrave Macmillan Ltd 2003

All rights reserved. No reproduction, copy or transmission of this publication may be made without written permission.

No paragraph of this publication may be reproduced, copied or transmitted save with written permission or in accordance with the provisions of the Copyright, Designs and Patents Act 1988 or under the terms of any licence permitting limited copying issued by the Copyright Licensing Agency, 90 Tottenham Court Road, London W1T 4LP.

Any person who does any unauthorised act in relation to this publication may be liable to criminal prosecution and civil claims for damages.

The authors have asserted their rights to be identified as the authors of this work in accordance with the Copyright, Designs and Patents Act 1988.

First published 2003 by
PALGRAVE MACMILLAN
Houndmills, Basingstoke, Hampshire RG21 6XS and
175 Fifth Avenue, New York, N.Y. 10010
Companies and representatives throughout the world

PALGRAVE MACMILLAN is the global academic imprint of the Palgrave Macmillan division of St. Martin's Press, LLC and of Palgrave Macmillan Ltd. Macmillan® is a registered trademark in the United States, United Kingdom and other countries. Palgrave is a registered trademark in the European Union and other countries.

ISBN 0–333–80438–4

This book is printed on paper suitable for recycling and made from fully managed and sustained forest sources.

A catalogue record for this book is available from the British Library.

Library of Congress Cataloging-in-Publication Data
The challenges of high command: the British experience/edited by Gary Sheffield and Geoffrey Till.
    p. cm. – (Cormorant security studies)
    Includes bibliographical references and index.
    ISBN 0–333–80438–4
    1. Command of troops – Case studies. 2. Leadership – Case studies.
3. Great Britain – Armed Forces – History – 20th century. 4. Great Britain – History, Military – 20th century – Case studies. I. Sheffield, Gary, 1961–
II. Till, Geoffrey. III. Series.
UB210.C477 2002
355.3′3041′0941–dc21   2002074818

10 9 8 7 6 5 4 3 2 1
12 11 10 09 08 07 06 05 04 03

Printed and bound in Great Britain by
Antony Rowe Ltd, Chippenham and Eastbourne

Contents

List of Tables and Figures	vii
Notes on the Contributors	viii
Acknowledgements	ix
List of Abbreviations and Acronyms	x

1. The Challenges of High Command in the Twentieth Century   1
   Gary Sheffield

Part I   The First World War

2. British High Command in the First World War: An Overview   15
   Gary Sheffield

3. Ratcatchers and Regulators at the Battle of Jutland   26
   Andrew Gordon

4. The Gallipoli Campaign: Command Performances   34
   Geoffrey Till

Part II   The Second World War

5. Scandinavian Disaster: Allied Failure in Norway in 1940   59
   Nigel de Lee

6. The Very Model of a Modern Manoeuvrist General: William Slim and the Exercise of High Command in Burma   73
   Duncan Anderson

7. The Art of Manoeuvre at the Operational Level of War: Lieutenant-General W.J. Slim and Fourteenth Army, 1944–45   88
   Robert Lyman

8. Lessons Not Learned: The Struggle between the Royal Air Force and Army for the Tactical Control of Aircraft, and the Post-mortem on the Defeat of the British Expeditionary Force in France in 1940   113
   David Hall

9 Sir Arthur Harris: Different Perspectives   126
   Christina Goulter

Part III   The Contemporary Scene

10 The Realities of Multi-national Command: An Informal
    Commentary   139
    General Sir Mike Jackson

11 Reinventing Command in United Nations Peace
    Support Operations: Beyond Brahimi   146
    Stuart Gordon

12 Reaching for the End of the Rainbow: Command and
    the Revolution in Military Affairs   177
    Mungo Melvin and Stuart Peach

Index   207

List of Tables and Figures

Tables

12.1	The Clausewitzian concept of friction	190
12.2	Facets of war	190

Figures

12.1	Spectrum of conflict	188
12.2	Tactical act, strategic impact	192
12.3	Military roles around the spectrum of conflict	194

Notes on the Contributors

Duncan Anderson is Head of the Department of War Studies, Royal Military Academy Sandhurst.

Andrew Gordon is Reader, Defence Studies Department, King's College London at the Joint Services Command and Staff College.

Stuart Gordon is Senior Lecturer, Department of Defence and International Affairs, Royal Military Academy Sandhurst.

Christina Goulter is Senior Lecturer, Defence Studies Department, King's College London at the Joint Services Command and Staff College.

David Hall is Lecturer, Defence Studies Department, King's College London at the Joint Services Command and Staff College.

General Sir Mike Jackson is Commander-in-Chief, UK Land Forces.

Nigel de Lee is Senior Lecturer, Department of War Studies, Royal Military Academy Sandhurst.

Robert Lyman is a former British Army officer and author of a forthcoming study of Field Marshal Slim.

Brigadier Mungo Melvin is Chief Engineer of the Allied Rapid Reaction Corps.

Air Commodore Stuart Peach is Commandant of the UK's Air Warfare Centre.

Gary Sheffield is Senior Lecturer, Defence Studies Department, King's College London at the Joint Services Command and Staff College.

Geoffrey Till is Dean of Academic Studies, Defence Studies Department, King's College London at the Joint Services Command and Staff College.

Acknowledgements

Many people have contributed in a variety of ways to producing this book. The editors would like to thank all those involved in the original conference held at Bracknell in 1997, and subsequently at Joint Services Command and Staff College (JSCSC) Shrivenham, and at Palgrave, both behind the scenes and in front of house. Mairi McLean and Lesley Adkin deserve especial thanks. The Strategic and Combat Studies Institute kindly gave permission to make use of material first published in Occasional Paper No. 38. Thanks we due to HMSO for permission to use Crown Copyright material in the Public Record Office.

Disclaimer

The opinions expressed in this book are those of the individual authors and do not necessarily reflect those of any institution or organisation.

List of Abbreviations and Acronyms

ADP	*Army Doctrine Publication*
ALFSEA	Allied Land Forces South East Asia
AOC-in-C	Air Officer Commanding-in-Chief
BAFF	British Air Forces in France
BAR	*British Army Review*
BCS	Battlecruiser Squadron
BDA	Bomb Damage Assessment
BDD	British Defence Doctrine
BEF	British Expeditionary Force
BMD	*British Military Doctrine*
C2	Command and Control
C3	Command, Control and Communications
CAS	Chief of Air Staff
CIGS	Chief of the Imperial General Staff
C-in-C	Commander-in-Chief
DAM	Department of Administration and Management
DCAS	Deputy Chief of the Air Staff
DHA	Department of Humanitarian Affairs
DPA	Department of Political Affairs
DPKO	Department of Peacekeeping Operations (UN)
DRC	Democratic Republic of Congo
DS	Directing Staff
ECPS	Executive Committee on Peace and Security
EISAS	ECPS Information and Strategic Analysis Secretariat
GHQ	General Headquarters
GMOs	Gratis Military Officers
GPS	Global Positioning System
IMTF	Integrated Mission Task Forces
IWM	Imperial War Museum
JFHQ	Joint Forces Headquarters
JSCSC	Joint Services Command and Staff College
MEW	Ministry of Economic Warfare
MoD	Ministry of Defence
MOU	Memorandum of Understanding
MTR	Military-Technical Revolution
NAM	Non-Aligned Movement

OODA	Observe, Orientate, Decide, Act
OTU	Operational Training Unit
PRO	Public Record Office
PSOs	Peace Support Operations
RAF	Royal Air Force
RDMHQ	Rapidly Deployable Mission Headquarters
RFC	Royal Flying Corps
RMA	Revolution in Military Affairs
SEAC	South East Asia Command
SHIRBRIG	Standby Forces High Readiness Brigade
SRSGs	Special Representatives of the Secretary-General
UNAMIR	United Nations Assistance Mission in Rwanda
UNAMISIL	United Nations Assistance Mission in Sierra Leone
UNDPI	United Nations Department of Public Information
UNMEE	United Nations Mission in Ethiopia and Eritrea
UNOSOM	United Nations Operations in Somalia
UNPROFOR	United Nations Protection Force
UNSAS	United Nations Standby Arrangements System
VLR	Very Long Range

1
The Challenges of High Command in the Twentieth Century[1]

Gary Sheffield

This collection began life as a series of papers given to a conference organised jointly by institutions with considerable interest in high command in an international context: the Strategic and Combat Studies Institute, the Joint Services Command and Staff College (JSCSC), and the Department of War Studies, Royal Military Academy Sandhurst. The conference was hosted by the JSCSC and held at Bracknell in October 1998. The authors were given liberty to focus on the aspects of command that they wished to highlight, and the result is a multi-faceted exploration of the subject of high command.

Definitions

There is often some confusion about what command actually is. In contrast to the literature on leadership, which is vast, and generalship, which is of similarly elephantine proportions, comparatively little has been written on the nature and practice of command. Some books draw little distinction between command and leadership. To pick just two examples, John Keegan's *The Mask of Command*, in spite of its title, deals to a very large extent with leadership (at least, as we have defined it here); while many of the articles in Michael Handel's edited volume, *Leaders and Intelligence*, deal with matters which are best described as coming under the rubric of 'command'.[2]

So, what is 'command'? The definitions in the British Defence Doctrine (BDD) will be familiar to many readers: 'Effective command and control comprises direction at the highest level necessary to achieve unity of purpose, combined with delegation of authority for achieving objectives to the lowest level possible for the most effective use of forces.'[3] This is amplified in *Army Doctrine Publication 2 (ADP–2)*, which defines command as 'the authority vested in an individual for the direction, co-ordination, and control of military forces'. In addition, control 'is the process through which a commander, assisted by his staff, organises, directs and co-ordinates the activities of the forces allocated to him'.[4]

An unofficial, but simpler definition of command formulated by John Pimlott is the 'direction, co-ordination and effective use of military force', while 'control' is 'the management of command'.[5]

The level of command that can be considered 'high' command differs according to circumstances. A divisional commander on the Somme in 1916 was not a high commander; his equivalent in Bosnia in 1997 most definitely would be. High command does not differ in principle from other types of command, but because it is characterised by interaction between military commanders and their political superiors, it involves its own set of challenges. Politicians and military commanders often have different agendas. One reason why this is so was articulated by an individual who had first-hand experience of both military command, albeit at a junior level, and also of political command at the highest level: Winston Churchill. Speaking in early 1916, he argued that: 'You cannot combine [parliamentary] politics and war. Politics require popularity, and the direction of war means inevitable unpopularity. The fighting men got all the popularity of success; the statesmen, the unpopularity of any ill-success.'[6]

Churchill was speaking from bitter personal experience, having been recently forced out of office in part because he was blamed for the failure of the Gallipoli operation. Of course, accountability to an electorate is not the only political spanner to be hurled into the military works. Military commanders sometimes have to operate in the absence of clear political direction: as General Sir Mike Jackson remarked (see below): 'Political guidance can be really helpful if you get it.' Of necessity, politicians must take a broad view of events, taking into account not just political but also economic, diplomatic, and many other factors. Military commanders below the level of high command are often spared the need to consider such aspects of strategy. The true military high commander must be as aware of these factors as his political superiors. Indeed, good commanders at the highest levels generally possess very highly attuned political skills. In spite of his carefully cultivated image as an inarticulate 'simple soldier', Sir William Robertson (Chief of the Imperial General Staff 1915–18) was a figure of considerable importance in Westminster, and had his fair share of skill as a political in-fighter. In the next war, Field Marshal Sir John Dill, the senior British representative on the Anglo-American Combined Chiefs of Staff, displayed diplomatic ability of the very highest order in his dealings with Americans and his own prime minister, Winston Churchill.

At some levels, leadership and command are best treated as distinct but related matters. In contrast to the managerial nature of command and control, leadership is, in Sir Michael Howard's words, 'the capacity to inspire and motivate; to persuade people willingly to endure hardships, usually prolonged, and incur dangers, usually acute, that if left to themselves they would do their utmost to avoid'. Some individuals display differing levels of competence as commanders and leaders. Horatio Nelson combined the attributes of an inspirational leader with those of an innovative and daring commander. Douglas Haig, by contrast, had some merit as a commander but was not, by any stretch of the imagination, an inspirational leader of men. Like Haig, Arthur Harris's strengths as a commander are a matter of debate among historians, but as Commander-in-Chief (C-in-C) of Bomber Command he had little opportunity to exercise 'leadership' in the traditional sense.

However, high command involves leadership of a different kind. High commanders need to exercise leadership over their senior subordinates: an army commander over his corps commanders, for example. This task becomes all the more difficult in joint and multi-national operations, where high commanders may have to impose their will in an atmosphere of political, legal and even moral confusion.

In his model of command, Joel S. Lawson argued that command has five aspects (or, as he describes them, 'functions'). *Sense* gathers:

> data on the environment, including friendly and enemy forces, allied forces, terrain, weather and so on. The *process* function draws together and correlates the data to give the commander information about the environment. The *compare* function juxtaposes the existing state of the environment – the relative strengths, weaknesses, positions etc. – with the desired state, the commander's view of what the state of the environment should be. The *decide* function chooses among available courses of action for reconciling the existing state of the environment with the desired state. The *act* function translates the decision into action.[7]

A similar, but better known, formula is the 'OODA loop' (also known as the Boyd cycle, after Colonel John Boyd, who formulated the theory). OODA is an acronym for *Observe, Orientate, Decide, Act*. In many ways, the key to the manoeuvrist approach to war is for a commander to go through these four processes more swiftly than his opponent: that is, 'get inside his OODA loop'. The Coalition ground forces in Operation Desert Storm achieved this in 1991, aided by the destruction of Iraqi command and control systems, superior doctrine and leadership, and the application of massive firepower from air, sea, and land. The Iraqi ground forces were always reacting to events, and were never able to seize the initiative. Physical destruction and systemic collapse brought about the Iraqi defeat.

Case studies

This book contains a number of case studies drawn from the British experience of high command in the twentieth century. What follows is a brief summary of some of the key arguments of each chapter, which leads into some reflections on the challenges of high command.

Gary Sheffield's contribution in Chapter 2 examines the evolution of British high command in the First World War. In recent years many revisionist historians, rejecting tired 'lions led by donkeys' stereotypes, have argued that the British army on the Western Front underwent a steep learning curve which turned it into a highly effective force by 1918. This study argues that this was as true for command as it was for tactics. On the home front, however, relations between the politicians and the military, the 'frocks and brasshats', remained the Achilles heel of the British war effort well into 1918.

In his discussion of command at Jutland, Andrew Gordon introduces the concept of 'ratcatchers and regulators', which he links to manoeuvrists and attritionalists. Beatty, the aggressive manoeuvrist who favoured 'initiative, resource, [and] determination', and Jellicoe, the micro-manager clutching at 'the comfort-blanket of "control"', stand at opposite ends of the spectrum. Lacking 'the doctrinal tenets of Manoeuvrism', the slow command and control system of the Grand Fleet ensured that at Jutland Jellicoe was never able to get inside the OODA loop of the German fleet.

The Gallipoli campaign, a recognisably modern expeditionary and manoeuvrist operation, is full of interest for today's forces. Geoffrey Till's analysis of command at Gallipoli (Chapter 4) demonstrates that the campaign lacked many of the essentials of a joint operation, ranging from the lack of adequate strategic direction to the lack of a Joint Force Commander and effective machinery for the co-ordination between the Royal Navy and the Army. Yet, as Till argues, goodwill and friendship between individual sailors and soldiers at times compensated for the failings of the system. This 'concealed the huge deficiencies in the mechanics of their co-operation'. Gallipoli, in short is a prime example of the 'muddle through' philosophy that has been all too typical of British military operations over the centuries.

Commenting on his experience in the campaign of 1794–5, the Duke of Wellington said that he had 'learnt what one ought not to do, and that is always something'.[8] As Nigel de Lee makes clear in Chapter 5, something similar might be said of command arrangements in the 1940 campaign in Norway. Of the many problems identified by the author, perhaps the most striking was that the operation was launched with grossly defective command structures in place. No amount of mere tinkering with command arrangements was going to improve the situation.

Bill Slim's name would have to appear on any shortlist of the greatest British soldiers to command at the operational level in the Second World War. Duncan Anderson argues in Chapter 6 that in recent years Slim has replaced Bernard Montgomery as the British army's favourite general of 1939–45, mirroring the doctrinal shift from attrition to manoeuvre. However, in a complementary chapter, Robert Lyman is less sure that Slim's brand of manoeuvrism has triumphed in the modern British army. Both authors address the issue of Slim as a manoeuvrist commander, although they take rather different approaches to the subject and differ in some of their interpretations. Lyman judges Slim against a template of modern military doctrine and concludes that 'Slim's experience of command in war provides an almost perfect model for the study of manoeuvre warfare and warrants, at the very least, its renewed attention today.' Anderson is no less admiring of Slim in this respect, describing him as 'the very model of a modern manoeuvrist general', but his discussion of Slim strips away some of the legends that have come to surround the commander of Fourteenth Army. Anderson highlights Slim's ruthlessness in dealing with some of his subordinates and his skill as a political in-fighter. Moreover, he questions the extent to which Slim practised the doctrine of mission command that he so eloquently preached in the pages of *Defeat into Victory*. Taken together, these two chapters provide stimulating insights into a great commander and into contemporary debates on the manoeuvrist approach to warfighting.

'Who should control aircraft on the battlefield and how and for what purpose should they be deployed?' David Hall, in Chapter 8, examines the British Army's response to this fundamental question in the aftermath of its defeat in France and Flanders in May–June 1940. The results of a 'post-mortem' on Army–Royal Air Force (RAF) co-operation demonstrated that, based on a misunderstanding of the victorious Luftwaffe, the Army wanted a tactical air force under its own control. This view clashed head-on with that of the RAF. The Air Staff argued that winning air superiority over the battlefield was the essential precondition for the fulfilment of the 'air support needs' of the ground forces. This, Hall argues, was essentially correct. Moreover, it took 'the laborious work of...many airmen and soldiers who overcame numerous conceptual, political, procedural and technical difficulties' before 'an effective army air support system' emerged. Lessons were learned, but the upper echelons of the British army 'were very slow and reluctant learners'.

Recently, 'Bomber' Harris has been described as the 'last of the RAF's great captains' although, as Christina Goulter comments, 'it all depends on how we define "greatness"'. The evidence in Chapter 9 places a large question mark against Harris's elevation to the premier league of commanders. Harris's antipathy to both Coastal Command and Army Co-operation Command showed a dangerous narrowness of vision in respect of the naval and land dimensions of Britain's war effort. Moreover, Harris's attack on Dominion and foreign aircrew in Bomber Command, quite apart from anything else, showed a blithe disregard for the realities of the coalition war Britain was fighting. In the current Joint and Combined environment of limited conflicts, Britain cannot afford the luxury of the Harris-figure.

This last point is amplified by the observation of General Sir Mike Jackson in Chapter 10 that although 'the single most efficient way of delivering military capability is for a single nation to do whatever needs to be done', in today's environment that is not possible. Rather, 'The trick is to get the right balance between political desirability and military feasibility.' His experience has shown that much of the commander's role lies in minimising inter-allied friction, in order to maximise cohesion and unity of effort. Recent Peace Support Operations (PSOs) have required military commanders to build unity of effort in a fractured political environment. Personal relationships and high-level leadership are all important, especially if (as is likely) there is no unity of command, and the use of the dreaded 'red card' by a national commander is to be avoided. Ultimately, his message is optimistic: 'multi-national command does work', but it involves more effort on the part of the commander than would a unilateral operation.

Problems of command and control in multi-national headquarters are also examined by Stuart Gordon in Chapter 11 on PSOs. Moreover, at the operational level it is far from easy to balance the requirements of military, political and humanitarian agendas. The structural problems presented by United Nations involvement are a further complicating factor.

The UN Department of Peacekeeping Operations (DPKO), for instance, has made valiant attempts to adapt to the new international environment but it still faces considerable problems. The UN remains institutionally ill-equipped to deal with the wider problems of policy and operational co-ordination as well as the specifically military concepts of command and control.

Finally, Mungo Melvin and Stuart Peach also touch on the Command and Control (C2) problems posed by PSOs as part of their discussion of command in modern operations, which is (or will be) complicated by the information-based 'Revolution in Military Affairs' (RMA). As an antidote to some of the more extreme enthusiasts for the RMA, they remind us that in terms of information more does not necessarily equal better. They also caution against neglecting the human element in command: 'technology and RMA systems assist commanders in their exercise of command, but they do not offer a substitute for it'.

High command in the twentieth century: some reflections

Some general themes on the nature of high command emerge from our discussions. One is that the success of operations depends to a great extent on the effectiveness of the administrative machinery of command. Two of the most famous military blunders in Anglo–American history, the charge of the Light Brigade at Balaklava (1854) and the battle of the Little Big Horn (1876), were caused in large part by personality clashes with which command systems were too inflexible to cope. Indeed, if one were to compile a list of military forces that have failed in war, a connecting thread would be failures of command.[9] As Chapter 4 makes clear, the command structure of the assaulting forces at Gallipoli in 1915, which was both multi-national (Anglo–French) and joint (armies and navies) was deeply flawed. During the German attack in the West in 1940, the French army and air force suffered from 'cumbersome' command structures, poor communications, and intelligence that proceeded at a snail's pace up the chain of command.[10] The command structure for US and allied forces in Vietnam did not so much resemble the classic chain or pyramid as a map of the London Underground.[11] The Iraqi forces in Kuwait in 1991 had a highly centralised command structure that was extremely vulnerable to Coalition air attack, and the list could go on.

Thus, effectiveness of command systems can materially affect the outcome of conflicts at the tactical and operational levels of war. The same is true at the military and grand strategic levels. As a recent study by an

American historian has demonstrated, the high command machinery established by the British during the Second World War was more effective than that of Germany. Hitler presided over 'an unwieldy decision-making system' in which he dealt with his subordinates and advisers individually rather than collectively, disliked hearing contrary views, and ruled by fear. Churchill dealt with the chiefs of staff as a body, took notice – however unwillingly – of views which contradicted his own, and 'a true sense of collegiality' grew up between the Prime Minister and Alan Brooke and his colleagues. 'In this respect, [Churchill and the service chiefs] ... served their nation more effectively than did their German counterparts.'[12]

Elsewhere, I have argued, one can identify three broad and simple (perhaps excessively so) principles of military command.[13] When considering the highest levels of command, we must add a fourth. First, there must be clear understanding between political masters and military subordinates. This provides the basis for our second principle, sound planning, which produces a situation in which all are aware of the commander's intent. Third, good communications are essential; this includes effective working relationships between individuals, military and civilian, as well as efficient means of communications. Finally, the plan and the command system must have sufficient flexibility to cope with 'friction', the things 'that makes the apparently easy so difficult'.[14] In the case of high command in the twentieth century, changes in political circumstances would appear under the heading of friction.

In part, these factors are dependent on technology. At the beginning of the Battle of the Somme in 1916, a technological hiatus rendered it exceptionally difficult to maintain communications. As a result, the British Expeditionary Force (BEF) relied on a plan that was characterised by a lack of flexibility.[15] However, military forces may have technologically advanced communications equipment but still fail to implement the principles of command. The Allied forces fighting in the north-west European campaign of 1944–5 had radios that would have appeared almost miraculous to their predecessors of only a generation before. This enabled quite junior commanders to call down air support or bring an impressive number of guns to bear on a single target. Yet on Omaha Beach on 6 June 1944, to quote from the US official history, 'Command was generally one of the gravest problems faced by assault troops, not only because officer casualties were high and mislanding of command groups had left many units leaderless, but also because of extreme difficulties of communication. Three-quarters of the 116th Infantry [Regiment]'s radios were destroyed or useless.'[16] The US command system on Omaha did not function properly, partly through sheer bad luck, partly through faulty decision-making, and partly because of the friction of war, with which it was unable to cope.

The American experience in Vietnam, where a proliferation of radios made it easier than ever for superior commanders, up to and including the president, to interfere with operations, further suggests that technology poses as many problems as it solves. Indeed high commanders, both civilian and military, should learn that the exercise of restraint is a vital part of the business; just because the technical means are available to allow high commanders to intervene in tactical or operational situations, it does not mean that individuals should feel obliged to do so. In terms of the supply of information to the commander, 'more' does not always been 'better'. As commander of the US Army's Training and Doctrine Command (TRADOC) in 1993, Lieutenant-General Fredrick M. Franks, Jr, issued a new doctrine for the US Army. As a result of his experience commanding VII Corps in the Gulf War, Franks reacted against the 'size and complexity of the information flow at a command post in the 1990s', stressing instead the importance of 'battle command', which emphasised leadership and decision making. In short, 'Commanders command while the headquarters and staff coordinate and make necessary control adjustments consistent with the commander's intent.'[17] This approach is also adopted by the British Army in *ADP*-2 Command. In some ways, this is a return to the nineteenth-century Prussian system in which a commander relied on a powerful chief of staff. Perhaps commanders in the information age must learn to delegate more than ever, leaving the details to their staff for, as Andrew Gordon comments, 'Great worriers can rarely be great warriors.'

Our case studies demonstrate the primary importance of creating effective command machinery. Sometimes forces have had to operate in the absence of coherent political guidance, or when politicians and service chiefs have been at loggerheads. While in a democracy it may be the case that the military can do little about that problem, inter-service disputes have also had a debilitating effect. Only in recent years have the British armed forces put into place the machinery for the command of traditional 'triphibious' joint operations. PSOs have brought yet further challenges to commanders. Indeed, Christopher Bellamy has recently argued that PSOs have:

> refocused attention on the senior commander as the prime mover in peace negotiations. His or her personality is absolutely crucial to the conduct of operations, the battle of wills with the other party and

public perception...no one military commander [of the two world wars] could exercise as much personal and rapid influence on events in the era of massed, impersonal destruction as they can now.[18]

One challenge is the need to persuade actors outside the normal chain of command and without a common doctrine – the media, relief agencies and so on – of the virtues of unity of effort. Bellamy's suggestion that officers should go on attachment to civilian crisis agencies, and that such a posting should be seen as enhancing rather than damaging their career prospects, deserves serious consideration.[19] Britain has a wealth of experience of operating in circumstances of multi-national command, some of it positive, some of it less so. The experience of recent PSOs, where some national contingents have been deployed at platoon level, suggests that the challenges of multi-national command are likely to intensify. In these circumstances, diplomatic and political skills are not additional extras for the commander: they are essentials.

The influence of dominant personalities can thus have a powerful influence for good or ill, as the studies of Norway, the Western Front and Gallipoli demonstrate. Operations in joint and combined environments only exacerbate this problem. Individual personalities and their previous experience can also have a profound influence on command styles, as the cases of Jellicoe, Beatty and Harris demonstrate. It is not a coincidence that Slim, the archetypal manoeuvrist, cut his military teeth during the First World War in mobile operations in Mesopotamia rather than on the Western Front.

Our final theme is command culture. One of the fundamental tenets of manoeuvre warfare is, of course, a philosophy of decentralised command, variously called *Auftragstaktik*, directive command or, in the British army, mission command. This stands in contrast to the more prescriptive *Befehlstaktik*, or 'top-down command'. We hear so much about mission command today that it is easy to forget that to have it as the standard doctrine of British forces is a considerable novelty. The principles of mission command were understood, at least in theory, at the beginning of the First World War. On 25 April 1915 Hamilton attempted to use a form of mission command at Gallipoli. Unfortunately, Hamilton lacked one of prerequisites of mission command: subordinates who can be trusted to operate with a loose rein.

Of course, devolved command has been successfully practised in the past, as Andrew Gordon's categorisation of naval commanders at Jutland into 'ratcatchers and regulators' reminds us, but it was far from universally accepted. The Montgomery style of war, for instance, did not exclude subordinates from exercising their initiative or taking risks, but neither did it particularly encourage this tendency.[20] Indeed, Montgomery's 21st Army Group in 1944 was at its best conducting set-piece, centrally controlled, attritional, firepower-intensive battles. These were an updated version of the highly successful 'bite and hold' operations carried out by Plumer's Second Army around Ypres in 1917, in which Montgomery played a minor role as a junior staff officer. Montgomery's style of warfare was partly influenced by lack of trust in subordinates. As Duncan Anderson shows, even Slim's espousal of mission command in Burma was partly forced upon him by circumstances, and he was quite ready to intervene in the decisions of his subordinates if necessary. Mungo Melvin and Stuart Peach's chapter brings the *Auftragstaktik/Befehlstatik* debate up-to-date. Advances in technology, some have argued, have created a situation where the Olympian commander, remote from the battlefield, is in a better position to judge events than the commander in the thick of the fight. While superficially attractive, this approach has many dangers, overreliance on technology being one of them. Melvin and Peach are surely correct to surmise that Mission Command will continue to have a role in the era of the RMA.

Finally, what is the role of doctrine in high command? The British tradition of ad hoc command arrangements, exemplified by Gallipoli and Norway, has, judged on the outcome of battles, campaigns and wars, been more successful than it deserved. Perhaps the flexibility displayed by British commanders at Gallipoli is an example of turning a virtue into a necessity, and thus creating a necessary 'coping mechanism'. One hopes that the adoption of doctrine by the British armed services in the last few years will reduce the likelihood of the command confusion of a 'Norway' or a 'Gallipoli' occurring in the future. At its best, doctrine institutionalises past experience and 'best practice', and provides the conceptual basis for exploiting new technologies. What must never be forgotten, of course, is that doctrine is not holy writ. Slavishly sticking to doctrine in inappropriate circumstances can be as fine a recipe for disaster as ignoring it altogether. Study of past operations – good, bad and indifferent – can provide the contemporary practitioner of high command with insight into both the limitations and the strengths of doctrine.

Notes

1 I would like to thank Colonel Archie Miller-Bakewell, late Scots Guards, Colonel Defence Studies, for his comments on an earlier draft of this introduction. Some of these papers were published (some in a slightly different form) in Occasional Paper No. 38 published by the Strategic and Combat

Studies Institute: Gary Sheffield and Geoffrey Till (eds), *The Challenges of High Command in the Twentieth Century* (Camberley: 1999).
2. John Keegan, *The Mask of Command* (New York: 1987); Michael Handel (ed.), *Leaders and Intelligence* (London: 1985).
3. BDD, JWP 0-01, 7.6.
4. *ADP*-2, 1-1, 1-2.
5. Editor's introduction, G.D. Sheffield (ed.), *Leadership and Command: The Anglo-American Military Experience since 1861* (London: Brassey's, 1997) p.1.
6. Remark recorded in the diary of Brigadier-General John Charteris, 4 January 1916, published as *At G.H.Q.* (London: 1931) p.130.
7. Thomas P. Coakley, *Command and Control for War and Peace* (Washington, DC: 1992) pp.32–3.
8. Philip Guedalla, *The Duke* (London: 1940 edn) p.44.
9. Elliot A. Cohen and John Gooch, *Military Misfortunes: The Anatomy of Failure in War* (New York: 1991).
10. Ibid., pp.221–5.
11. For the problems of US command and control in Vietnam, see Peter M. Dunn, 'The American Army: The Vietnam War, 1965–1973', in Ian F.W. Beckett and John Pimlott, *Armed Forces and Modern Counter-Insurgency* (London: 1985).
12. Alan F. Wilt, *War from the Top: German and British Military Decision Making during World War II* (Bloomington: 1990) pp.287–8.
13. Sheffield, *Leadership and Command*, p.3.
14. C. von Clausewitz, M. Howard and P. Paret (eds), *On War* (Princeton, NJ: 1976) p.121.
15. See Martin van Creveld, *Command in War* (Cambridge, MA: 1985) and Martin Samuels, *Command or Control? Command, Training and Tactics in the British and German Armies, 1888–1918* (London: 1995).
16. Gordon A. Harrison, *Cross Channel Attack* (New York: nd; first published 1951) p.319.
17. John L. Romjue, *American Army Doctrine for the Post-Cold War* (Fort Munroe, VA: 1996) p.118.
18. Christopher Bellamy, *Knights in White Armour* (London: 1996) p.202.
19. Bellamy, *Knights*, p.202.
20. Stephen Hart, 'Montgomery, Morale, Casualty Conservation and "Colossal Cracks": 21st Army Groups Operational Technique in North West Europe, 1944–1945', in Brian Holden Reid (ed.), *Military Power: Land Warfare in Theory and Practice* (London: 1997) pp.139–40, 143.

Part I
The First World War

2
British High Command in the First World War: An Overview

Gary Sheffield

The First World War presented Britain with military challenges unique in its history. It is the only time Britain has ever played in the 'premier league', fielding as part of a coalition a Continental scale army that took on the main enemy force. In the years 1916–18 Britain was, in a way that was not true before those years and has not been true since, a military superpower. The first challenge of high command was to develop, from scratch, effective administrative machinery for conducting a total war. There was little in the way of informal doctrine and next to nothing in recent British history to guide the soldiers and statesmen of 1914. Not surprisingly, the relationship between the politicians and the military was to cause major problems throughout the war.

For the first few months of the war in 1914–15 Asquith's Liberal administration attempted to maintain 'business as usual'. The Committee of Imperial Defence (CID) – 'essentially an organisation for peacetime pontifications' – lapsed, and Britain's war effort was run by a system of cabinet government little different in principle from that of peacetime. The principal innovation on the outbreak of war was to appoint Britain's most prestigious active soldier, Field Marshal Lord Kitchener of Khartoum, as Secretary of State for War with greatly enhanced powers. Overall, this experiment was not a success. Another individual might have made a greater success of this role, but 'K of K' was a natural autocrat rather than a team player, and he did not find it easy to adjust to the demands of cabinet government. He was too much of a soldier for his cabinet colleagues, while the fact that Kitchener was 'double-hatted', as both a politician and a soldier (for field marshals never formally retire), led to friction with the British Expeditionary Force's first Commander-in-Chief (C-in-C) Sir John French, not least because Kitchener was the senior to French in the Army List; in 1914 French was deeply offended that Kitchener came to France dressed in uniform, rather than a frock coat, to deliver a rebuke. Perhaps the basic problem was that Kitchener saw himself as the de facto Commander-in-Chief of the Army, in the mould of the Duke of Cambridge, Queen Victoria's cousin, who had held the position from 1856 to 1895.[1] This post had been abolished as part of the reforms that brought in a general staff a mere ten years before.

Asquith's cabinet, in which neither the Chief of the Imperial General Staff (CIGS) nor the First Sea Lord had a place, was lacking in military experience, knowledge or even interest. A former 4th Hussars subaltern, Winston Churchill, the First Lord of the Admiralty, was an exception but he rapidly used up his political capital in the first year of the war and fell from power. Moreover, the Liberal government that fell in May 1916, the Asquith coalition that succeeded it, and the coalition led by David Lloyd George that came to power in December 1916 were all aware that 'their mandate to govern' was by no means accepted by all.[2] These two facts placed both Asquith and Lloyd George at a moral disadvantage in dealings with their military and naval advisers, the general public 'regard[ing] the war as the business of experts'.[3] Both set about 'creating consensus' but at the cost of not always being able to 'impose their own wishes on their professional advisers'.[4] It is therefore not surprising that Asquith at first paid Kitchener excessive deference. The drawbacks of this system soon became apparent to Kitchener's political colleagues; having given him enormous power at the beginning of the war, they devoted over the succeeding eighteen months much time and energy to clawing it back. Kitchener's death in May 1916 came as a relief to many in Westminster and Whitehall.

In 1915 the British military and civilian decision-making elite was divided into contending schools of strategic thought. Traditionally these have been identified as the 'Westerners' who stressed military commitment to the Western Front, where the main enemy was to be found, and the 'Easterners' who believed that Britain should exploit her seapower to effect a decision in other theatres of war, notably the Dardanelles. A more recent interpretation sees the real division as those who wanted limitations on Britain's commitment to the war, and the advocates of 'total war'. The most likely explanation of Kitchener's own strategic ideas (he never fully explained them) demonstrates that the traditional categories of Easterner and Westerner are too restrictive. It seems that Kitchener aimed to limit British commitment to the Western Front until his newly raised volunteer divisions of 'Kitchener's Army' could be committed en masse to bringing the war to an end on British terms, ensuring that Britain would have the primary role at peace conference.[5] However, the circumstances that developed on the Western Front in 1915 forced Kitchener to commit divisions to the Western Front in a piecemeal fashion. As Kitchener himself stated in 1915, 'We must make war as we must; not as we should like.'[6] The victory of the Westerners and total warriors in 1915 ensured that the British Expeditionary Force (BEF) in France and Belgium would continue to grow in size, and the Western Front would remain the main theatre of operations.

In 1932, the Kirke Committee on the lessons of the First World War drew attention to the unfortunate consequences of the general staff packing up and heading off to France with the BEF in August 1914. While this was an asset to Britain in the short term, in the medium and long term – for contrary to prewar expectations, the war did not prove to be a short one – it caused problems. It left something of a command vacuum at home, which Kitchener attempted to fill. This situation helped to promote at best rivalry and at worst a power struggle between London and GHQ on the Western Front, the clashes between Sir John French and Kitchener being the most obvious example.

The reconstitution of the general staff in London in September 1915 was part of the process of weaning the government away from its reliance on Kitchener. The appointment of General Sir William Robertson as CIGS in December 1915 was an important step. 'Wully' Robertson, the first man to rise, as the title of his autobiography put it, 'From Private to Field Marshal' had a powerful intellect and was a formidable political in-fighter. He took over many of the powers previously held by Kitchener, becoming the War Committee's only source of 'military advice'. Robertson insisted that he must 'present to the War Committee his reasoned opinion as to the military effect of the policy which they propose, and as to the means of putting this approved policy into execution'.[7]

Robertson's appointment as CIGS coincided almost exactly with the elevation of General Sir Douglas Haig to C-in-C of the BEF. Arguably, Haig bore a greater burden than any other twentieth-century British commander. Effectively, Haig was both commander of the British Army in the main theatre and an army group commander; and, unlike the situation in the Middle East in 1942, he had no Alexander to his Montgomery. In his relationship with Robertson, Haig was very much the senior partner: this was the mirror image of the Alanbrooke/Montgomery relationship in the Second World War.[8] The period from Kitchener's death in May 1916 to Lloyd George becoming prime minister in December of that year, despite encompassing the Somme offensive, was a relatively placid period in civil military relations. This resulted from the fact that Asquith generally deferred to Robertson on military matters. Indeed, the Somme took place against the background of something of a leadership vacuum in London.[9] This situation was to change when David Lloyd George became prime minister.

In contrast to the final months of Asquith's tenure at 10 Downing Street, Lloyd George's premiership was dynamic. In the Second World War Britain had a prime minister who was politically secure, knowledgeable about military affairs and who played an important and mostly positive role in strategic decision making. In the First World War, Lloyd George's situation was rather different. Ironically, Lloyd George, the radical Liberal, was sustained in office by the Conservatives, who generally supported the generals and thus sharply circumscribed the Prime Minister's freedom of action in dealing with the military. As Secretary of State for War during the Somme campaign, Lloyd George recognised that he knew little of military matters but resented what he regarded as the military attitude that it was 'his duty to find the men, but that after they have been thrown into the cauldron, he has no further responsibility'. While disclaiming the entitlement to dabble in tactical issues, Lloyd George argued: 'I am entitled to consider the general conduct of the campaign. That is one of my duties.'[10] As prime minister he was soon at loggerheads with his senior military commander over strategy.

Lloyd George held a paradoxical position: he was both a total warrior and an instinctive Easterner who was horrified by the vast 'butcher's bill' on the Western Front. He mistrusted Haig, and all this led to a series of serious clashes, most notably the 'Calais plot' of February 1917 (when he attempted to sideline Haig and place the BEF under operational control of the French commander, Nivelle) and the arguments over manpower in late 1917 and early 1918. Lloyd George succeeded in ousting Robertson, but not Haig, in February 1918. His relationship with 'Wully's' successor as CIGS, Sir Henry Wilson, was far from ideal despite the fact that Wilson was regarded by his military peers as the consummate political general: one once claimed that the sight of a politician could send him into 'a state of sexual excitement'.[11]

Both the Asquith and, especially, the Lloyd George administrations made considerable strides towards establishing the effective machinery for the conduct of war. By November 1914 Asquith had accepted that the large, peace-time style cabinet was far too unwieldy to deal effectively with the demands of directing Britain's war effort. A cabinet committee, the War Council, was established, to be succeeded by the Dardanelles Committee and, in November 1915, the War Committee (Lloyd George's War Cabinet). In addition, both Asquith and his successor made increasing use of other committees to handle particular war-related matters. A former Royal Marine officer, Maurice Hankey, emerged as a key player as secretary of the War Cabinet between 1916 and 1919. He brought in many innovations, including the taking of minutes, that represented major strides towards the establishment of modern cabinet government.[12] The effectiveness of the higher direction of Britain's war effort should not be exaggerated. As Hew Strachan has recently written, while 'In the hands of Hankey, the war cabinet pointed forwards to the notion of integrated [i.e. civilian–military] control', Lloyd George had a 'contempt for the generals that stood in the way of an harmonious relationship and blocked the establishment of an effective machinery for the co-ordination of strategy and policy'.[13] The generals, of course, did not have entirely clean hands when it came to politicking. Yet in spite of what Lloyd George professed to believe about the dangers of a military dictatorship, the administrative and governmental machinery that emerged between 1914 and 1918 did enable a liberal and fairly democratic state to fight and win a total war while remaining a liberal democracy. This in itself was a considerable achievement.

From a contemporary perspective, the higher direction of Britain's war effort poses a number of interesting and relevant questions of democratic accountability. In terms of casualties, how much pain can a democratic state bear? What are the problems of conducting military operations in a period of weak political leadership or, worse, when the political leadership is at odds with the military leadership, but is unable to impose its authority? To what extent should the military be included in the political decision-making process? What is clear is that the interface between the military and the politicians represented a serious weakness in Britain's war effort.

High command on the Western Front was complicated by the fact that Britain was the junior military partner in a Coalition. Kitchener's instructions to Sir John French in August 1914 emphasised that his 'command is an entirely independent one' but that 'every effort must be made to coincide most sympathetically with the plans and wishes' of the French.[14] Both French and Haig had to walk this difficult tightrope, which circumscribed the British C-in-C's freedom of action without giving the compensatory benefit of unity of command. During the war there was never a 'united' command structure (like that of SHAEF (the Supreme Headquarters Allied Expeditionary Force) in 1944–5), and until March 1918 there was not even a 'unified' structure, involving co-ordination of national chains of command. In 1915, the need to keep the French sweet led to the British conducting operations at Neuve Chapelle in March to prove the British willingness to fight. At Loos in September, against the wishes of both French and Haig, the BEF fought to support the French campaign in Champagne. In 1916 Haig would have preferred to fight at Ypres, where there were genuine strategic objectives and where he believed, possibly correctly, he stood a real chance of achieving success. Instead he had to bow to French pressure and fight on the Somme, which was bereft of major strategic objectives but where the French and British armies joined. Finally the battle of Arras in April 1917 was fought in support of the French Chemin de Dames offensive.

Britain's military position within the alliance strengthened as her numbers of divisions increased. From the summer of 1917 onwards, thanks to the widespread mutinies in the French army, the BEF took on main burden of fighting on the Western Front. If anything, this further complicated the command situation. The establishment in November 1917 of an inter-Allied Supreme War Council with, to quote a British liaison officer, 'a view to the better co-ordination of action on the western front',[15] was a small step in the right direction. However, it took the 'doomsday scenario' of the German offensive in March 1918 to bring about a modest degree of unity of command. The German attack, which broke through the British lines and threatened to split the French forces from the BEF and send them retreating on divergent axes towards Paris and the Channel ports, served to concentrate the minds of Allied commanders.

At the Doullens conference of 26 March 1918 the first steps were taken to place General Ferdinand Foch in overall control of Haig's BEF and Petain's French forces. As a Supreme Commander, Foch was not directly comparable with Eisenhower in the Second World War. Unlike Ike, Foch was a co-ordinator rather than a commander and, crucially, he did not possess a large, integrated staff. However, Foch made a success of his position. A unified command structure made it possible to avert a calamity in spring 1918: a senior British liaison officer with the French commented in April, after the French commander Petain resisted some of his troops being sent to Flanders, 'Thank goodness we have got a central authority to fight the battle as a whole.'[16] Unified command also allowed considerable co-ordination of Allied operations, thus making the rudiments of operational art a reality. This culminated in the series of attacks along virtually the entire Western Front between 26 and 29 September 1918, a classic example of the sequencing of assaults that unhinged the entire German position. Perhaps the experience of 1918 offers a potential model for future coalition operations where there is no one overwhelmingly dominant partner and therefore no framework nation, or where political sensitivities preclude placing national forces directly under the control of a foreign commander. Such a situation might occur in a North Atlantic Treaty Organisation (NATO) or UN context, where US forces are present, but not (as in the 1991 Gulf War) in such large numbers as to be able to claim command as of right.

Relations with the French posed the main problems for British high command, but from 1917 onwards the arrival of American forces created a new set of difficulties. The US commander, General Pershing, was determined to create a national force under his command rather than agree to 'amalgamation', sending American units piecemeal to serve under the British and French, who were desperate for reinforcements. In keeping with the USA's somewhat semi-detached status as an Associated Power rather than a full ally, President Wilson was determined that the USA should create a fully 'independent army'. This would serve in its own discrete sector under its own commanders. Wilson's wishes eventually came about, but at the price of disharmony among the Allies.[17] A further problem for the British high command had been virtually unimaginable in 1914, and this was the emergence of the Dominions, especially Canada and Australia, as 'junior but sovereign allies'[18] rather than as mere overseas extensions of Britain. This development was facilitated by the emergence by 1918 of the Canadian and Australian corps as elite formations, with a consequent spur to nationalism: 'To Haig, the Canadian Corps was simply the part of the British Expeditionary Force that happened to speak with flat North American accents; to Canadians, however, it was the country's national army.'[19] Much the same point could be made about other white Dominion contingents. As both Lloyd George and Haig discovered, Dominion acquiescence in 'Imperial' plans could no longer be taken for granted.

Before 1914, the British army had possessed a semi-formal doctrine in the shape of the Field Service Regulations (FSR). These contained much sensible material, but were to prove woefully inadequate on the Western Front. There the British army, like its allies and enemy, was forced to grapple with the implications of a Revolution in Military Affairs (RMA), as between 1915 and 1918 warfare moved from a quasi-Napoleonic form to something recognisably modern. In matters of command, as in tactics, solutions were evolved over time, on the spot, and largely by a process of trial and error. In the process, the army developed an up-to-date semi-formal doctrine; 'semi-formal' because, although vast numbers of pamphlets and training documents were issued, doctrine was never properly codified (understandably in view of the dynamic nature of the conflict). Nevertheless, while semi-formal, the offensive doctrine that evolved during the war proved highly effective in 1918 and on occasions even earlier. Command at the tactical and operational level was bedevilled by a simple problem. By 1914 armies were too large and too dispersed to be commanded by a general in person, as had been possible as late as the American Civil War of 1861–5. Voice communications, as exercised by Wellington or Lee in the nineteenth century, were no longer possible in 1914–18 forward of the front line. A sophisticated and comprehensive field telephone system linked commanders with troops – a chateau, linked by wire to forward units, was as good a place as any for a general to be located – but once the troops went over the top his line-based system was next to useless. This deprived high commanders of information on which to base their decisions and made transmission of orders immensely difficult. To take but one example, in July 1916 Horne, the commander of XV Corps, believed for about 24 hours that the whole of High Wood had been captured by his troops, when that was not the case.[20]

The communications problem was never 'solved' during the First World War, but some steps were taken to mitigate it. First, a greater degree of decentralisation and devolution of command allowed important decisions to be taken at a much lower level, which shortened the command cycle considerably. Second, improved technology was introduced including primitive radio; by 1918 the BEF's communications were, for the period, remarkably sophisticated, but wireless was morse- and not voice-based. The development of radio came in time to restore the facility of voice communication to high commanders, but it was the generals of 1939–45, not their predecessors of 1914–18, who benefited from this innovation.

These problems were linked to another one: the size of the BEF grew inexorably from 1914 to 1916 from six to 60 infantry divisions (in addition to large numbers of other troops, including 500,000 artillerymen). None of the BEF's senior commanders had had any experience of handling forces of this size. They were trained in the ways of the small pre-war colonial gendarmerie and had to adjust to commanding much larger forces. Perhaps even more difficult, they had to find large numbers of officers capable of controlling large subordinate formations of corps, division and brigade. Setting aside the important issue of personalities, much of the debate about the command and control of the BEF revolves around whether GHQ attempted to 'overcontrol' lower formations, a process that led to a lack of flexibility.

This is the argument of a number of historians, who have tended to focus on the beginning of the Somme campaign in July 1916. According

Gary Sheffield 23

to van Creveld, 'carefully laid plans rigorously and undeviatingly carried out' were GHQ's answer 'to the inevitable confusion of the battlefield'. '[S]trict centralization', and 'proper order and control' was to be regained 'at the end of each phase'; 'opportunism' was 'discouraged if not prohibited'.[21] Martin Samuels has described the 'umpiring' approach of British commanders. A form of Mission Command, it gave the local commander a high degree of discretion, but the higher commander gave little guidance to his subordinates and would not intervene during action.[22]

These pictures are somewhat overdrawn, and can be criticised in detail, but they contain an element of truth. However, they fail to acknowledge that 1 July 1916 was not the end of the British army's experience of mass warfare on the Western Front; it was the beginning of it. The Somme marked the beginning of a steep learning curve, in Command and Control (C2) as in many other areas. Even on the notorious First of July 1916 commanders at all levels were experimenting with tactics, disregarding or modifying advice issued from above and delegating command. Yet, rather than compare the Command and Control of the BEF of 1916 with that of the BEF of 1918, van Creveld and Samuels compare it (unfavourably, naturally) with German C2 in March 1918. This is simply not comparing like with like.

In reality, the BEF's C2 evolved and improved. By the time the Allies went on to the offensive in July–August 1918, Haig and GHQ had become less significant and 'real power' was wielded by the Army commanders, who in turn leaned on their subordinates and their staffs at corps and divisional level. Mission Command was extended further down the command chain, giving the brigade commanders and even more junior leaders considerable discretion in their conduct of the battle.[23] Haig was at last able to conduct operations in the way he had wanted to as far back as 1916, setting broad objectives and letting his subordinates fill in the details. In 1916 and 1917 this approach had not been a success. However, in 1918 his subordinates and forces were more experienced and competent. Haig and GHQ remained important. GHQ's role throughout the war in disseminating new ideas, and its willingness to embrace a technological solution over a manpower-oriented approach, should not be underestimated. Moreover Haig's grasp, however rudimentary and incomplete, of the operational level of war and his inevitably wider perspective than that of his Army commanders was an important factor in the Allied victory.

The BEF's learning curve in C2, as in other areas, was far from even. Nevertheless by 1918 the BEF's C2 system was resilient enough to withstand a tremendous battering in the German offensives of the spring and early summer, and flexible enough to adjust rapidly to the demands of open warfare in the late summer. In the Hundred Days campaign of August to November 1918 the BEF was the spearhead of the Allied armies, and played the pre-eminent role in the German defeat. To build, virtually from nothing, within four short years, a C2 system capable of carrying such a vast army to victory was a major achievement that has not been properly recognised by historians.[24]

The British experience of high command in the First World War has much to offer the modern practitioner. It encompassed Britain's first experience of modern total war, the first and only time that Britain has fielded a Continental-sized army, and it also raises issues of alliance politics, civil–military relations and democratic accountability with a distinctly contemporary flavour.

Notes

1 I owe this point to Dr Stephen Badsey.
2 David French, '"A One-Man Show"? Civil–Military Relations in Britain during the First World War', in Paul Smith (ed.), *Government and the Armed Forces in Britain 1856–1990* (London: 1996) pp.76–7; Hew Strachan, *The Politics of the British Army* (Oxford: 1997) pp.127, 142.
3 Lord Riddell, *Lord Riddell's War Diary 1914–1918* (London: 1933) p.266 [27–28 August 1917].
4 French, 'Civil–Military Relations', pp.76–7.
5 David French, *British Strategy and War Aims, 1914–16* (London: Allen & Unwin, 1986).
6 Michael Howard, 'British Grand Strategy in World War I', in Paul Kennedy (ed.), *Grand Strategies in War and Peace* (New Haven, CT: 1991) p.31.
7 Robertson to Lloyd George, 7 December 1915, quoted in French, 'Civil–Military Relations', p.95.
8 David Fraser, *Alanbrooke* (London: 1983) pp.286, 531.
9 George H. Cassar, *Asquith as War Leader* (London: 1994) pp.182, 194–7, 205, 236.
10 Riddell, *War Diaries*, p.216 [14 October 1916].
11 C.R.M.F. Cruttwell, *A History of the Great War* (Oxford: 1936) p.501.
12 French, 'Civil–Military Relations', pp.79–84; Strachan, *Politics of the British Army*, p.123.
13 Strachan, *Politics of the British Army*, p.142.
14 Major the Hon. Gerald French, *The Life of Field-Marshal Sir John French* (London: 1931) p.201.
15 Quoted in W.J. Philpott, *Anglo-French Relations and Strategy on the Western Front, 1914–18* (London: 1996) p.91.
16 Diary of Maj. Gen. GS Clive, 18 April 1918, CAB45/210, Public Records Office.
17 David F. Trask, *The AEF and Coalition Warmaking, 1917–1918* (Lawrence, KS: 1993) pp.168, 176–7.

18 Desmond Morton, 'Junior but Sovereign Allies: The Transformation of the Canadian Expeditionary Force, 1914–1918', in Norman Hillmer and Philip Wigley, *The First British Commonwealth* (London: 1980).
19 S.F. Wise, 'The Black Day of the German Army: Australians and Canadians at Amiens, August 1918', in Peter Dennis and Jeffrey Grey, *1918 Defining Victory* (Canberra: 1999) p.9.
20 Horne to wife, 15 and 16 July 1916, Horne papers, Imperial War Museum.
21 Martin van Creveld, *Command in War* (Cambridge, MA and London: 1985) pp.155–68.
22 Martin Samuels, *Command or Control? Command, Training and Tactics in the British and German Armies, 1888–1918* (London: 1995) p.284.
23 Tim Travers, 'The Army and the Challenge of War 1914–1918', in David Chandler and Ian Beckett (eds), *The Oxford Illustrated History of the British Army* (Oxford: 1994) pp.236–7.
24 For an elaboration of this theme, see G.D. Sheffield, 'The Indispensable Factor: The Performance of British Troops in 1918', in Dennis and Grey, *1918 Defining Victory*, pp.88–95.

3
Ratcatchers and Regulators at the Battle of Jutland

Andrew Gordon

The alliterative terms ratcatchers and regulators come from *The Rules of the Game*. Such simplistic labelling of officer types can be defended on three grounds.[1]

First, the pairing of 'ratcatcher' and 'regulator' is unoriginal in that it is merely a re-flagging of Norman Dixon's alliterative 'autocrat and authoritarian' in his hugely entertaining *On the Psychology of Military Incompetence*. It is more usable than 'autocrat and authoritarian', because in their customary usages those words are too close together in meaning for their intended juxtaposition to be obvious: you have to remember which is which and explain to your audience, before proceeding.

Second, the highest military top cover is claimed for one of them. The term 'ratcatcher' was first invented by Admiral of the Fleet Sir Walter Cowan (who commanded *Princess Royal* at Jutland) in allusion to his then battlecruiser senior, David Beatty. He referred to Beatty's 'ratcatching instinct for war', and that is the meaning attached to it here. Since 'ratcatcher' was first coined in reference to Beatty, one is inclined to treat Beatty as its personification, although he is by no means the only naval candidate which that war threw up. Lewis Bayly, Reginald Tyrwhitt, Reginald Plunkett (on whom Beatty relied for his doctrinal thought) or perhaps even Howard Kelly may be mentioned. In the next war one could of course name Cunningham, Philip Vian or Johnny Walker (although Tyrwhitt and Cunningham represented a balanced blend of ratcatcher and regulator).

Nonetheless, this chapter will take Beatty as the ideal ratcatcher. Jellicoe, with whom Beatty is so naturally and often contrasted, and whom Fisher described as 'saturated in discipline', is an obvious 'regulator', although there were very many others.

This leads into the third defence for the title. Such a polarisation *is* actually what was happening in the Royal Navy at the time. To borrow a well-known device, it was an evolving 'thesis, anti-thesis, synthesis' process, with time then favouring the anti-thetic ratcatchers. The 'rat-catching' forces of anti-thesis were to be greatly boosted by the empirical experience of war, especially Jutland; but the process was quietly happening anyway, and by (say) the early 1920s the Service would probably have been dominated by a senior officer corps with distinct rat-catching tendencies.

First, however, where did the 'regulators' come from? They came from long years of peacetime, and from too much technological change, which both claims too much for itself and curtails the development of *warrior technique*. The industrial revolution had naturally brought to the fore those officers who could most easily ride the wave of technical change. The Navy's past appeared to have been rendered spectacularly irrelevant, and it was not unreasonably assumed that the new warfare of machinery and science could only be responsibly managed by scientific, automated techniques of command and control, and by comforting processes of tabulation, automation and *regulation*.

This belief, and this generation of technicians (of which Jellicoe was a prominent member), ascended their peak of supremacy in the 1890s, exactly a century after the Navy had achieved so much by harnessing precisely opposite means. The 'regulators' immersed themselves in detail, at the expense of their clarity of view of principles. Jellicoe was a classic example. When Beatty succeeded him as Commander-in-Chief (C-in-C), he found his quarters filled with mounds of paperwork and complained to his wife that:

> there seems to be an enormous amount of time wasted on details which can be much better performed by others than by me and so free me for the more important things. I fancy the late C-in-C loved detail and messing about finicky things, and consequently the big questions got slurred over or overlooked altogether.[2]

The new C-in-C ejected tons of office equipment from HMS *Iron Duke* and replaced it with a curious sort of Turkish bath!

The supremacy of this group – their unquestioned 'broker' status in relation to Command and Control (C2) issues – was boosted by the Armstrong 12-inch breech-loading rifle, and the gyroscopically guided Whitehead torpedo, which between them forced battlefleets into line-ahead beam-firing stand-offs, and was then prolonged by wireless telegraphy, turbines, and so on, and by the daunting technical leap represented by the *Dreadnought* revolution. This situation lasted for some 20 years.

By about the time *Dreadnought* came into service in 1906, there was already a small but growing body of mostly middle-ranking officers (not quite the same people as the anti-Fisher 'Syndicate of Discontent', but there was certainly some overlap) which held that the Navy, dominated as it was by technologists, was 'losing the plot' in terms of the realities of war. A few of its members were probably frauds, men who were seeking to dignify their technical disorientation; but it became known as the 'Historical School', and it broadly held that many empirical lessons of the past had been too glibly discarded. In terms of seniority, the group's centre of gravity was at captain and commander level: too junior to be calling the shots in 1914, but they had enough patronage to prompt the creation of *The Naval Review* in 1913, the off-the-record journal which Jellicoe would suppress while he was First Sea Lord. At about this time, as it happens, faith in the march of technology was being questioned in the wider maritime world following the *Titanic* disaster.

The naval Historical School actually had two entrenched mindsets to tackle: the Victorian ethic of chivalry, and the overweening technocracy. Captain William Boyle took them both on in *The Naval Review* in its first year of publication. He said: 'It may be that Waterloo was won on the playing fields of Eton, but for us it is of more interest to know where Trafalgar was won ... Probably no class of Englishmen have been less sportsmen than the naval officers of the eighteenth century',[3] and he attacked the materialists with: 'The fact that we know how to handle our ships and manipulate her armament does not indicate that we are ready to play our part in war.'[4]

Beatty had gained accelerated promotion not through technical competence, not by particularly efficient ships, and certainly not through high exam passes, but through extraordinary luck followed promptly by initiative and courage, as a lieutenant in command of gunboats on the Nile in the Omdurman Campaign in 1898.

When Churchill gave Beatty command of the Battlecruiser Squadron (BCS) in the spring of 1913, his unorthodox style became apparent to his prospective flag-captain even before they met. For several days after his tenure had started, there was no sign of him. Captain Chatfield was perplexed:

> most people who had been signally honoured with a great command over the heads of others, would have made the occasion one for

showing great zeal and attention to duty; even if of no great value, it would have 'created a good impression'. Little did I know the peculiarities of his ways... he cared for none of these things.

His steward, Mr Woodley, who came down to look after the crockery etc; told me he thought the admiral had gone to Monte Carlo. Sure enough, I received a letter from him in a day or two, from that place. He would have his holiday and arrive just when he, and no-one else, considered it right and opportune.[5]

Beatty himself cannot really be described as an active member of the Historical School (a 'country member' perhaps). It is not clear how vigorous his thought processes ever were. But (unlike Jellicoe) he did read history, and he gave house-room and staff jobs to thinkers and would-be reformers. One of his first actions in 1913, on returning from Monte Carlo, was to circulate a BCS memorandum which was headed: 'From a Study of Great Naval Wars'.[6] It said:

It is impressed upon one that Cruiser captains – which includes Battlecruiser Captains – to be successful must possess, in a marked degree, initiative, resource, determination and no fear of accepting responsibility. To enable them to make best use of these sterling qualities, they should be given the clearest indication of the functions and duties of the unit to which they belong, as comprehended by the Commander of that unit. They should be completely comprehensive of his mind and intentions.

This was amazing. He had just been given the latest, largest, fastest, sexiest war machines in the world, and here he was looking back to the Navy of scurvy and weevils and creaking timbers for doctrinal guidance. 'Luddism on stilts!' the technocrats might have said, and probably did; but Beatty was seeking enduring *principles*, by which to lead his elite squadron, without deferring to the common conceits of *process*; or rather his staff-commander, Reginald Plunkett, was, and Beatty gladly put his name to the paper (and many others like it over the next five years). Even the *inclination to use a staff* could be mooted as a facet of rat-catching. Jellicoe, be it noted, exhausted himself through worry and overwork, with his inability to delegate (a frequent fault among British admirals). Great worriers can rarely be great warriors.

Beatty's role in relation to the rising groundswell of discontent with the overrationalised Edwardian Navy bears some comparison with that of John Jervis in relation to the Nelson generation: they both actively sponsored the philosophy of command by doctrine, by delegation and negation, and sought to lift their juniors above the need of constant supervision. Jervis, needless to say, had much more promising and battle-tested raw-material to start with.

As Cowan noted, Beatty's ratcatching was mostly instinctive, but he was patron and client to officers such as Plunkett, Osmond Brock and Herbert Richmond (in whose age group Beatty loosely belonged), who did the serious headwork which Beatty himself was too lazy or unfocused to bother with.

Jellicoe has already been located amongst the hitherto supreme 'materialists', whose card was being marked by the emergent Historical School; and unsurprisingly, therefore, he liked, employed and trusted quite different sorts of officers from those favoured by Beatty (who maliciously remarked that 'Jellicoe is absolutely incapable of selecting good men because he dislikes men of character who have independent views of their own').[7]

Whereas Beatty was rather drawn to other loose cannons, Jellicoe feared the damage they might do on the Battle Fleet's neat and orderly deck, and either sent them away or securely lashed them down. Lewis Bayly (who would win the first Battle of the Atlantic in 1917) was one such he was glad to see depart in late 1914. Frederick Sturdee, the celebrated winner of the Falklands Battle, thought so much that Jellicoe considered him subversive and stationed him in the middle of the battle-line in such a way that whichever way the fleet deployed Sturdee would have another vice-admiral both ahead and astern of him, curbing his potential for spontaneity. Both Bayly and Sturdee were rejected as possible Senior Officers of the new 'Fast Battle Squadron', when that group came to be formed in the autumn of 1915, on grounds of their supposed unreliability.

The Historical School Jellicoe cordially disliked. He tended to favour and trust the sort of admiral Richard Hough has described as 'dear blockheads': efficient, decent, amiable, aged or prematurely aged Paddington-Bear-like figures, whose actions or ideas would pose no threat to the carefully constructed applecart of Grand Fleet Battle Orders. Vice-Admirals George Warrender, Cecil Burney and Martin Jerram all came into this category. The first was 'deaf and absent-minded' but kept on for the incredible reason that he as 'excellent as a squadron admiral in peace'. The second 'ha[d] always been unwell', in Lady Beatty's view. Beatty wanted to have the third court-martialled for failing to pursue the enemy at Jutland (how could he, since Jellicoe had not told him to?). And among Jellicoe's Rear-Admirals, we find his old friend Hugh Evan Thomas, whose 'professional attainments were highly regarded', who was steady, loyal, lacking in imagination, and to whom he gave the Fast

Battle Squadron; and his old friend Herbert Heath, who was said to have had 'a pumpkin on his shoulders instead of a head'.[8]

Churchill's comment that in 1914 we 'had more captains of ships than captains of war',[9] is nowhere better illustrated than by the officers with whom Jellicoe felt comfortable. That is an indictment of Jellicoe, of the rationalising technocrats who were assumed to have all the answers in their machine-age Navy, and of the peacetime 'regulating' mindset. The only glowing – horribly glowing – spark in the Battle Fleet's flag-officer retinue was Robert Arbuthnot, the Grand Fleet's *Beserker* who was (colloquially, if not clinically-speaking) insane and who led 1,000 men to their deaths in a gallant, shockingly ill-judged suicide charge at the German fleet.

When Beatty had a Christmas party in 1916, just after assuming command-in-chief and replacing some of Jellicoe's favourites with his own, his flag-lieutenant was struck by how different the group seemed to the last time he had seen all the Grand Fleet officers together: 'none of them deaf or in any way aged or infirm'.[10]

Perhaps the most important difference between the regulators and the ratcatchers of the Great War (and perhaps more recently) was their approach to matters of Command, Control and Communications (C3).

Disregarding more recent upgrades, the term 'C3' is dangerously misleading. What is wrong with it is that it appears to present a trinity of three equal commodities, whereas in reality the first two are necessary military functions, while the third is merely a means to an end, a service provider. Communications are a way of achieving effective C2, but not the only way: the other way is doctrine. Obviously only the simplest operation can be C2'd either solely by Communications or solely by doctrine, but they both have a role and there is an obvious pay-off between them: the more doctrine, the less communications you need; the more communicating, the less doctrine.

However, there it is, in the acronym C3: communications masquerading as the equal and only partner of C2, and inviting the conclusion that the practitioner might as well abdicate C2 theory to the communicators. Strictly speaking, it is none of their business since they are servants, not masters. The late Victorian and Edwardian regulators fell into just that trap (without having the 'C3' acronym to prompt them).

The 'regulators' believed that signalling could be the reliable and sole enabler of C2. The 'ratcatchers' perceived this as dangerous nonsense. Beatty tried to liberate his Battlecruiser Fleet, and later the Grand Fleet, from the tyranny of the signalling process. He tried to teach his captains and junior flag-officers to act on doctrine. In some cases it was uphill work; but the experience of Jutland made graphically plain the 'action–reaction cycle' costs inherent in the command, control and communications trinity, if unassisted by doctrine.

Finally, regulating and ratcatching should be connected with attrition and manoeuvre. These are hotly argued concepts and, no doubt, the Jargon Police are already whipping out their notebooks. But attrition and manoeuvre are in the dictionary, and we should neither avoid their use, nor get ensnarled in verbose 'try to please everyone' definitions from doctrine theology. They are only tools for debate, after all. Attritionalism, if it means anything, must mean seeking victory by harnessing the weight of arithmetic when you perceive it to be in your favour. It rests on rational, 'estimate-driven' planning (as opposed to skill) and deliberate formalised (or *formula*-ised) decision-making cycles. It also requires the enemy to be either willing or obliged to fight on the same terms. 'Regulator' and 'attritionalist' are substantially synonymous, because the comfort-blanket of 'control', beloved of regulators, is permissible by attrition. That is how Jellicoe framed his Grand Fleet Battle Orders, and how he sought to lead his fleet to victory off the coast of Jutland.

The numerically-superior side is wise and safe to stick to attrition, if the enemy (as Rommel at Alamein) can be forced to compete on those terms. But the German fleet at Jutland could not be so forced, and declined an attritional confrontation. Why should it do otherwise? If the arithmetic were allowed to prevail, it would be sunk. So it manoeuvred. Jellicoe, preoccupied with micro-managing his own unwieldy fleet, and in spite (or because) of executive signals at a rate of one every 67 seconds, never got inside the German action–reaction cycle. And so, in spite of monumental blunders by Admiral Scheer, the German fleet escaped not once, not twice, but (if you count the events of the night) three times, and got back home to claim victory.

Nicholas Rodger, the most respected naval historian of what is still called (with increasing euphemism) the Younger Generation, argues that naval warfare is inherently attritionalist. In strategic terms he is probably right, certainly where the defence of trade is concerned, and perhaps elsewhere. But the open sea, by its very nature, lends itself to manoeuvrism. As far as fleets are concerned, the sea is in effect flat. There are no front lines, no ramparts, no hills or bocage country, no uncrossable obstacles, no *rivers*. The sea is natural cavalry country: hence perhaps the success of Prince Rupert as an admiral in the Restoration Navy.

Churchill described tanks in North Africa as land-ships in the sea of sand. Rommel or Patton or Guderian would probably have made good fleet commanders. Haig (a cavalryman remembered as the archetypal attritionalist infantryman) would not. Jellicoe did not lose the war, as he famously could have done in an afternoon, at Jutland. But he was a 'Haig' in his approach to fleet-action; and if the Grand Fleet seriously wanted to do battle with the German High Seas Fleet, it was going to have to speed up its laborious signal-dependent action–reaction cycle, and adopt the doctrinal tenets of manoeuvrism.

Enter Beatty, and the Historical School, or 'ratcatchers', or manoeuvrists. Beatty succeeded Jellicoe six months after Jutland, and ousted his control-intensive standing orders in favour of his own battlecruiser C2(CD)[11] philosophy. It was too late for that war, but it informed a generation of future admirals (eight future First Sea Lords were present at Jutland), and heavily influenced the *Fighting Instructions* of 1939.

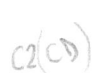

Notes

1 Andrew Gordon, *The Rules of the Game: Jutland and British Naval Command* (London: 1996).
2 Beatty to Lady Beatty, 4 December 1916, *Beatty Papers*, Vol. 1 (London: 1989) p.385.
3 *The Naval Review*, 1913, pp.77–8.
4 Ibid.
5 Lord Chatfield, *The Navy and Defence* (London: 1942) pp.104–5.
6 To be found in Drax papers 4/1, as cited in Gordon, *Rules of the Game*.
7 Beatty to Lady Beatty, 13 May 1917, *Beatty Papers*, p.241.
8 Quoted in Arthur Marder, *From Dreadnought to Scapa Flow*, Vol. IV (London: 1968) p.223.
9 Winston Churchill, *World Crisis*, Vol. 1 (London: 1923) p.93.
10 22/12/16 BTY 13/34, as cited in Gordon, *Rules of the Game*.
11 Command and Control (by Communications and Doctrine).

4
The Gallipoli Campaign: Command Performances
Geoffrey Till

The Fleet and Army acting in conjunction seem to be the natural bulwark of this kingdom.[1]

Introduction: Gallipoli as an expeditionary and manoeuvrist campaign

There can hardly be any doubt but that the Gallipoli campaign was 'manoeuvrist' in *strategic conception*; it was part and parcel of the so-called 'British Way in Warfare', an approach to conflict which maximised Britain's maritime advantages and avoided pitched battle on the continent of Europe, but called instead for the imaginative use of an expeditionary army against the exposed vulnerabilities of a land-bound adversary. General Sir Ian Hamilton, Commander-in-Chief (C-in-C) of the Mediterranean Force, was well aware of the advantages that British seapower had to confer in this respect. A convinced Easterner, he advocated a defensive in the West and an offensive in the East. Otherwise, it would be a case of 'not exploiting our own special characteristics, mobility and sea power!'[2]

In terms of *operational execution* it was also manoeuvrist, at least as far as intentions went. The notion of the Navy by-passing Turkey's western army and storming through the Narrows to reduce Constantinople and paralyse Turkey in one fell swoop was arguably the best idea of the First World War.[3] When this failed, the allies had to resort to joint and combined action in an amphibious assault against Turkey's defences in order that the Navy could try again later. Even here, the intention to use a bit of imagination, to avoid the enemy's strength, to shatter his will and coherence, to put him off balance and prevent his being able to stop the allies from doing what they wanted was absolutely clear. Thus Hamilton:

> the first and foremost step towards a victorious landing was to upset the equilibrium of Liman von Sanders...I must try to move so that he should be unable to concentrate either his mind or his men against us...I have to separate my forces and the effect of momentum, which cannot be produced by cohesion, must be reproduced by the simultaneous nature of the movement.[4]

Or here, later in the campaign:

> K[itchener] sees in a flash what the rest of the world does not seem to see so clearly: viz, that the piling up of increased forces opposite entrenched positions is a spendthrift, unscientific proceeding. He wishes to know if I mean to do this. To draw me out he assumes if I get the troops, I *would* at once commit them to trench warfare by crowding them in behind the lines of Helles or Anzac. Actually I intend to keep the bulk of them on the islands, so as to throw them unexpectedly against some key position which is *not* prepared for defence.[5]

Of course, when the manoueuvrist approach failed, it did seem, at least to the troops ashore, that the subsequent land operations were a question of frontal assault and of the attritional destruction of Turkish forces. According to the Official History, it was a case of 'definite trench warfare' by the Third Battle of Krithia in May.[6]

Nonetheless, the essential idea was manoueuvrist. It was a demanding form of war since it required the closest co-operation of the Army and the Navy: joint action in a maritime environment, to coin a phrase. Moreover, as Hamilton was perfectly well aware, 'the operation of landing in face of an enemy is the most complicated and difficult in war'.[7] Things could easily go wrong; the pursuit of operational manoeuvre from the sea brings risks as well as opportunities.

The requirements of manoeuvrist command

Modern doctrine is quite clear that to make the manoeuvrist approach (as exemplified by the Gallipoli campaign) work, the main commanders would need to adopt a distinctive approach to the business of command. There seem to be three key requirements.

1. Obviously at both the strategic and the operational levels, the commander and his subordinates would all need to know what the object of the exercise actually was.
2. To keep the momentum going once the operation was in progress, command would need to be 'decentralised through the use of directives which give a considerable degree of freedom of action to subordinate commanders'. It needed to be a question of mission-oriented *Auftragstaktik* rather than top-down *Befehlstaktik*. Subordinate commanders, such as Birdwood and Hunter-Weston, needed to know what was, in the modern jargon, 'the Commander's intent' and to be confident that they knew what they had to achieve and why.
3. For their part, Hamilton and de Robeck as commanders needed good communications so they could respond rapidly to the needs and concerns of their subordinates and to the movements of the adversary.[8]

How far, then, did practice conform to theory in the Gallipoli campaign of 1915? We should start with the grand strategic level of war.

The absence of strategic direction

Despite the extent to which amphibious operations had been a feature of British strategic practice for several centuries, it was a rather neglected area of defence at the beginning of the twentieth century. The two services were, in consequence, quite unable to agree a vision of the future role of amphibious operations in modern warfare. The Admiralty as a whole tended to be wary of diverting too much of the fleet away from its true purpose into the support of amphibious operations (unless, that is, these operations could themselves be seen as a way of improving the prospects for winning command of the sea). Before the war, army reactions could be more sceptical still, especially of the idea of opposed landings in modern conditions, but Army thinkers such as Charles Callwell, the Director of Military Operations, were surprisingly keen on subsidiary operations against the Turks, outside Europe.

Despite such hesitations, and despite the immediate preoccupations of the war on the Western Front and/or the North Sea, there was soon (in Sir Julian Corbett's words) 'a stirring of the old instinct' for combined (joint) operations, once it became clear that there was no prospect of a quick decision on the Western Front, and provided not too many resources were committed. But when it was realised that the required investment of resources was going to be heavier than was at first thought, elements in both the Army and the Navy began to backtrack.

The absence of previous consideration of the strategic possibilities of such maritime possibilities and of the consequent institutional requirements for a joint approach to war contributed to a lack of clarity about the whole aim of the Gallipoli enterprise. The ambiguity of the War Council's order of 13 January is well-known: 'The Admiralty should also prepare for a naval expedition in February to bombard and take the Gallipoli Peninsula with Constantinople as its objective.'[9] Hamilton's account of the idiosyncratic way in which Kitchener told him about his mission and the sparse nature of his subsequent directives is equally familiar. 'The Admiral [de Robeck] asked to see my instructions and Braithwaite read them out. When he stopped, Roger Keyes, the Commodore, inquired, "Is that all?" And when Braithwaite confessed that it was, everyone looked a little blank.'[10]

Given all this, the lack of clarity about the mission is hardly surprising. Was this a joint operation, or was it a naval operation with a degree of Army support? Was it just a question of the fleet turning up off Constantinople, or would the army have to garrison the hinterland and/or the peninsula? Were the Russians to be involved, or were they not? These issues were nebulous in themselves and, worse still, constantly shifted throughout the campaign.

Explaining the absence of strategic direction

So why were there such failures in the strategic direction of the Gallipoli campaign? Some of the difficulties derived not from the necessity for co-operation between the two services, but from the intrinsic characteristics of the situation itself.

Gallipoli as a dependent variable

The Gallipoli campaign was something of a dependent variable; its parameters were set by other events, which irritatingly changed as events unfolded. The strategic environment against which the planners conceived and conducted the campaign was not static but, on the contrary, constantly shifted in a way which undermined the original strategic assumptions upon which it had been built. Perceptions of Russian vulnerability, for example, did much to inspire early action, but worries about French resilience limited the number of troops thought to be available. Later it became clear that neither worry was justified.

Nowhere were such strategic uncertainties more evident than in the closing stages of the campaign when, as the Official History rather nicely puts it, 'the councils of the Entente were perplexed by conflicting theories' in the debate about whether to reinforce Gallipoli, to pull out and concentrate on the Western Front or to open another campaign from Salonika.[11] Strategic uncertainty and change impeded clear command throughout the campaign, but did not originate in the problems of inter-service co-operation.

Moreover, the essential issues cut right across service lines. Some of the most strident arguments, for example, were inside the Admiralty, between Fisher and Churchill. Both were masterful, peremptory, and decidedly not 'organisation men'. They had a warm regard for each other, compounded by long association. Even after the debacle of May 1915, Fisher could write of Churchill: 'I backed him up till I resigned. I would do the same again! He had courage and imagination! He was a War Man!'[12] Despite this, Fisher eventually cracked for a variety of reasons, amongst them a growing sense that the Dardanelles campaign was putting too many ships and men at risk, sucking resources away from the war against the High Sea Fleet, and also because of a growing sense of frustration at the way in which Churchill increasingly interfered in the Admirals' business. Their argument percolated downwards too. Keyes, ardently for the campaign, was dismissed by Fisher as 'very shallow... [and] a special pet of the First Lord'. Their dislike and distrust were plainly mutual.[13] For his part, Churchill was frustrated by the reluctance of his subordinates, first Carden and then de Robeck, to initiate and then to resume the scheme to force the straits. Curiously, in some of these intra-naval quarrels, the Army could sometimes act as mediator, as happened most famously at the War Council of 28 January when only Kitchener's intervention prevented Fisher from resigning and storming out of the meeting, there and then.

Later, when Keyes fought his last-ditch campaign to prevent the evacuation and came to argue his case over the head of his local naval commander, he found Kitchener, not the new Admiralty Board, to be most sympathetic to his point of view. But it all came to nothing and, as he later remarked, 'Thus the Admiral [de Robeck] and the General [Monro] who were really entirely responsible for the lamentable policy of evacuation left the execution of this unpleasant task to an Admiral [Wemyss] and a General [Birdwood] who were strongly opposed to it.'[14]

Service competition

It was nonetheless true that each service had its own agenda and that their priorities were sometimes hard to reconcile. There were quarrels between the dark blue and the khaki at all levels. Kitchener was in favour of Eastern operations so long as whatever was done would not suck so many forces away from the Western Front that the allied position in France could be jeopardised. He was prepared to support a campaign led and mainly fought by the Navy. Fisher's view was similar, although played out in a different dimension. He would support an operation in the Dardanelles just so long as it did not threaten the naval balance in the North Sea. He could spare a squadron of old surplus warships to blast their way through the straits; if more effort were required, he would support a joint operation in which the Army predominated. He was therefore reluctant to send the valuable *Queen Elizabeth* in the first place, and later insisted on its withdrawal despite the army's protests.

The third of the three Titans, Churchill, also representing the maritime dimension of British defence, took a different line from either of the others. He thought the Turkish empire a ripe fruit ready to fall if the branches were shaken a little. In the Dardanelles, British seapower could affect the outcome of the whole war, much more cost-effectively than would feeding yet more men into the slaughter of the Western Front. Churchill remained confident that the Navy could get through on its own, with perhaps a little help from the Army on the way in and for garrisoning purposes afterwards.

Service difficulties

The apparent inability of both services clearly to articulate their perspectives on the matter made successful co-ordination of these two dimensions of what should have been a joint national strategy prohibitively difficult. Two reasons can be adduced for this. First, both services suffered from internal bureaucratic deficiencies which prevented them from developing a real understanding of the requirements of joint operations and of the strengths and weaknesses of the enemy. The Admiralty's War Staff was embryonic at best and failed even to identify the crucial differences in strategic approach between Churchill and Fisher. Kitchener had a much more developed staff, but largely ignored it. Key figures in the War Office, who might have restrained him, had already gone to France leaving him (in the generally admiring Hamilton's words), 'like a powerful engine from which we have removed all controls, regulators and safety valves'.[15]

In both Departments of State, military professionals (such as Callwell in the War Office and Richmond in the Admiralty) were at best lukewarm about the project. But their advice, such as it was, went largely unheeded. All the careful work and meticulous arrangements that had produced the really rather impressive 1913 Manual of Combined and Military Operations, and the clear recommendations on the conduct of landing operations contained within the Army's Field Service Regulations of the same year, were ignored. The Admiralty had always been much less aware of these recommendations than the War Office anyway. The result was inevitable. As Roger Keyes told the Dardanelles Commission, the division of responsibility at Gallipoli was decided impromptu, on the basis of 'some army book' and the King's Regulations, and much of the detail had to be re-learned in combat.[16]

This failure in jointery derived from the complete independence of the Admiralty and the War Office, the uncertain provenance of the operation and the haste with which it was eventually put into effect. But it also owed much to the fact that so much of the conduct of the affair was in the hands of the amateurs in the War Council rather than the professionals in the Admiralty and War Office.

Failures in the mechanisms of strategic co-ordination

The War Cabinet/Council was certainly grievously defective as an agency for strategic direction. It met rarely and was dominated by Kitchener and Churchill. Its military advisers were expected to attend but to keep their mouths shut. Kitchener in particular was extremely secretive about his intentions. 'It is repugnant to me,' he is supposed to have said, 'to have to reveal military secrets to 23 gentlemen [of the cabinet] with whom I am hardly acquainted.'[17] The cabinet, with the collapse of the Liberal Government and its replacement by a coalition, was in any case in a state of political chaos at key moments. The War Council only met irregularly when the Prime Minister summoned it, kept its proceedings in manuscript, did not work to an agenda, received few Departmental memoranda and did not forward its conclusions, if any, to the Cabinet.[18]

The machinery for high-level strategic co-ordination between the services also left a great deal to be desired, as was recognised even at the time. Hankey noted in his diary on 19 March: 'Wrote a memo to Prime Minister imploring him to appoint naval and military technical committee to plan out military attack on Dardanelles in great detail, so as to avoid repetition of naval fiasco, which is largely due to inadequate staff preparation.'[19] But, sadly, too little was done. Inter-service co-operation at the strategic level remained largely a matter of the interaction of key personalities, rather than of the workings of an established machinery.

At this exalted level, it was a question of deciding the overall approach to the Dardanelles campaign, of weighing strategic options and of making choices. Control seemed to be in the hands of a number of patrician war-lords who hoped to function with autocratic, almost Olympian, certainty.[20] In fact those conducting the war at this level found the burden of exercising their responsibilities in the 'miasma' (as Fisher called it) created by continual change and continual uncertainty hard to bear. However energetic they might otherwise be, the strain was considerable for men such as Fisher at 74, Kitchener at 65 and Asquith at 63. Only the youthful Churchill, at 41, seemed to revel in the pulse of day-to-day events. But, in the end, both he and Fisher fell victim to their circumstances. Even the hugely prestigious and magisterial Kitchener found himself thwarted (such as over Fisher's insistence on bringing home the *Queen Elizabeth*), his opinions disputed by his own War Office; and, towards the end of the campaign, he lost his personal sense of certainty, eventually going out to the Dardanelles not as supreme arbiter, but more as an umpire between the 'evacuators' (led by General Monro) and those who wanted to carry on, led by Commodore Keyes. 'I could not help feeling sorry for him,' Keyes noted afterwards. 'He looked so terribly weary and harassed.'[21] In their own way, Britain's strategic leaders were also victims of the Dardanelles campaign.

Nonetheless, the deficiencies in strategic direction derived less from the difficulties of mounting joint operations than from the differing, and changing, perceptions of the strategic issues and on the crucial interaction of personalities under acute strain. Not surprisingly, perhaps, and given the absence of an effective inter-service machinery to manage this necessary process effectively, the result was an incremental, unsure, approach to the campaign which left those conducting it in theatre with the dismaying (indeed, demoralising) impression that their leaders were making up their strategy as they went along. In the Commons, Lord Charles Beresford pointedly asked: 'Who is responsible for the operations in the Dardanelles?'[22] Whatever his motives, it was a good question.

Results of absence of strategic direction

The consequence of all this indecision was an incremental campaign in which the objectives constantly changed, in which fundamental questions and issues were not addressed and in which both naval and land forces were fed into the theatre too late and in dribs and drabs. Naval and Army commanders regularly complained that the campaign would have been won had the forces in theatre at the end of the campaign been present at the beginning. Thus Lord Moyne (then plain Walter

Guinness), on 8 November 1915:

> We heard this morning that Lord Kitchener is on his way out. It is difficult to see how we can withdraw from here without great losses. Never can a campaign have been worse managed. Although 17 Divisions have been sent out here, it has always been by driblets which have not even sufficed to replace the wastage. If all the men who have been out here could have been available simultaneously, something might have been done.[23]

The absence of strategic direction was also at least partly responsible for a range of additional failures at the tactical level. The failure correctly to load ships departing from England, for example, reflected a lack of clarity about the strategic tasks that lay before their occupants.[24] Again, the inadequacy of naval gunfire support [despite superficial appearance] illustrates the same point. All too often, the Navy's fire was inaccurate, or ineffective when it was accurate. The latter was a function of having the wrong sort of shells: the ones appropriate to a sea battle. The former derived in large measure from Fisher's entirely understandable preoccupation with the strategic situation in the North Sea and consequent reluctance to risk ships such as the *Queen Elizabeth* which had modern fire control systems. In this way command failures at the top cascaded down to failure on the beaches.

The demands of command at Gallipoli

What was particularly worrying was the fact that amphibious operations were recognised to be inherently difficult since their success depended on the closest operational co-ordination between participating services. As Hankey warned, 'It must be remembered that combined operations require more careful preparation than any other class of military enterprise.'[25] Moreover, even as amphibious operations went, this was an ambitious exercise in that it was opposed from the start, and conducted in a distant area in the most demanding of climatic and topographical conditions.

In addition, the operational conditions at Gallipoli were particularly difficult for all the commanders. What Hamilton called 'the strain of waiting' was not 'softened by distance. Here we see the flashes, we hear the shots; we stand in our main battery and are yet cut off from sharing the efforts of our comrades. Too near for reflection, too far for intervention: on tenterhooks, in fact, a sort of mental crucifixion.'[26] The commanders were debilitated by a variety of stomach disorders, physical ailments and nervous strain, and several had to be invalided home (including Admiral Carden and General Hunter-Weston). They did not, of course, share the daily privations and dangers of the troops ashore, but occasionally came uncomfortably close to it. Hamilton, being rowed about from ship to ship, was personally shelled on several occasions. Compton Mackenzie, then working in the Intelligence section on the *Arcadian*, went ashore regularly. On one visit he recalled: 'Looking down I saw squelching up from the ground on either side of my boot like a rotten mangold the deliquescent green and black flesh of a Turk's head.'[27] More generally, the restricted area of the battlespace (a term intended to cover both the sea and the land) resulted in considerable losses amongst commanding officers. In the first day or so of the 29th Division's assault on Helles, for example, it 'lost two out its three brigadiers, two of its three brigade majors, and the majority of its senior infantry officers in the four and a half battalions of the covering force that landed at X,W and V beaches]'.[28] Losses of this sort would strain any military command system.

However, this was a campaign, to repeat the point, in which both sets of commanders had their own separate tasks to perform and in which each was crucially dependent on the other.

How to cope? A combination of equals

Famously, there was no single in-theatre joint force commander at Gallipoli. Corbett was rather proud of this since he preferred a 'combination of equals'.[29] The Army and the Navy went about their complementary business largely in isolation. Consultations were largely a matter of telling each other what was going to be done. Hamilton was absolutely clear that he had no right to interfere in the naval side of the campaign: 'Obviously I cannot go out of my element to urge the Fleet to actions, the perils of which I am professionally incompetent to judge.' Even when de Robeck was plainly hoping for a steer from Hamilton, it was not forthcoming. De Robeck for his part was equally scrupulous in not interfering in the General's affairs. Interestingly, Hamilton clearly thought there should have been a theatre commander on the *medical* side of the campaign, but did not apparently extend this logic to the operational area.[30]

The rationale for this approach was the argument that the nature of fighting ashore was fundamentally different from that at sea, and that the command system needed to reflect this inescapable fact. Thus Hamilton:

> In sea warfare, the Fleet lies in the grip of its Admiral like a platoon in the hands of a Subaltern. The admiral sees; speaks the executive word and the whole Fleet moves; not, as with us, each Commander carrying out the order in his own way, but each Captain steaming, firing, retiring to the letter of the signal.[31]

But in land warfare, on the other hand, all was chaos and disorder. To cope with these circumstances army command would need to be delegated. The notion of a theatre commander operating in such a way that the colour of his cloth did not matter was, quite simply, inconceivable in 1915.

The nature of naval command

Certainly, the conditions of naval warfare were different: 'a huge mystery hedged in by sea-sickness', as Fisher described it.[32] Outside commentators frequently noted that the difference between naval and land commanders was that the former were always in the thick of the action, as vulnerable as anyone else:[33] a factor bound to affect (and perhaps differentiate) their command style.

However, naval command style itself differed. Although this issue is to be debated more fully elsewhere in this book, it was the familiar aspiration of many naval commanders to keep a tight hold on the fleet at sea lest all degenerate into chaos. Jellicoe has often been accused of this. In Fisher's words: 'Jellicoe had all the Nelsonic attributes except one – he is totally wanting in the great gift of Insubordination. Nelson's greatest achievements were all solely due to his disobeying orders! ... Any fool can obey orders!'[34] Nonetheless, Fisher also recognised the decisive role of the Admiral in command:

> Every telescope in the fleet ... is looking at the Admiral as he goes to the topmost and best vantage spot on board his flag ship to see the enemy, and sees him alone outlined against the sky – neither time nor room for a staff around him ... and the people of the Fleet watch him with unutterable suspense to see what signal goes up to alter the formation of the fleet – a formation on which depends Victory or Defeat.[35]

With such expectations it is perhaps not too surprising that sometimes the Navy generated a very centralised system of command which could easily stifle initiative. Keyes was not immune to this tendency himself but criticised it in others. Thus, of Backhouse, he said: 'He is a charming fellow, but is not a very strong character – and I'm told can't use a staff – must do everything himself. Like so many Admirals!'[36] While Hamilton doubtless had this conception of naval command in mind, there was an alternative style, however, associated with people such as Beatty. Here the difficulties of exercising close control in a fast moving maritime environment required commanders to make their intentions clear and to delegate authority to meet them to the extent that circumstances required:

> From a study of the great naval wars, it is impressed upon one that cruiser Captains...to be successful must possess in marked degree: initiative, resource, determination, and no fear of accepting responsibility. To enable them to make the best use of these sterling qualities, they should be given the clearest indication of the functions and duties of the unit to which they belong, as comprehended by the Commander of that unit. They should be completely comprehensive of his mind and intentions.[37]

Beatty went on in this 1913 description of the function of the battle-cruiser squadron to quote von Clausewitz on the inevitable uncertainties of war and the consequent inability of the commander to foresee every eventuality. Accordingly:

> Captains should be supplied with all the information available, to enable the admiral to rely upon them to grasp the situation and pursue it with resolution, using their own discretion how to act under conditions which could not have been anticipated by him. Instructions issued should be such as not to interfere with the exercise of the judgement of the captains and should – except in very exceptional cases – be of a very general character.[38]

Beatty tinkered with these instructions in the light of unfolding experience, particularly after the Battle of Jutland, and always in the direction of allowing subordinates to exercise their discretion in anticipating the commander's order.[39]

The Navy's command performance at Gallipoli

Relations between naval commanders on the spot were good and de Robeck did much to confirm Beatty's view of him: 'He might not have been a genius...but a born leader of men, of great energy and determination; in fact with those qualities that only come to the front in war.'[40] De Robeck's style of leadership was liberal enough to allow Keyes to go back to London in November to argue for the retention of the land campaign and for a renewal of the naval attack, although he himself had concluded that neither was desirable. Hamilton himself made the point that at Gallipoli, where the fleet was disaggregated around the coast supporting various activities ashore, de Robeck hardly had any choice but to allow his subordinates to exercise initiative. The naval style of command also allowed brilliant acts of individualism in the shape of Lieutenant-Commander B.C. Freyberg's extraordinary feats off Bulair on 15 April, aircraft exploits over the peninsula and submarine attacks beyond it. Such free-wheeling derring-do was widely admired in the fleet, despite its centralising proclivities.

Perhaps the biggest deficiency in the maritime command system was the lack of what we would now call a Joint Force Amphibious Component Commander, presumably on the assumption that all of this could be confidently left to orthodox naval types, and reflecting the curious fact that at this time there was no particular association between the Royal Marines and amphibious warfare. Commodore Wemyss was generally in charge of the amphibious side of the landing operation, but had no special competence or experience in this area. He provided genial and effective leadership, although mistakes were inevitably made. The consequences of this deficiency, arguably, were a great many problems, especially on the logistical side of the landing operation: the failure to combat load the transports coming out from the UK, insufficient attention to ship-to-shore movement, poor naval gunfire support, inadequate supplies of everything on shore, and so on and so forth.

Of course, there were naval failures and confusions, but it is not clear whether they reflected a naval command at Gallipoli that was too centralised or too decentralised. Often people had to make up their own minds as to what it was best to do in situations of ambiguity and with varying results. For instance, it now appears that one of the reasons why the ANZAC forces were landed at the wrong place was because of a decision made by a midshipman approaching an unfamiliar shore, and taking it upon himself to seek his own solution. Another example took place during a meeting on the *Euryalus* on 21 April when the fleet's gunnery officers convened to discuss the provision of gunfire support for the landings. The meeting closed ambiguously. Some attendees concluded that they had been ordered to keep their ships well back (which would generally degrade the quality of their fire support), while others felt that they had been given discretion to go closer in. Captain Lockyer of the *Implacable* was one of the latter fraternity; he took his ship almost to the water's edge of X beach, blasting everything in sight. For ever afterwards he was convinced that if everyone else had followed his example, things would have been very different on 25 April.[41]

Army command performance at Gallipoli

Hamilton's vision of Mission Command

Hamilton has often been accused of being too deferential towards Kitchener, of excessive loyalty, of not querying ambiguous direction or putting the case for reinforcements and re-supplies more strongly. Perhaps this derived from excessive loyalty, or from treating Kitchener more as his military commander than as Secretary of State for War. There is something in all this although, in his diaries, Hamilton's exasperation about Kitchener's lack of sufficient support is at least as evident as is his admiration for his former leader.

In performing his task, Hamilton plainly believed that the circumstances of land warfare demanded a delegated system of command. The apparent failure of the commander ashore (General Hunter-Weston) to exploit the unexpected opportunities of Y beach in the initial landings tempted him to go against this:

> Braithwaite was rather dubious from the orthodox General Staff point of view as to whether it was sound for G.H.Q. to barge into Hunter-Weston's plans, seeing he was executive Commander of the whole of this southern invasion. But to me the idea seemed simple common sense...
>
> My inclination was to take a hand myself in this affair but the Staff are clear against interference when I have no knowledge of the facts – and I suppose they are right.[42]

His supposition was no doubt strengthened by the fact that Braithwaite, unlike Hamilton himself, was one of the exalted ones who had not only been through Camberley, but had actually been a member of the

Directing Staff there. Accordingly, he was thoroughly imbued with the doctrine of delegated command, and authoritative in its expression.[43]

Hard though it would doubtless have been for Hamilton to withstand such views, the officers of the *Queen Elizabeth*, to judge by the wardroom scuttlebutt, were deeply dismayed by his evident failure to do anything very decisive about Roger Keyes' suggestion that the landings at Y beach should be reinforced, rather than abandoned:

> Hamilton...had a deckchair on the bridge down below the rails. He couldn't see anything. He didn't want to see anything. He wouldn't look at anything... [Keyes] said shouldn't you stop them [evacuating]... and the answer was that General Hunter-Weston was in charge of the operation and he couldn't do anything without consulting him.[44]

In the event of course, Hunter-Weston denied all knowledge of any order to evacuate Y beach.[45] It is at least arguable that his communications were so bad that he knew even less of what was going on at Y beach than Hamilton did. Certainly command arrangements below him (where two Lieutenant-Colonels at Y beach, Koe and Mathews, both thought they were in command) left a good deal to be desired.

Things were even worse at Suvla in early August, where confusion rather than command was being delegated.[46] Stopford's unexpected decision not to go ashore until the evening of 8 August further aggravated the confusion since it deprived him of an opportunity to sort matters out ashore; moreover, his command ship, the tiny sloop HMS *Jonquil*, was simply not equipped to deal with the large number of signals the command function required.

Stopford was by no means entirely responsible for the indecision and inactivity at Suvla, and it is worth pausing on this point. A good deal of uncertainty derived from inherent ambiguities about what Stopford was supposed to do. Latter-day critics often seem to assume that he was expected to lead a large-scale flanking operation through open country to undermine Turkish resistance to the allied position at Anzac from the rear, but this was not the case. Hamilton's orders were certainly ambiguous (perhaps especially after he and Stopford had re-negotiated them), but the main effort was to be made *from* Anzac, not towards it; Suvla was to provide first a secure port and only then a degree of support for the expected break-out from Anzac. In this case 'the Commander's intent' was more misinterpreted by Stopford's critics than by Stopford himself.

Nonetheless the command system in place at Suvla was at fault in that it did not encourage subordinates (including Stopford) to use their own initiative in order to make the most of the unexpected opportunity to reach the hills quickly, thereby helping to achieve the required objective. Finally, as far as Hamilton was concerned, poor communications from Suvla obscured the *extent* to which things were going wrong, and required intervention from on high.

Gallipoli difficulties

Many of Hamilton's command difficulties derived from the specific circumstances of the Gallipoli campaign. First, and most obviously, it was a very rushed affair: and the administrative machinery was scrabbled together at the last moment. Hamilton's initial dismay at his own ramshackle staff was clear:

> My staff still bear the bewildered look of men who have hurriedly been snatched from desks to do some extraordinary turn in some unheard-of theatre. One or two of them put on uniform for the first time in their lives an hour ago. Leggings awry, spurs upside down, belts over shoulder straps! I haven't a notion of who they all are.[47]

There was a further problem. The force had originally been despatched to the Mediterranean with the expectation that troops would face little resistance when they eventually landed on the peninsula. Once it became clear that the landing would be seriously opposed, the force needed to be sorted out and restowed at Alexandria. Hamilton's administrative staff had little choice but to stay in Egypt while this was going on. They did in due course arrive in the Gallipoli area, but the logistics failures of the landings of 25 April can largely be ascribed to these initial confusions and delays.

The geographic circumstances of the campaign were important too. This was not like the Western Front where the commander was positioned back from the line, remote, comfortable and best able to plan and administer. Said Hamilton: 'What a contrast we must present to the Headquarters in France! There the stately Chateau; sheets, table-cloths and motor cars. Here the red tabs have to haul their own kits over the sand.'[48]

In modern theory, 'quick reaction will be paramount and there will always be the need to reach a timely decision in relation to an opponent's own decision-action cycle'[49] and this depends on good communications. Hamilton had high hopes of these at the beginning: 'Never... has a Commander-in-Chief been so accessible to a message or appeal from any part of the force. Each theatre has its outfit of signallers, wireless etc and I can either answer within five minutes, or send help, or rush myself upon the scene.'[50] But in fact communications at Gallipoli turned out to be very slow and unreliable, and this played a major role in the frustrations at Y beach and, later, at Suvla. Hamilton felt he was therefore neither one thing nor the other: 'neither a new fangled Commander sitting cool and semi-detached in an office; nor an old-fashioned Commander taking personal direction of the show'.[51] Moreover, this was again in modern parlance a 'combined' operation in which the French played an important but largely independent part. Communications between them and the British were rudimentary, and Hamilton was not in a position to direct them, say (for example) over keeping the Kum Kale bridgehead in April or launching simultaneous attacks in June. In Hamilton's view it was better for the French to be physically separated from their allies rather than be 'mixed up together on [the] Peninsula'[52] for this reason.

These two circumstances aggravated command problems that had nothing to do with the nature of the theatre or the campaign. For instance, Hamilton's relaxed attitude to the fact that his administrative staff were down in Alexandria owes much to his obsession with the supposed benefits of a small headquarters staff. Even in the immediate theatre he separated it from his administrative staff, clearly regarding the latter as a tedious encumbrance.[53]

Keyes was sometimes incensed at what he regarded as the inefficiency of the Army, regarding them as suffering from 'over-staffing and the water-tight compartments and miles of red tape which tightly bound them up and add enormously to *our* difficulties'. Supplying the troops ashore, he thought, was made unnecessarily difficult 'if his [Hamilton's] people are so absolutely careless and callous'.[54]

To sum up, Hamilton had a consensual command style, neither Napoleonic nor ego-centric, that depended on eliciting a full spectrum of opinions in collaborative discussion before a decision emerged. He quite consciously took an apparently very modern, non-interventionist view of his command function. But the problem seemed to be that, despite a century of experience of small colonial wars and distant interventions, the British Army had not yet really grown the degree of initiative in its subordinate commanders that *Auftragstaktik* required. The Army of the late Victorian period was personalised and improvisatory rather than an exponent of what we would now call Mission Command.[55] In consequence, as the commander of the land side of the Gallipoli expedition, Hamilton was well served neither from above nor from below.

The lack of a Joint Forces Headquarters and its effects

There was no equivalent at Gallipoli of a Joint Force Commander able to talk to all service interests both above and below him. Hamilton was quite clear about this. He did not feel he could appeal directly to Churchill for support against Fisher's reluctance to despatch proper landing craft, because this might have lacerated Kitchener's sensitivities. '[A]lthough the sailors [in the theatre] want me to pull this particular chestnut out of the fire, it is just as well they should know I am not going to speak to their Boss even under the most tempting circumstances.'[56] Hamilton was 'not even supposed to have knowledge, much less an opinion, as to what passes between the Fleet and the Admiralty'.[57]

Worse still, there was also only rudimentary machinery for co-ordination between the two services. Hamilton was usually on one ship, the *Arcadian*, at Alexandria or Lemnos, but was later at Imbros.[58] De Robeck was usually somewhere at sea. During the landings on 25 April Hamilton joined de Robeck on *Queen Elizabeth* but this meant 'his staff being incarcerated in gun turrets and other clanging recesses where they were quite useless'.[59] Putting the staffs of both Rear-Admiral Wemyss and General Hunter-Weston on the *Euryalus* off W beach was certainly a mistake. The latter's Chief of Staff operated in a chart room 20 yards from A turret. 'The 9.2" gun was firing about every five minutes and whenever it went off, it made chaos of the divisional signals and reports which had been laid out in neat rows on the chart table.'[60] In these circumstances it was not surprising that the General should have lost track of what was happening at Y beach away to his left and so failed to answer Hamilton's anxious queries.

At Suvla, Hamilton once again had his own ship, but this was apparently immobilised with boiler trouble for six frustrating hours while, as he suspected, Stopford frittered away the possibilities of victory ashore. This failure in communications, coupled with his inherent unwillingness to interfere in the actions of his subordinates, meant that Hamilton lost the initiative and Kemal Ataturk won the crucial race to reinforce the position. In today's inelegant terminology Hamilton failed to get inside his adversary's OODA loop,[61] largely because of the deficiencies of his command system.

Such physical separation encouraged both services to take decisions independently. On 9 May the Navy held a big conference aboard *Queen Elizabeth* to consider the prospects for a renewed naval assault on the narrows without the presence of a single soldier, even though the Army might well have been virtually marooned on the peninsula if such an attack had gone badly wrong.[62]

With the wisdom of hindsight, it would seem that the lack of a Joint Forces Headquarters (JFHQ), which could talk the issues through and facilitate effective Command decisions, contributed to key decisions often later considered to have been mistakes. These include:

- independent naval operations at the beginning of the campaign conducted without the presence of immediate available land forces should their use be proved necessary
- initial landings at the tip of the peninsula, in order directly to facilitate the naval passage, instead of at easier sites further to the north (perhaps Suvla)
- dispersing forces between seven beaches, rather than three or four, in a manner which made it difficult for success to be reinforced[63]

For all these reasons, it would indeed:

> probably have been better if, for the first few days of the landing, both the admiral and the military Commander-in-Chief, with all their respective Staffs, could have been accommodated on a specially equipped unarmed vessel, fitted with all the signalling apparatus necessary for the control of the fleet and for issuing orders and receiving messages from the shore.[64]

But a note of caution...

Despite such criticisms, though, the system in place actually sometimes worked surprisingly well given the circumstances of a campaign in which what Corbett called the 'relative primacy of the land and sea element'[65] shifted backwards and forwards. This greatly complicated the co-ordination process, and made it difficult to see who really should have been in charge at any particular point.

Many of these potential inter-service deficiencies were, however, compensated for by the fact that the Naval and Army leaders got on so well together. This was partly a function of deliberate policy by all concerned. Keyes was quite insistent that 'this was going to be an expedition in which there should be no quarrels and the Admiral would send home anyone responsible for friction [with the Army] at once without the slightest hesitation'.[66] Keyes was already a friend of Hamilton's Chief of Staff, General Braithwaite, and Hamilton, too, was a family friend. Everyone liked and admired de Robeck, and all these close personal relationships do much to explain why the two services were not at loggerheads despite such difficult circumstances. But the fact that they did get on so well, and came to complementary conclusions (if by independent routes), rather concealed the huge deficiencies in the mechanics of their co-operation.

Curiously enough, it was much the same story when things began to go badly wrong and the end of the campaign came into sight. As we have seen, service affiliation played little part in determining positions for or against evacuation. Keyes was as angry with de Robeck as he was with Monro for their decision to withdraw, but in neither case did this disagreement become personal.

In the theatre of operations, inter-service co-operation was better than it was in London since decisions were consciously and deliberately made, and many of them look sensible even in retrospect. For instance, after the failure of the Navy on 18 March, a joint conference was held on *Queen Elizabeth* in Mudros harbour of all the admirals and generals; it was agreed that combined action was now necessary but 'must be postponed until plans had been developed and perfected'. Arrangements for the next few weeks were agreed. 'And so the meeting came to an end with perfect accord between the Navy and the Army, and we each went our way to our several tasks.'[67]

It is indeed important not to be seduced by the advantages of hindsight into failing to recognise the scale of the administrative achievement involved in improvising at such short notice so large and difficult an amphibious undertaking.[68] The tendency to focus on the problems of the campaign should not blind observers to the fact of its successes. Getting the Army ashore in such numbers and keeping them there for so long remains an impressive achievement. The Suvla landing, and even more the final evacuation, showed how much had been learned during the course of the campaigns by both services, separately and jointly. As so often, Corbett put the point particularly well:

> In that marvellous evacuation we see the national genius for amphibious warfare raised to its highest manifestation. In hard experience and successive disappointments the weapon had been brought to a perfect temper, and when the hour of fruition came to show of what great things it was capable, it was used only to effect a retreat.[69]

Conclusion

Not surprisingly, therefore, the British generally concluded that there was nothing necessarily and theoretically wrong with the command system that was put into effect for the joint operations at Gallipoli; it was the way it had been implemented that was at fault. Accordingly, during the inter-war period the need to prepare for amphibious exercises played a significant part in the establishment of the Chiefs of Staff system and for a level of preparation for combined operations that has frequently been underestimated by historians. The Interservice Planning Staff that was set up in February 1940 to consider the prospects for a British invasion of Norway discussed the setting-up of a single theatre commander to co-ordinate the work of three junior component commanders, a joint Signal Board to supervise all communications, a joint Security Board for intelligence and so on.[70] In the end this failed to materialise in the rush to respond to the German pre-invasion, but how, why and with what consequences is another story.

Notes

The author is grateful for permission to use and to quote material from the Imperial War Museum and the Liddle Collection, Brotherton Library, Leeds University.

1. Thomas More Molyneux, *Conjunct Expeditions, or Expeditions that have been carried on by the Fleet and Army* (London: 1759).
2. General Sir Ian Hamilton, *Gallipoli Diary* (London: 1920), Vol. II, pp.141–2, 183. The title of this book is in some respects misleading; its contents were plainly written-up well after the events described.
3. Arthur J. Marder, *From the Dardanelles to Oran* (London: 1974) p.1.
4. Hamilton, *Diary*, Vol. I, pp.95–6.
5. Ibid., p.207.
6. Brig.-General C.F. Aspinall-Oglander, *Military Operations: Gallipoli*, Vol. II (London: 1932).
7. Hamilton, *Diary*, Vol. I, p.46.
8. *Design for Military Operations – The British Military Doctrine* (London: Ministry of Defence, 1989) Army Code 71451, pp.48–9; *United Kingdom Doctrine for Joint and Combined Operations*, Joint Warfare Publication 0–10. Section VI, para. 0222.
9. Conclusions of War Council Meeting 13 Jan 1915, Public Record Office (PRO) CAB 42/1/6.
10. Hamilton, *Diary*, Vol. I, pp.1–3 and for the meeting of 17 March 1915, p.23.
11. *Military Operations*, Vol. II, p.375.
12. Admiral of the Fleet Lord Fisher, *Memories* (London: 1919) p.57. The disputes between the two men are fully if somewhat tendentiously described in Geoffrey Penn, *Fisher, Churchill and the Dardanelles* (London: 1999), esp. pp.170ff and 186.
13. For Fisher's views on Keyes see his letter to Beatty of 3 February and to Jellicoe 4 April 1915, in A.J. Marder (ed.), *Fear God and Dread Nought*, Vol. III (London: 1959). See also *The Keyes Papers*, Vol. I (London: 1972) p.229.
14. Quoted in Alan Moorehead, *Gallipoli* (London: 1983) p.271.

15. Hamilton, *Diary*, Vol. I, p.13.
16. Dardanelles Commission, Evidence p.1,453, PRO, CAB 19/33. Much of this paragraph is derived from the work of Dr David Massam of Oxford University.
17. Quoted in J. Laffin, *Damn the Dardanelles: The Story of Gallipoli* (London: 1980) p.23.
18. General Sir Hugh Beach, 'The Murderous Responsibility', Gallipoli Memorial Lecture Series, 1985, p.14.
19. Sir Maurice Hankey, *The Supreme Command 1914–1918*, Vol. I (London: 1961) p.293.
20. For evidence see Violet Bonham Carter, *Winston Churchill As I Knew Him* (London: 1965) pp.239–40 et seq, and pp.350–76.
21. Moorehead, *Gallipoli*, pp.269–71; *Keyes Papers*, diary entries for 17–24 November 1915, pp.243–55.
22. Quoted in Penn, *Fisher, Churchill*, p.166.
23. Entry for 5 November 1915 in B. Bond and S. Robbins (eds), *Staff Officer: The Diaries of Lord Moyne* (London: Leo Cooper, 1987) p.49.
24. T.H.E. Travers, 'Command and Leadership Styles in the British Army: The 1915 Gallipoli Model', *Journal of Contemporary History*, Vol. 29 (1994), pp.403–42.
25. Quoted in Laffin, *Damn the Dardanelles*, pp.40–1.
26. Hamilton, *Diary*, Vol. I, pp.192–3.
27. Compton Mackenzie, *Gallipoli Memories* (London: 1929) p.83.
28. *Military Operations*, Vol. I, p.251.
29. Sir Julian Corbett, *Naval Operations* (London: 1921), Vol. III, p.7.
30. Hamilton, *Diary*, Vol. II, p.32. Also see their discussion of 20 August, pp.124–5. For his medical point see Vol. I, p.367.
31. Hamilton, *Diary*, Vol. I, p.127.
32. Fisher, *Memories*, p.110.
33. This was a common view at the time. See Colonel John Buchan, *A History of the British Navy During the War* (London: 1918) p.228; and for an unadmiring commentary on the nature of Army Command, *War Memoirs of David Lloyd George* (London: 1936) p.2,042.
34. Fisher, *Memories*, p.38.
35. Ibid., p.107.
36. Keyes to Chatfield, 14 August 1937, in Paul Halpern, *The Keyes Papers*, Vol. II (London: 1980) p.371.
37. 'Functions of a Battle Cruiser Squadron', 5 April 1913 in B.McL. Ranft (ed.), *The Beatty Papers*, Vol. I (London: 1989) p.59 et seq.
38. Ibid., p.60.
39. For evidence of this see Beatty's 'Grand Fleet Battle Instructions', 1 January 1918 in ibid., pp.459, 462, 469.
40. Beatty to Churchill, 17 October 1914 in ibid., p.142.
41. For this claim, and related correspondence, see Capt. H. Lockyer, RN, 'The Tragedy of the Battle of the Beaches', privately published pamphlet of 1936, in Lockyer MSS at Imperial War Museum 75/56/1.
42. Hamilton, *Diary*, Vol. I, pp.133, 147.
43. Travers, 'Command and Leadership Styles', p.414.
44. Diary entry Lord Strathclyde papers, Liddle collection: University of Leeds.
45. Hamilton, *Diary*, Vol. I, p.63.

56 *The Gallipoli Campaign: Command Performances*

46 Travers, 'Command and Leadership Styles', pp.423–5; and *Military Operations*, Vol. II, p.233.
47 Hamilton, *Diary*, Vol. I, p.16.
48 Ibid., p.226.
49 *Military Operations*, p.43.
50 Hamilton, *Diary*, Vol. I, p.152.
51 Ibid., p.43.
52 Ibid., pp.159, 319, 193.
53 Beach, 'Murderous Responsibility', p.16.
54 *Keyes Papers*, Vol. I, pp.165, 167.
55 See Ian Beckett, 'Command in the Late Victorian Army', in G.D. Sheffield (ed.), *Leadership and Command: the Anglo-American Experience Since 1861* (London: 1996) pp.37–56.
56 Hamilton, *Diary*, Vol. I, p.45.
57 Ibid., p.228.
58 Ibid., pp.104–5.
59 Beach, 'Murderous Responsibility', p.16.
60 J.H. Godfrey, 'The Naval Memoirs of Admiral J.H. Godfrey', unpublished, 1964, Vol. II, p.4.
61 For an interesting discussion of the Obervation–Orientation–Decision–Action loop, see David S. Fadok, 'John Boyd and John Warden: Air Power's Quest for Strategic Paralysis' (SAAS, Maxwell Air Force Base, Alabama: 1995) p.16.
62 Godfrey, 'Naval Memoirs'.
63 Callwell, for example, believed strongly that all the troops should have been landed on the littoral north of Gaba Tepe in the area subsequently known as Anzac Cove: Major-General Sir Charles Callwell, *The Dardanelles* (London: 1919) pp.128–9.
64 *Military Operations*, Vol. I, p.254.
65 Corbett, *Naval Operations*, Vol. II, pp.177–8.
66 Keyes, letter to his wife, 2 July 1915, *The Keyes Papers*, Vol. II, p.157.
67 Admiral of the Fleet Lord Wester Wemyss, *The Navy in the Dardanelles Campaign* (London: 1924) pp.40–2.
68 Peter Liddle, *Men of Gallipoli* (London: Allen Lane, 1976) p.98.
69 Corbett, *Naval Operations*, Vol. II, p.245.
70 See the work of Dr David Massam, already referred to.

Part II
The Second World War

5
Scandinavian Disaster: Allied Failure in Norway in 1940

Nigel de Lee

In spring 1940 Allied attempts to lure Germany to diversionary expeditions and defeat in Scandinavia ended in a defeat for the Allies and the German conquest of Norway. This chapter will concentrate upon the deficiencies of co-ordination in the Allied policy and operations, ally to ally, service to service, and force to force, which played an important part in these catastrophic events. Particular attention will be paid to developments in central Norway. Five main areas of interest will be examined: defects in command structure; political interference in the planning and conduct of military operations; the corporate autism of the services, leading to conceptual dissonance and divergences of military policy; practical and technical difficulties in communication; and the impact of significant personalities.

Defects: command structure

Allied command structures were improvised and highly complicated at international and national levels. The procedures for planning were so involved that a proposed course of action which affected or impinged upon the French would have to pass through six 'gates' before it could be approved. This cumbersome arrangement produced misunderstanding, confusion, delay and paralysis.[1] The multiplicity of bodies engaged in the process generated friction, which according to Clausewitz was always the most dangerous threat to efficiency.[2] At the highest level, the Supreme War Council and Allied Military Committee were supposed to formulate and execute joint military policy and strategy. These bodies were convoked ad hoc regarding membership, location and timing of meetings, and in effect were reactive in nature.[3]

The British command structure was not founded on any philosophical or functional principle. The organs of control evolved by adaptation to political pressures and compromises with each other. They were not controlled or guided by defined or reconciled aims or functions. One of the British official historians, J.R.M. Butler, remarked that there was no proper division of labour between the major organs, which meant that war policy, strategy, and operational planning were confused. In particular, there was no effective machinery to connect strategic policy to battle plans.[4] The weaknesses of the command machinery were acknowledged, and simultaneously compounded, by the creation of the Ministerial Co-ordination Committee in 1939. The formation of this committee was intended to reduce the excessive burden of paperwork of which the War Cabinet and Chiefs of Staff had been complaining since the outbreak of hostilities. The permanent members were the Service Ministers, Ministers of Supply and Co-ordination of Defence, and the Chiefs of Staff. Other persons could be summoned to attend at the will of the committee. The terms of reference required the committee to keep important strategic matters under review, and to make *recommendations* to the War Cabinet.[5] These terms determined that the committee had no executive powers. In operation, it simply produced even more paperwork for the War Cabinet and Chiefs of Staff, and required them to spend more of their valuable time attending meetings.[6] What was worse was that the committee frequently lapsed into disputes over strategic policy, producing disunity, acrimony and fragmentation rather than a common policy. A great deal of time and energy was expended in these disruptive and damaging activities.[7]

The power of decision remained with the War Cabinet, which was unwilling to delegate control, whilst the work of preparing advice and plans was diffused to a series of subsidiary bodies.[8] The War Cabinet tended to concentrate on minor issues to the neglect of the general questions of strategic policy.[9] Subsidiary organs, such as the Joint Planners, were exasperated by the consequent delay and indecision. To mitigate the effects they began to generate draft directives in anticipation of approval by the Chiefs of Staff.[10] The weaknesses in the machinery also made the planning process vulnerable to distortion by the actions of strong and energetic personalities intent on political interference in strictly military matters. For example, senior French and British politicians such as Paul Reynaud and Winston Churchill were desperately impatient for offensive action, and ready to overrule their military advisers to get their own way.[11]

At lower levels the system of command was designed to achieve 'Co-ordination by Liaison' rather than 'Unified Control'. In autumn

1939 it was intended that the Chiefs of Staff should serve as a Battle Headquarters, issuing orders to commanders in the field. This intent proved impractical because the Chiefs were overworked and disunited.[12] In response to the perceived need, informal planning organisations were created ad hoc to serve urgent requirements. In March 1940 the Joint Planners set up an Inter-Service Planning Staff consisting of Staff Officers from the forces, French Liaison Officers, and officials from the Ministry of Shipping. The task of this staff was to draw up outline plans with a particular concern for logistics. The overall aim was the negative one of avoiding clashes of interest between individual service plans that were envisaged as 'Independent but Co-ordinated'. A subsidiary body, the Inter-Services Signals Board, was created to provide for communications between the services in the field.[13]

According to the final version of the plans for operations in Norway, R4, the expeditionary forces, *Avonmouth* (later renamed *Rupert*), which was bound for the north, and *Stratford*, which was intended to seize Stavanger, Bergen and Trondheim, were to act as independent forces directly under the War Office, once ashore.[14] The troops assigned to *Stratford* began to land on 16 April, initially with rather fragmentary and obscure command arrangements. On 22 April Lieutenant-General H.R.S. Massy, General Officer Commanding of V Corps, took overall command of land forces in central Norway. He had no staff specifically earmarked for this responsibility, so employed officers from HQ V Corps and Military Operations 8 for the purpose.[15]

Before landing, the expeditionary forces were under naval command. The Admiralty was also entrusted with the duty of initiating the operation because it was recognised that the chances of success depended heavily upon good timing. On 4 April the Chiefs of Staff remarked in support of this decision that it was intended 'to ensure that the action of the Service Departments is unified and simultaneous ... [the Royal Navy] ... being the senior partner in the first phase'.[16] These command structures were fractured and incomplete. A subsequent commentator, Alfred Vagts, remarked that the Allied Forces in Norway were 'quantities forming a sum in the addition of which several persons took a fumbling hand'.[17]

Political interference

The lack of a strong rational structure for making decisions and planning operations made military policy vulnerable to domestic and foreign political pressures. These prevented the selection and maintenance of a consistent aim, as well as distorting planning and disrupting the conduct of operations. Fear of adverse public opinion, driven by boredom with the hardships of war unrelieved by the vicarious excitement of action was a significant factor.[18] So were the wishful thinking, impatience and pathological activism of certain political leaders. These factors combined to exert an irresistible demand for offensive action in Scandinavia, with priority being given to operations in the north. This demand succeeded despite the competent and realistic advice which was offered against it.

In spring 1940 Edouard Daladier, who was the French prime minister until March and remained as war minister thereafter, and Paul Reynaud (a key cabinet member who succeeded his rival Daladier as prime minister), were desperate to embark upon a spectacular and successful adventure. They were oppressed by a sense of failure because the Allies had failed to prevent the defeat of Poland, and all too aware that volatile public opinion in France had already decided that the *Drôle de Guerre* was not really funny. They also wished to impress and attract neutrals to the allied cause by positive action.[19] Their anxiety and sense of shame were intensified on 13 March by the capitulation of Finland, which seemed to reinforce the impression that the Allies were militarily impotent.[20] The political crisis precipitated by the failure to help the Finns led to Daladier's resignation. The new prime minister, Reynaud, was a natural activist, spurred to greater efforts by the causes of Daladier's downfall.[21]

Political considerations were reinforced by strategic calculations. The French Government and High Command were anxious to avoid a decisive clash of arms in north-west Europe, so were keen to lure the Germans into diversions, to Scandinavia, the Balkans, or the Near East. They were quite prepared to obtain Scandinavian[22] co-operation by forceful coercion if necessary. In March French proposals included seizures of strategic points in the North Cape, by descents on Narvik, Petsamo and Murmansk. They also supported plans for Operation *Paul*, in which naval aircraft would bomb Lulea, the Swedish port on the Gulf of Bothnia through which iron ore was exported from Gallivare to Germany.[23] In April the French gave a warm welcome to *Wilfred*, the British plan to close the Norwegian leads by sowing mines, and the R4 plan for a contingent intervention in Norway if the Germans were provoked to invade.[24] In the British government the main proponent of offensive action in Scandinavia was Churchill, the First Lord of the Admiralty. He was determined to exercise a major influence over the planning and conduct of operations.[25] Churchill held that offensive action was essential, as the only means to obtain a favourable decision in war.[26] He believed that in taking strategic decisions it was best to rely upon instinctive judgement rather than rational calculation, because no statesman could ever count upon having complete and accurate current information.[27]

This belief made Churchill impatient for action, and much inclined to dismiss the criticisms and objections raised against his schemes by the Joint Planners and Chiefs of Staff. Indeed, he condemned the Joint Planning staff as 'the machinery of negation'.[28] Opposition simply made Churchill more determined to have his own way. The prime minister, Neville Chamberlain, remarked that 'in his enthusiasm [Churchill] put more intense pressure on his advisers than he realised, and reduced them to silent acquiescence'.[29]

In spring 1940 a majority of the War Cabinet, the Chiefs of Staff, and the Joint Planners were all sceptical of the feasibility of schemes for operations in Scandinavia. The Chief of Imperial General Staff (CIGS) advised the War Cabinet in January that offensive actions must be postponed until such time as the Allies had secured the sea lines of communications, and the Western Front.[30] This view that the Allies must postpone offensive action until their base was secure and their latent power fully mobilised was shared by the Prime Minister.[31] The Joint Planners held that 'we cannot organise for a long war and try to win a short one at the same time', and warned against the diversion of scarce military resources to theatres of secondary interest.[32]

The Chiefs of Staff and Joint Planners combined to advise the War Cabinet along the following lines: first, there could be no chance of successful operations in Scandinavia without the active co-operation or acquiescence of the Scandinavian governments.[33] Second, the original plans for operations based in Norway but extending into central Sweden would require the employment of nine divisions, much shipping, and substantial Air Defence equipment. These resources were simply not available.[34] The Chiefs of Staff remarked, damningly, that even if the requirements for forces and other assets were met the proposed operations 'considered in themselves are not militarily sound'.[35] Third, *Avonmouth*, *Stratford* and *Plymouth* would be separate but interdependent operations, and it was highly desirable that they should be simultaneous.[36] *Stratford*, the operation projected for central Norway, could be carried out before *Avonmouth*, but on no account should *Avonmouth* precede *Stratford*.[37] Fourth, militarily, central Norway was of vital importance whilst north Norway was of marginal significance.[38] Moreover, in order to have any prospect of success the Allies must preempt the arrival of German forces, particularly at Sola (the airfield near

Stavanger) and at Trondheim. But there was a distinct possibility that Allied operations would be anticipated by the Germans. In that case the expeditionary forces would attract devastating attacks by the Luftwaffe in the early stages.[39]

The politicians set all this sound advice aside. Operations were planned despite the absolute refusal of the Scandinavians to co-operate or contemplate the friendly reception of uninvited help.[40] The plans were revived, in a hasty and improvised manner, despite the lack of necessary resources.[41]

In April 1940 Chamberlain was persuaded to favour active operations in Scandinavia. He was strongly attracted by the notion of a strategic plan based on economic factors, and the project for action in Scandinavia was based on an intention to interrupt the supply of iron ore to Germany from Gallivare in northern Sweden.[42] Although dismayed by the necessity for war, the Prime Minister was convinced that Hitler had to be defeated and removed.[43] In addition, he was concerned by the state of popular opinion and civilian morale: people in Britain were becoming bored and discontented with the combination of hardship and inactivity.[44] Finally, he was stung by Reynaud's sharp criticisms of the apparent passivity of Allied strategic policy.[45] Once Chamberlain had been won over, the opponents of offensive action in Scandinavia in the War Cabinet, such as the Foreign Secretary, Lord Halifax, were overwhelmed.[46] With Churchill triumphant and Chamberlain acquiescent, the War Cabinet authorised offensive operations: *Wilfred*, a scheme to mine the Norwegian leads, and R4, the plan to send expeditionary forces to Norway to pre-empt any German attempt at invasion.[47]

The actual conduct of the operations in Norway was also subject to distortion by political interference. Halifax remarked that the War Cabinet tended to neglect its proper sphere of the grand strategic issues and take refuge in consideration of operational details.[48] The CIGS complained that the politicians insisted on exercising control, but were too ignorant, hesitant and divided to do so effectively.[49]

Alarmed by British activity in Norwegian waters, on 9 April the Germans mounted Operation *Weserubung*, the protection of Norway against a projected British invasion. At once, the War Cabinet insisted on giving absolute priority to operations in north Norway, the primary objective from the economic point of view.[50] On 14 April they changed their minds, and assigned priority to central Norway.[51] But the shift in emphasis was too late, and plan R4 was doomed to failure. The operations in the Narvik area culminated in the first Allied victory, and inflicted a great humiliation on General Dietl's German Mountain

Corps. However, in the overall context of the theatre it was immaterial and, because central Norway had been neglected, north Norway was lost. The War Cabinet had failed to apply the nineteenth-century Swiss military theorist Jomini's fundamental principle of war, concentrate the main effort at the decisive point, and this guaranteed a defeat in Norway.[52]

Corporate autism

The weaknesses of the institutions and structure for planning and command also allowed freedom of action, almost absolute liberty, to the armed forces. Each of these was inclined to pursue its own interest with considerable indifference regarding others' interests. Butler remarked that there was no mechanism 'to ensure the mutual understanding between the services'.[53] According to 'Pug' Ismay, Churchill's close adviser, 'The Chief of Naval Staff and Chief of Imperial General Staff acted with sturdy independence...appointing their respective commanders without consultation,...and gave directives without harmonising them.'[54] In the words of the British official historian of the Norway campaign, T.K. Derry, 'directives came from an Admiralty which had a greater immediate interest in blockade measures, a War Office all too conscious of its heavy commitments in France, and an Air Ministry whose first concern was the Air Defence of Great Britain'.[55]

The Royal Navy did have an active interest in using the south Norwegian ports and denying them to the Germany Navy,[56] but its most compelling interest was in a general fleet action.[57] On 9 April reconnaissance reports indicated substantial German naval movements. These reports, which were of sightings of German vessels on their way to Norway, should have triggered plan R4. Two infantry brigades, 146 and 148, had been ready to move since 5 April, and were loaded on cruisers waiting to carry out the plan for *Stratford*. Instead, they were disembarked in a rapid and disruptive manner in order to free the cruisers, which then sailed off into the Atlantic hoping to intercept a naval breakout by the *Kriegsmarine*. This precipitate action compromised plan R4, and all chance of seizing Stavanger, Sola, Bergen and Trondheim was lost.[58]

On 14 April the War Cabinet issued orders for a direct attack on Trondheim. The Royal Navy resisted these orders on the grounds that there were German destroyers in the fjord and probably German garrisons in the coastal fortifications, which would make such an attack extremely hazardous. As the Navy was short of expendable old ships suitable for such an operation, the proposed assault was judged not to be a practicable operation.[59] The strategic plans were changed accordingly.

On 16 April orders were issued for a pincer movement on Trondheim by land forces to be put ashore north and south of the town.[60] The following day Royal Marines seized Aandalsnes, and a detachment moved inland to Dombås, where they helped some Norwegian troops to seize the railway junction from a force of German paratroopers.[61] Subsequently, the Royal Navy provided support for the land forces ashore in a number of ways. The most important of these were the provision of communications facilities for the rear link to London, some air cover from the Fleet Air Arm, Air Defence for the bases at Aandalsnes, Molde and Namsos, and, eventually evacuation.[62]

The British army had intended to send five battalions to the south of Norway, to make surprise landings at Bergen, Stavanger and Trondheim. The CIGS had wished to follow up these landings with two divisions, to consolidate inland. Subsequently, two brigades, one of them of French *Chasseurs Alpins*, were to have landed at Narvik.[63] In the event, all these plans were deranged, and the landing forces were diverted and delayed. 146 Brigade, originally earmarked to seize Bergen and Trondheim, was diverted towards Narvik, then sent back to land at Namsos, north of Trondheim.[64] 148 Brigade's orders were to go ashore at Stavanger, then proceed inland to seize the airfield at Sola. On the way this brigade was diverted towards Namsos, transhipped at sea, sent to disembark at Aandalsnes, ordered to advance via Dombås to Trondheim, but then directed to move south towards Lillehammer.[65] 146 Brigade was reinforced by a force of *Chasseurs Alpins*; 148 Brigade was followed up by 15 Brigade, to form Sickleforce.[66]

Once the British troops had landed, they ran into severe difficulties in attempting to co-ordinate their efforts with those of the Norwegians. There had been no staff talks or official contacts with the Norwegian forces because of Norway's adherence to the policy of strict neutrality.[67] Having been both surprised and shocked by the German invasion of 9 April, the Norwegian troops greeted the soldiers of 148 Brigade with relief, and evidently greatly overestimated the capabilities of this Territorial Army force.[68] Wishful thinking and desperation on the Norwegian side, combined with a lack of timely clear directions from London about command arrangements, led to catastrophe for 148 Brigade. The brigade commander, H. de R. Morgan, was sent orders from the War Office at 19.55 on 16 April. He was instructed to land at Aandalsnes, advance inland to seize the strategic railway junction at Dombås, then move northwards to attack the German force at Trondheim. Transport was to be obtained locally from the Norwegians. With regard to command, the orders stated: 'your force independent command under War Office until receipt further orders. Intention later place you under Commander General Operations Trondheim area.' The final paragraph stated: 'previous instruction re co-operation with Norwegians and reports to War Office unchanged'.[69]

In sum, Morgan was to act in support of the Norwegian forces rather than under their command. But the Norwegian Chief of Staff, General Ruge, assumed that the British reinforcements would be subject to his authority. On 18 April he signalled, via the Admiralty, 'I presume first troops now landed at Aandalsnes are at my disposal.'[70] Next day the difference of opinion was resolved by a meeting between Ruge and Morgan. Ruge insisted that the 148 Brigade must accept command by General Hvinden Hauge of the Second Division, or the Norwegian forces would cease their resistance to the German invasion at once. Morgan was under intense pressure, for British officials at the Norwegian HQ advised him that the Norwegians were exhausted and would cease firing unless he accepted Ruge's demand. Morgan signalled to the War Office for advice and support, but the only reply he got from the CIGS simply repeated his instruction to 'co-operate', which did not clarify the vital issue. In the face of Ruge's demands, and in the absence of support from his own seniors, Morgan gave way.[71] This concession sealed the fate of 148 Brigade. The two battalions were sent south, to reinforce Norwegian troops holding a defensive line based on the Lundehogda. They were divided up into detachments, the Sherwood Foresters being deployed on either side of Lake Mjosa. As the British soldiers approached the front, Norwegian troops withdrawing through them greeted them: 'Hello Tommy, thank you Tommy, goodbye Tommy'. The mixed force of Norwegian and British troops was insufficient to hold the Lundehogda position, and was pushed back. On 23 April, at Tretten, the 148 Brigade made a final stand; its positions were penetrated, outflanked and overrun, and it was reduced to a strength of 9 officers and 300 other ranks.[72]

The day before, General B.C.H. Paget had been appointed GOC Sickleforce, under the command of General Massy. Paget's orders addressed the question of command relations very specifically, stating: 'You will not be under the orders of the CinC Norwegian Army.' Indeed, on 26 April General Ruge put his troops under Paget's command. The Norwegian ski troops and artillery provided excellent support, even after Paget had informed Ruge of the decision to evacuate Sickleforce.[73]

Despite the great difficulties the army experienced over command relations with the Norwegians, co-operation was easier with them than it was with the RAF. The adverse air situation in Norway was of critical importance to the Allied failure in the centre and south. Persistent and almost unopposed attacks by the Luftwaffe wrecked the bases at Aandalsnes and Namsos, and degraded the mobility and morale of field units.[74] The Air Ministry and Air Staff had never shown any positive interest in operations in Scandinavia, which they believed would be hazardous and unprofitable. They felt that the proposed operations would be diversionary and contrary to the principles of the conservation and concentration of force, and were likely to distract attention from their own schemes for decisive attacks on the Ruhr and German oil plants. The Air Staff manifested a praetorian contempt for politicians, and resisted strong pressures to get involved in the operations in central Norway.[75] Eventually one squadron of Gloster Gladiators was sent to fly combat air patrol from a temporary base on Lake Lesjaskog. This embryonic station was immediately spotted and bombed out by the Luftwaffe. The RAF resisted proposals to co-ordinate plans with the Fleet Air Arm, and ignored urgent pleas from the British and Norwegian ground forces to mount attacks on Luftwaffe bases and German lines of communications in Norway.[76]

Communications

Throughout the campaign in central Norway communications were generally unreliable and poor. Most signals between the UK and Norway were passed by Royal Navy ships, some by a wireless set removed from the British Embassy in Oslo when the diplomatic staff fled before the German invaders. In the interior of Norway field units had to use the civil telephone system, which was suspected of being infiltrated by quislings. The only available methods within units were despatch riders and runners. These technical and human limitations made co-ordination very difficult, and above battalion level it was almost impossible to concert action swiftly. Within battalions companies were often cut off from their headquarters for considerable lengths of time, and there were many cases of failure to deliver orders of critical importance.[77] The lack of regular and reliable communications not only prevented effective co-ordination down to a low level, but also created a sense of isolation, anxiety and demoralisation amongst the troops.[78]

Personalities

Personalities also had important effects on the fate of the Allied expedition to Norway. Strong characters, such as Churchill, Reynaud and

Ruge, disrupted the planning process and the conduct of operations. The main incidents of their agency have already been mentioned. The absence of key personalities, caused by accidents, also took effect. The first nominated commander of Sickleforce, General Hotblack, suffered a seizure on 18 April. His successor, Brigadier Berney-Ficklin, was hurt in an air crash *en route* to Norway. These accidents deprived Sickleforce of an overall commander for days at a time when hours were important.[79]

The Allied military performance in central Norway was mixed, but overall it was ragged and ineffective. Failures of command and co-ordination were important to the outcome of the Allied operations. Defective command structures were compounded by the coalition nature of the war and Clausewitzian friction. French and British politicians paid scant regard to sensible and realistic advice from the military. Strong personalities placed their stamp on the planning and execution of strategy. In sum, political, structural, conceptual, technical, personal and accidental factors contributed to the Scandinavian disaster of 1940.

Notes

1 A. Vagts, *Landing Operations* (Harrisburg, PA: 1946) p.597; F. Kersaudy, *Norway 1940* (London, 1990) p.93; Ismay, *The Memoirs of General The Lord Ismay* (London: 1960) p.109; J. Mcleod and R. Kelly (eds), *The Ironside Diaries* (London: 1962) pp.189–90; J.R.M. Butler, *Grand Strategy*, Vol. II (London: 1957) p.129.
2 C. von Clausewitz, *On War*, edited by M. Howard and P. Paret (Princeton, NJ: 1989) pp.119–21.
3 Vagts, *Landing Operations*, p.597; Butler, *Grand Strategy*, p.108; AMC DF No. 72, JPC CAB 84/10; COS(40)2 33(JP)(S) CAB 80/104; MO1 Note, JP(40) 48(S) WO193/772; all in Public Record Office, London (hereafter PRO).
4 Butler, *Grand Strategy*, p.129.
5 Ismay, *Memoirs*, p.109.
6 S.W. Roskill, *Hankey, Man of Secrets*, Vol. II (London: 1974) p.450; T.K. Derry, *The Campaign in Norway* (London: 1952) p.59.
7 Derry, *Campaign*, pp.59, 237; K. Feiling, *The Life of Neville Chamberlain* (London: 1946) p.435; Butler, *Grand Strategy*, p.130; Ismay, *Memoirs*, p.111.
8 Kersaudy, *Norway 1940*, p.93; Derry, *Campaign*, p.59.
9 Mcleod and Kelly, *Ironside Diaries*, pp.189–91, 209, 213, 218, 221, 224, 227; Note on WP(40)100, WO 193/772, PRO.
10 JP(40)82(S) (COS(40)268(JP)(S) CAB 84/11, PRO.
11 J. Colville, *The Fringes of Power, Downing Street Diaries 1939–55* (London: 1985) p.108; Ismay, *Memoirs*, 110,122; WP(40)111 CAB 66/6, PRO.
12 Ismay, *Memoirs*, p.111; Butler, *Grand Strategy*, p.131.
13 JP(40) 29(S); JP(40)39(S) CAB 84/10; JP(40)80; JP(40)81(S) CAB 84/11, PRO.
14 Annexe to JP(40) 12; JP(40) 15(S) (COS(40) 214(JP)(S) JP(40) 6(40) 194(JP) CAB84/10; JP(40) 81(S) CAB 84/11; DDMO and P to DSD; CIGs to AQ, QMG and PUS; SWC Decision, in DMO Collation, WO193/773; COS Directive,

30 March 1940, COS(40) 281(S) (WP(40)122) in DMO COS Reports WO106/5732, PRO.
15. 13 May 1940, Despatch of Lt-General H.R.S. Massy, C-in-C Central Norway, in supplement to *London Gazette* of 29 May 1946.
16. COS(40)281(S) (WP(40)122) in WO 106/5732, PRO.
17. Vagts, *Landing Operations*, p.597.
18. Feiling, *Chamberlain*, pp.424–6; McLeod and Kelly, *Ironside Diaries*, p.236; Colville, *Fringes of Power*, pp.92,197; Butler, *Grand Strategy*, p.121.
19. Colville, *Fringes of Power*, p.37; WP(40)109 CAB 66/6.
20. Templewood, *Nine Troubled Years* (London: 1964) pp.426, 430–1.
21. Butler, *Grand Strategy*, p.121; P Reynaud, *In the Thick of the Fight 1930–45* (London: 1955) pp.258–9; WM(40)70; CAB 65/6; WP(40)109, CAB 66/6, PRO.
22. Kersaudy, *Norway 1940*, pp.53–4; Derry, *Campaign*, p.81; Reynaud, *Thick of the Fight*, pp.264, 268; WP(40) 109, CAB 66/6, PRO.
23. COS(40)233 (JR) (S); COS(40)241(S) (WP(40)53) CAB 80/104; AIR 36/39: PRO.
24. JP(40)81(S) Note, CAB 84/11, PRO.
25. Colville, *Fringes of Power*, pp.102, 104, 105; Ismay, *Memoirs*, pp.116, 159, 163.
26. Colville, *Fringes of Power*, pp.58, 60.
27. Ibid., p.125; WM(40)5th concs, CAB 65/5, PRO.
28. Colville, *Fringes of Power*, p.70; Ismay, *Memoirs*, p.122; Mcleod and Kelly, *Ironside Diaries*, pp.194, 196, 222, 228; Templewood, *Troubled Years*, p.427; S.W. Roskill, *Churchill and the Admirals* (London: 1977) pp.93–4.
29. Butler, *Grand Strategy*, pp.130, 150; Mcleod and Kelly, *Ironside Diaries*, p.192.
30. JP(40) 19(S) (COS(40)216(S) CAB 84/10, PRO.
31. WP(40)111, CAB 66/6, PRO.
32. MO1 note of 21 Feb 1940, No. 193/772; JP(40)61, CAB 84/11, PRO.
33. COS(40)283(JP)(S); COS(40)262(S) (WP(40)90) CAB 80/104; JP(40)88(S) Revised Draft CAB 84/11, PRO.
34. Annexe, JP(40)12; JP(40)15(S) COS(40)214(JP)(S) JP(40)6(40)194(JP), CAB 84/10, PRO.
35. COS(40)215 CAB 80/104, PRO.
36. COS (40) 215 CAB 80/104; JP(40)12, Note, CAB 84/10, PRO.
37. COS(40)256(S) (WP(40)78), CAB 80/104; JP(40)82 (S) COS(40)268(JP)(S) CAB 84/11; ISPS 26th, WO.166/1972 DMO Instructions, WO 106/183, PRO.
38. MC(40)30 (COS(39)168) CAB 83/2; JP(40)49(S) (COS(40)254(JP(S)) CAB 84/11; COS(40)262(S) (WP(40)90) CAB 80/104; JP(40)95(S) (COS(40)285 (JP)(S)) CAB 84/12, PRO.
39. Mcleod and Kelly, *Ironside Diaries*, pp.192, 194–5; JP(40)34(S) (COS(40)242 (JP)(S); JP(40)40(S) (COS(40)243(JP)(S)) CAB 84/10; DMO Collection, WO 193/772, PRO.
40. Butler, *Grand Strategy*, 108, 112; Mcleod and Kelly, *Ironside Diaries*, p.225; WP(40)103, CAB 66/6; WO Note on WPC(40)100, WO 193/772, PRO.
41. JP(40)81 (S); DDMO and P to DSD; CIGS to AQ, QMG and PUS; WO 193/773, PRO.
42. COS(40)271(S) CAB 80/105, PRO; Feiling, *Chamberlain*, p.428.
43. Feiling, *Chamberlain*, p.428; Colville, *Fringes of Power*, pp.34–5.

44 Feiling, *Chamberlain*, pp.424, 426; Colville, *Fringes of Power*, p.92; Templewood, *Troubled Years*, pp.430–1; Butler, *Grand Strategy*, p.117.
45 Mcleod and Kelly, *Ironside Diaries*, p.236, Butler, *Grand Strategy*, pp.117, 121, 123–4; WP(40)109, CAB 66/6, PRO.
46 Colville, *Fringes of Power*, pp.96, 108; WP(40)107, CAB 66/6 WM(40)70th, CAB 65/6; WM(40)50th, CAB 65/5, PRO.
47 JP(40)81(S) CAB 84/11, PRO.
48 Note on WP(40)100, DMO Collation, WO 193/772, PRO.
49 Mcleod and Kelly, *Ironside Diaries*, pp.189, 221.
50 M(40) 87th, 88th, 89th, CAB 65/12, PRO.
51 14 April 1940, Admiralty to General Mackesy and Brigadier Phillips, DMO Sickleforce plans, WO 106/1897, PRO.
52 A.-H. Jomini, *The Art of War* (London: 1971) pp.70–1.
53 Butler, *Grand Strategy*, p.131.
54 Ismay, *Memoirs*, p.111.
55 Derry, *Campaign*, p.80.
56 Lord Strabolgi, *Narvik and After* (London: 1946) pp.18–19, 30–1; Derry, *Campaign*, pp.10–11; Roskill, *Churchill and the Admirals*, pp.93–4.
57 Ibid., p.99.
58 Note on COS(40)205(JP)(S), WO 193/773; JP(40)61, CAB 84/11; COS Directive, WO 106/5732; G.S. Short Appreciation, WO 106/1831; Naval Staff History, No.106/1959; PRO.
59 13 April 1940, CIGS Memo, Operations, Trondheim Area, 18 April 1940; DMO and P, to HQ, Force Hammer, plan of operations; WO 106/1895; undated, proposals for combined operations against Trondheim, WO 106/1815; 1945, Naval Staff, Battle Summary No. 17; WO 101/1959 WM(40) 198 Min 3 CAB 65/12; MC(40)81, CAB 83/5 NC(40)80 CAB 83/3, PRO.
60 Admiralty to Mackesy and Phillips, DM6, Sickleforce plans, WO 106/1897, PRO.
61 Interviews with Mr Sveen, Major H.B. Dowson, Sound Archive, Imperial War Museum (hereafter IWM); W.K. Laing, 'Account of Experiences in Norway in the 8th Foresters', 77/54/1; Department of Documents, IWM.
62 1943 Naval Staff, Battle Summary No.17 WO 106/1959, PRO.
63 JP(40)82(S) COS(80)268(JP)(S) CAB 84/11, ISPS 26th WO 166/1972; MO2 to WC, Note on WP(40)115, 116 DMO collation, WO 193/1773, PRO.
64 WO Administrative History of Operations in Scandinavia, No 198/17; ISPS, 29th, WO106/1972; ISPS, Meeting, 24 April 1940, WO 106/5848; Narrative of Events on Namsos Front, WO106/1815; CIGS Instructions for Carton de Wiart, 14 April 1940, WO106/1831; 14 April 1940, 18.00, Admiralty to Mackesy and Phillips, WO106/1897, PRO.
65 Colonel E.G.C. Beckwith 'The 8th Battalion of the Sherwood Forresters, TA, Campaign in Norway, April 1940' (unpublished paper); Major A.H. Dowson, 'Account of the Activities of the 8th Forresters between leaving Shildon, Co Durham, on Saturday 6 April and returning to Clydebank on Tuesday 7 May 1940' (unpublished paper); L.G.J. Sheppard, 'The Royal Leicestershire Regiment in Norway 1940' (unpublished paper); interviews with RQMS L.G.J. Sheppard, Major J.G. Shields, Major B.H. Dowson, Lieutenant H.B. Dolphin, Corporal A.C. Carter, Private S. Barthorpe, Sound Archive, IWM.

66 WO Administrative History of Operations in Scandinavia, WO 198/17; 3 May 1940, Narrative of Events on Namsos Front, WO 106/1815 Hq NWEF ORBATS, WO 198/1; HQNWEF, Sickleforce Narrative of Operations of 15 Infantry Brigade, 22 April–2 May 1940 WO 198/11.
67 London, PRO, 14 May 1940, Draft Letter, HMG to Norwegian Minister in London, WO 106/1959; WO Administrative History of Operations in Scandinavia, 1940, WO 198/17, PRO.
68 W.K. Laing, 77/54/1, Documents Department, IWM; Beckwith, 'The 8th Battalion'.
69 WO to Brigadier Morgan, sent 1955, 16 April 1940, WO 106/1939, PRO.
70 18 April 1940, Norwegian HQ to Admiralty, WO 106/1939, PRO.
71 19 April 1940, SICKLE to WO; 19 April 1940, MI6 to MI2(b); 20.30, 20 April 1940, WO to Sickleforce; WO 106/1916; 02.29, 22 April 1940, Morgan to WO, WO 106/1854, PRO; Dowson, 'Account of', Documents Department, IWM; Interviews, Dowson, Dolphin, Sound Archive, IWM.
72 Supplement to the *London Gazette*, 29 May 1946; L.G.J. Sheppard, interview, 8773/6, Dept of Sound Records, Imperial War Museum; Beckwith, 'The 8th Battalion'; Dowson, 'Account of the Activities'; Laing, 77/54/1, Documents Department, IWM.
73 Supplement to *London Gazette*, 29 May 1946; General Paget, Report on the Operations of Sickleforce in Norway 25 April–1 May 1940; General Sir Cameron Nicholson, Personal Account of the Operations of Sickleforce, in Nicholson papers, DS/MISC/7, Documents Department, IWM.
74 WO Administrative History of Operations in Scandinavia 1940, WO 198/17; 13.38, 23 April 1940, Carton de Wiart to CIGS; 17.16, 25 April 1940, Sickle to WO; 07.10, 20 April 1940, Paget to Massy; 20.45, 20 April 1940, Massy to Paget, WO 106/1916, PRO; Interviews; Brigadier A.W. Vickers, Colonel A.D. Mackenzie, Sound Archive, IWM.
75 Colville, *Fringes of Power*, p.93; Templewood, *Troubled Years*, p.426; JP(40)12, CAB 84/10; WP(40)111 CAB 66/6; 7 October 1939, DAP to CAS; 12 April 1940, DDAP to DAP; DAP to CAS; undated, unsigned, memo 'Restriction of Offensive Air Operations', AIR 8/292, PRO.
76 J.L. Moulton, *The Norwegian Campaign of 1940* (London: 1976, p.208); COS(40)100M, WO 106/5732; 14 May 1940, Draft Letter, HMG to Norwegian Minister in London, WO 106/1939; Air Component, NWEF, Review of Campaign in Norway, AIR 36/39; 27 April 1940, Discussion of Telegram from Paget; WO 106/5732, PRO.
77 5 May 1940, Lt-Col. Royal Signals, Report, Signals Communications, Paget Force; WO 198/11, PRO; General notes on Norwegian Campaign, Cass papers, 87/28/1; Laing, 77/54/1; Nicholson, Personal Account; Paget, Report; Nicholson papers, DS/MISC/7, all Documents Department, IWM.
78 Interviews, RQMS Sheppard; Lieutenant Dolphin; Private Barthorpe; Corporal Carter; Lance-Corporal Cowling; Sergeant Ryalls, Sound Archive, IWM.
79 17 April 1940, WO Instructions for Hotblack; 10 April 1940, WO Instructions for Berney-Ficklin; Supplement to *London Gazette* of 29 May 1946, PRO.

6
The Very Model of a Modern Manoeuvrist General: William Slim and the Exercise of High Command in Burma

Duncan Anderson

In the bar of the old Army Staff College at Camberley the portraits of Britain's two greatest army commanders of the Second World War once hung directly opposite each other: Montgomery in his black beret faced Slim in his bush hat. Neither commander would have considered the honour at all appropriate. Montgomery was *British* Army and Slim was *Indian* Army; Montgomery was the son of a bishop and Slim the son of a failed Birmingham ironmonger. Montgomery had gone to Sandhurst and Slim, in 1914 a clerk in a metal tubing factory, had been commissioned only because of service in the Territorial Force. And, as Slim himself was only too aware, when in 1947 Montgomery relinquished the post of Chief of the Imperial General Staff (CIGS), he did all in his power to prevent Slim becoming his successor.

The proximity of the portraits also seemed to suggest that, like Montgomery, Slim was one of Camberley's chosen sons. This impression was so convincing that officers today are sometimes surprised to learn that only eighteen months before the war the 47-year-old Slim was still a major at a time when many of his Indian army contemporaries had made full colonel, several had become brigadiers, and two were close to promotion to major-general. Although later writers have attempted to impose an inevitability upon Slim's progression from major (February 1938) to lieutenant-general (February 1942) in just four years, it is clear that in 1938 Slim was not regarded as a 'high flyer'.

Montgomery (were he still alive) would have been mortified by a visit to the mess of the new Joint Services Command and Staff College (JSCSC) at Bracknell. There, hanging alone, is Slim's portrait: for, as

Montgomery's reputation has declined, Slim's has risen steadily. On the surface this reversal of fortunes seems extraordinary. When Montgomery won at Alamein, Slim was known only as a corps commander who had led (many said mishandled) the longest retreat in British military history. When Montgomery broke the Mareth Line, Slim was being blamed for the disastrous First Arakan campaign. And when Montgomery set up his headquarters in Normandy, Slim was trying to fend off criticism of his handling of the Kohima–Imphal battle, which the CIGS still thought might end in disaster. Yet with the passing of the years it is Slim who is now deemed the very embodiment of military virtue, the general whose 'mask of command' never slipped. Always calm in a crisis, his subtle, flexible intelligence allowed him to extract the best from his subordinates and his superiors, to read battles and outwit his enemies. He has become the very model of a modern manoeuverist general.[1]

Slim's reputation has not always seemed so unassailable. So rapid was his rise that at times he found himself, at least initially, out of his depth: some contemporary criticism of his conduct was indeed justified. Inevitably he made enemies. Montgomery's resentment toward him emerged only after 1945 (he had little to do with Slim during the war itself). Far more troublesome was the hostility displayed by Slim's immediate superiors, which bedevilled his exercise of high command. Both the Commander-in-Chief (C-in-C), Wavell, and Slim's corps commander, Quinlan, were deeply ambivalent about his performance at brigade and divisional level in Ethiopia and in the Middle East between the autumn of 1940 and the spring of 1942. His command of a corps in the retreat from Burma (March–May 1942) for a time convinced Auchinleck, the new C-in-C India, that Slim had peaked at divisional level.[2] This opinion was shared by Alexander, Slim's commander during the retreat,[3] and by the commander of British Eastern Army, General Noel Irwin.[4] In the spring of 1943, Irwin regarded Slim's handling of the latter stages of the First Arakan campaign as so inept that he attempted to have him sacked. Six months later the commander of the 11th Army Group, General George Giffard, was sufficiently unsure of Slim's abilities at the highest levels that he attempted to block his promotion to army command. And in May 1945 the new commander of 11th Army Group, General Sir Oliver Leese, convinced that Slim lacked the ability to command the complex amphibious operations that the reconquest of south-east Asia would require, sacked him from command of Fourteenth Army. Slim was variously described as 'conventional', 'slow', 'a bellyacher', and 'a megalomaniac'. Moreover, he had 'a chip on his shoulder', he 'was not straight', and was 'a twister'.[5]

Slim will be compared with Haig, Jellicoe, Beatty and Harris. Like these men, Slim, too, had his critics, and his career often hung by a thread. The difference between Slim and the others is that Slim's critics were wrong. At Sandhurst, British Army officer cadets are presented with a list of qualities embodying the desirable attributes in a leader. Such a list can (up to a point) also be formulated for high command. There are certain prerequisites which will allow an officer in certain circumstances to perform effectively in high command, and if he does not have these it is unlikely he will succeed. Part of Slim's success was due to luck: he was almost as lucky as Harold Alexander. But, as Slim made clear in a famous lecture given to the US Army Staff College in 1952,[6] a general can be lucky once or twice (for example, Harold Alexander's near miraculous escape from Rangoon in March 1942); an unbroken chain of 'luck' suggests something more. Slim was not simply lucky: he also possessed the physical, psychological and intellectual attributes which allowed him to excel in the conditions posed by the Burma theatre between 1942 and 1945.

A degree of physical robustness is obviously desirable for an air or naval commander, just as it was for a 'chateau general' on the Western Front during the First World War, but it is not absolutely essential. Such robustness was, however, a crucial possession for a land force commander facing the Japanese in the Asia–Pacific theatres between 1941 and 1945. In the Philippines the 61-year-old Douglas MacArthur, suffering from massive hernias, was rarely able to surface from something akin to a catatonic trance during the First Philippine campaign. In Singapore Arthur Percival and Lewis Heath quickly succumbed to heat exhaustion in the stifling confines of Fort Canning during the first two weeks of February 1942. And in Burma Hutton, painfully injured in an air crash in December 1941, decided to apply for sick leave as he lost control of the campaign, and thereby effectively ended his career.

Slim was different. He was built and looked like a middle-weight boxer[7] and his basically sound constitution, coupled with extraordinary stamina, enabled him to cope with the debilitating effects of three war wounds, the last received as recently as January 1941, and two of the chronic conditions common in male middle age, haemorrhoids and prostate trouble. These conditions could sometimes make travelling by jeep over corrugated roads, or landing in an aircraft on a bumpy strip, nothing short of excruciating. Like every other soldier in Burma, Slim suffered occasional bouts of 'Delhi belly' (acute bouts of dysentery) and, at a particularly inconvenient time at the end of the Imphal–Kohima battle, a severe bout of malaria. In fact, during the Second Arakan and Imphal–Kohima battles Slim was afflicted successively by dysentry, malaria and prostate trouble, the latter requiring his hospitalisation in August 1944.

Most men with physical ailments of this sort would have taken to their bunks, but there were many times when Slim simply could not. He was constantly on the move, flying between widely separated subordinate and superior headquarters. By one rough calculation during 1944 he spent one week in every five airborne, often flying in atrocious conditions. Accidents were frequent – that which killed Wingate on 25 March 1944 was in no way exceptional – and there was always the prospect of an encounter with enemy aircraft or groundfire. Attempting to fly to Rangoon on 29 April 1945, for example, Slim's Dakota took heavy flak, and was just able to make it back to an emergency airfield near Pegu, where doctors saved the life of a severely wounded member of Slim's staff by amputating his leg.

When operations were not going well Slim at times had to go without sleep for 50 hours or more (for example, the crisis at the outset of the second Chindit operation) but he tried not to make shortage of sleep a habit. He knew that he had to conserve his energy, and did so by following the carefully regulated regime of the Indian Army. Except when beset by a crisis his day started at 06.00, with a long break – often more than three hours – from midday to mid-afternoon, followed by work and then bed at 22.00. This was his routine, his aides having strict instructions not to wake him unless there was an emergency. Like Montgomery,[8] and unlike Leese, Ritchie, Cunningham, Mountbatten and many younger men, Slim saw himself as a runner in a very long race: he knew he would need to pace himself in order to finish.

Though he often felt tired and washed-out, Slim never appeared exhausted. He looked tough and pugnacious – just the sort of man one would like to have on one's side in a fight – and his physical appearance proved to be a considerable asset in his exercise of high command. Slim became a corps commander at the very point at which generals in all armies, even those of Germany and Japan, were increasingly expected to behave towards their men like politicians campaigning with constituents. One not only had to look the part but one also had to be able to communicate in a way which most generals of the First World War would have found impossible.[9] Years of writing short stories for money had given Slim the ability to reduce complex ideas to their basic essentials. He had also been a schoolteacher and knew something about holding the attention of an audience. In addition, his accent was virtually classless (much more Mountbatten than Montgomery) with only a slight flatness of some vowels betraying his humble Birmingham origins.

Unlike Percival in Malaya, whose first and only foray into mass communication was a disastrous press conference on 7 February 1942, and who then responded to a worsening crisis by cutting himself off from his men in the fastness of Fort Canning, Slim invariably made for the closest front-line formation, knowing his presence would have the effect of both calming and stimulating troops. And, also unlike Percival, he could address them not just in English, but in Hindi, Urdu, Ghurkali and Pushtu.

A robust constitution and a gift for communication would have fitted Slim for many occupations, including that of politician, but neither were of themselves sufficient to explain success in high command. Slim had also undergone a thorough intellectual preparation, in part thanks to his years as Indian Army DS at Camberley and his time at the Imperial Defence College, but even more due to his private immersion in military history. All successful generals share this trait: they are voracious readers of campaign histories and military biography, and most could themselves have been successful writers and academics had they chosen a different career path. Slim's library was not as extensive as those of Archibald Wavell or Douglas MacArthur, but for a major it was impressive enough. Slim managed to take his profession seriously; he deepened and broadened his knowledge without being ostracised by his mess as a 'military shit', the fate that befell many intellectual officers in the 1920s and 1930s.

None of these attributes, of course, was unique to Slim. They were shared to a great extent by officers such as 'Punch' Cowan, Bruce Scott, 'Pete' Rees and hundreds more in the British and Indian armies. Slim was a little luckier than most. Just fourteen months before his first appointment to corps command Slim discovered that he had not yet developed what was later to be called the 'mask of command',[10] the ability to exude confidence and appear calm when everything is going to blazes. The great majority of officers who later excelled in high command in the First and Second World Wars usually had some experience of catastrophic military failure, often as battalion commanders. Slim was already a brigadier when he managed to mishandle his first battle as a formation commander: the attack on Gallabat on 10 November 1940. He was to write a disarmingly honest account of the battle, but not until 1958, when he was Field Marshal Sir William Slim, the governor-general of Australia.[11] The key lesson he learned from this battle was not, as he claimed in 1958, the necessity always to be bold, but rather the necessity always to keep his emotions under control. There was nothing particularly original about this – several generations of British public schoolboys had been exhorted to do exactly the same thing by their headmasters and by Henty, Masefield, Kipling and dozens more – but knowing it and experiencing it were two entirely different things. When the 1st Essex cracked at Gallabat, Slim also cracked. Rushing into the path of the headlong flight, he grappled with soldiers and then, grabbing hold of the battalion commander, he punched him to the ground.

Gallabat became a running sore in Slim's future relationship with officers of the Essex Regiment, but the battle had taken place far enough south of Cairo and east of Khartoum for nobody who mattered to have noticed. In this respect Slim was far more fortunate than Ritchie and Cunningham in the Western Desert, Percival, Heath and Lloyd in Malaya, Hutton in Burma, Fredendall in Tunisia, and a host of others. From his arrival in Burma in March 1942 until the fall of Rangoon in May 1945, all commentators on Slim, even his worst enemies, remarked on his iron self-control in the midst of crises. Two instances out of the dozens available will suffice. On 30 April 1942 Slim's corps headquarters (HQ) received reports that the Japanese had occupied the western bank of the Chindwin opposite Monywa, thus blocking the route by which Slim intended to withdraw. During the preceding six weeks he had been constantly on the move between subordinate HQs and he was very tired, yet all those present affirm that Slim was quite unshaken by the news. He studied his maps, quickly assessed the implications of the Japanese thrust, and within fifteen minutes had issued orders to restore the situation.

What is perhaps the best known incident occurred on the night of 5–6 March 1944, when Slim was visiting Wingate's HQ for the launch of Operation Thursday.[12] The arrival, late in the afternoon, of aerial reconnaissance photographs showing one of the three landing grounds blocked by logs, threw the highly-strung Wingate into a panic. He now demanded the cancellation of the operation, contending it would be murder to fly the Chindits into the obstructed landing grounds. Slim's assessment was much less pessimistic – he felt it was probably Burmese loggers – and he overruled Wingate's objections. The worst moment came in the small hours of 6 March, when a signal arrived (incorrect, as it turned out) that the Chindits had indeed flown into an ambush. Wingate's staff officers, watching Slim's reaction, had nothing but praise. For example, Colonel Claude Rome, Brigadier Calvert's second in command, recalled that: 'Slim was a tower of strength – absolutely calm, absolutely in the picture and worth a guinea a minute to the staff whose nerves became badly shaken as they realised how badly astray some of the gliders were going.'[13] A constant theme in Slim's postwar lectures and writings is that the failure of a commander in his first battle should not be judged too harshly; all must be given a chance to learn from mistakes, just as Slim had so evidently done.

The British Army contained many men who were physically fit, intelligent and professionally well read, who could inspire confidence in others and who did not flap in a crisis, and yet who could never have been effective in high command. In his postwar writings and lectures Slim poured scorn on the 'first person singular generals – the I's',[14] who failed to acknowledge that their success (or failure) was in large part due to the quality of the collective brain they had at their disposal in their headquarters. Slim knew that all headquarters reflect the personality and prejudices of the man at the top. George Giffard's 11th Army Group HQ, for example, was very Indian Army, with all the strengths and all the infuriating delays which that term implies. When Oliver Leese took over in October 1944, and its name changed to HQ Allied Land Forces South East Asia (ALFSEA), it was quickly transformed into an Eighth Army-cum-London District club, where the atmosphere was a little like that of the Eton prefects' common room. Mountbatten's South East Asia Command (SEAC) HQ at Kandy resembled a cross between an oriental court and a 1920s open-house party (open, that is, to socially well-connected 'bright young things'),[15] where Lord Louis, presiding over frenetic but sometimes pointless activity, conducted seminars in which visiting professors, political advisers, admirals and generals all shouted at each other. The environment was intellectually stimulating but the staff work was frequently abysmal. Mountbatten's chief of staff, General Pownall, confided to his diary:

> The Staff machine is creaking along. I suppose someday it will become really efficient but it certainly isn't now... we have among the British *no* really trained staff officers. There is I think not one PSC [Passed Staff College] below the rank of Major General. So the most absurd and annoying mistakes are made and I have to do a lot of hunting myself.[16]

Slim felt his way towards creating an effective HQ. Like everyone else he had quirks: he insisted on clean desks at the end of the day and burning all documents which were no longer of immediate relevance (sensible precautions in a theatre in which a HQ might have to move very quickly). He also decided very early against the appointment of a chief of staff. This was in part because he did not want to place a barrier between himself and other members of his staff, with whom he wished to deal individually, in part because he was loath to create an overmighty subject like, for example, MacArthur's Richard Sutherland, the 'lord chamberlain of the South West Pacific'. At best a chief of staff was unnecessary, at worst he could inhibit the free flow of information. And if the information did not flow freely a headquarters could never be successful because Slim had also decided that the key to an effective organisation lay not in elaborate wiring diagrams but in the fostering of a co-operative and intellectually creative culture. Within the headquarters Slim would not tolerate a 'need to know' mentality except for the most sensitive information. All headquarters function as brains, but in Fourteenth Army HQ this was to be true in more senses than one.

Slim also railed against 'travelling circuses', army commanders who carried their staff with them whenever they moved. His particular hate figure was Oliver Leese, who had brought virtually his entire Eighth Army staff with him when he took over HQ ALFSEA in Barrackapore at the end of 1944, and had then set about sacking every Indian Army officer above the rank of major, but Montgomery, MacArthur and many others were just as guilty. It was Slim's boast that he had never succumbed to cronyism of this sort, preferring instead to use the staff he found in position.

Slim's sentiments were laudable, but it is very easy to show that Slim, too, had a ring, at the core of which was a group of Gurkha officers who had served with him in the Middle East, in Burcorps, IV Corps, and finally in Fourteenth Army. The difference between Slim, and Leese and Montgomery, was that his officers were often contemporaries, or close contemporaries; they were men of whom Slim had the measure and whom he could trust implicitly. These were officers who could go to Slim informally after a meeting and say 'Bill, I think you're making a howling cock of such and such.' The mind boggles when trying to imagine Montgomery or MacArthur in such a situation.

Slim's HQ was dominated by Gurkha officers, men with decades of experience of soldiering in difficult environments. It was inclined to be clannish, a tendency which increased markedly once Leese took over 11th Army Group HQ. In a letter to his wife Leese wrote of an early meeting with Slim: 'I said how glad I was to come to his great XIV Army. He showed no signs of wanting to see me!'[17] Leese's Eighth Army officers visiting HQ Fourteenth Army soon discovered that if they wanted to eat they had to bring their own rations. And only three weeks after Leese had arrived at Barrackapore outside Calcutta Slim moved HQ Fourteenth Army from Comilla to Imphal, increasing the distance between himself and Leese from 200 to 400 miles.

Slim's HQ could respond very self-protectively towards those it perceived as alien predators, but it could be welcoming to officers of other services who were clearly fighting the same battle. The most notable achievement was the co-location of the HQs of Baldwin's 3rd Tactical Air Force and Brigadier General Old's American and British Troop Carrier Command with Fourteenth Army HQ at Comilla. In *Defeat into Victory*, Slim wrote: 'We pooled intelligence resources, our planners worked together, and, perhaps most effective of all, the three commanders and their principal staff officers lived in the same mess.'[18] This was a true air–land headquarters, and doubtless would have become properly tri-service if Slim had been nearer the sea.

Of all British Army wartime HQs, Fourteenth Army's seems to have come closest to operating as what would today be called a 'think tank'. Commander's conferences were not unlike postgraduate university seminars, with Slim as chairman, guiding but not dominating discussion. His technique was to say very little until the end, when he would summarise the discussion, analysing the strengths and weaknesses of the various arguments. He welcomed disagreement, even when he felt the arguments were unsound; the only thing he would not tolerate was mindless, sycophantic agreement with his point of view. Anthony Brett James, who attended one of these conferences, felt that Slim in action was as good as the very best of Oxford dons. Under Slim, then, HQ Fourteenth Army became a collective brain, capable of creative responses to apparently intractable problems. The decision to switch from Operation Capital to Extended Capital, for example, involved an elaborate deception operation and a massive movement of men and vehicles, as an entire corps crossed over the lines of communication of another corps, and began an advance on a new axis. It did not spring fully formed from Slim's brain, but was rather the product of the collective headquarters' brain, with Slim as controller. The move, which involved an immense amount of staff work, was completed in just two weeks, an achievement which the headquarters of Manstein or Patton would have had difficulty matching.

How did this brain communicate its intentions to the rest of the Army? Much is written today about Slim's employment of 'mission command' as distinct from *Befehlstaktik*, which a general such as Montgomery employed, at least in part because *Defeat into Victory* contains one of the most concise descriptions of mission command yet penned. Slim encouraged his corps and divisional commanders:

> to act more on their own; they were given greater latitude to work out their own plans to achieve what they knew was the Army

Commander's intention. In time they developed to a marked degree a flexibility of mind and a firmness of decision that enabled them to act swiftly to take advantage of sudden information or changing circumstances without reference to their superiors.[19]

It is precisely this approach to which all would-be manoeuvrists aspire, but Slim's description requires two caveats. First, 'mission command' was the only means of conducting operations over the great distances of the Burma theatre: Montgomery's fronts were rarely more than 100 miles while Slim's were rarely less than 1,000. Second, despite the fact that Slim had known his corps and divisional commanders for a fairly long time, his frequent flights around battlefields are a clear indication of his willingness to intervene. Slim knew his commanders' strengths, and he also knew their weaknesses. Scoones would never move fast enough and thus Slim spent time prodding him. By contrast, Messervy would move too fast, taking too many risks. Slim sought to control Messervy by imposing on him as chief of staff a level-headed sapper, Brigadier Cobb. When Messervy protested against this imposition Slim signalled famously, 'NO COBB NO CORPS'.

It would be wrong to portray Slim and his corps commanders as a happy band of brothers. Problems in the conduct of the Imphal–Kohima battle led Slim to relegate Scoones to the backwater of Central India Command, and to lasting bitterness, at least on the part of Scoones. During the dash for Rangoon Stopford avoided a similar fate when he was able to convince a furious Slim that complaints emanating from his headquarters about the unfair distribution of logistic support had been made without his authorisation. And Christison was deeply unhappy that Slim appointed him to command Twelfth Army, the force destined to garrison Burma, when Leese had promised him Fourteenth Army, the formation which was to reconquer south-east Asia. When he had to be, Slim could be a bastard, but he always did his own dirty work, consistently refusing to pass the unpleasant jobs on to junior officers.

Slim encountered greater problems when dealing with other commands, namely Wingate's Chindits and Stilwell's Sino–American forces in the north east. Both Wingate and Stilwell were for operational purposes technically subordinate to Slim, but both had powerful external sources of support. Of the two, Wingate was by far the more difficult. Slim and Wingate had entirely different personalities. Slim, a Catholic who had lapsed into atheism, instinctively distrusted Wingate, a member of the fundamentalist Plymouth Brethren, who pressed his theories of airmobile assault as though they were revelations from the Almighty.

He treated Slim as his logistics officer, made increasingly heavy demands for men, material, and air transport, and threatened, when Slim failed to respond with sufficient enthusiasm, to appeal directly to Churchill, a right the prime minister had conferred on him at the Quebec conference in 1943. Displaying great moral courage (since in a showdown Churchill would certainly have backed Wingate rather than the commander of Fourteenth Army), Slim called Wingate's bluff, refusing to weaken Fourteenth Army to support an operation he regarded as inherently unsound. Relations with Stilwell proved easier. Slim and the notoriously anglophobic American had taken each other's measure during the retreat, and Stilwell had been outraged when the British publicity machine gave Alexander the credit for the successful extraction of Burcorps. In addition, Stilwell knew that Slim and he were fighting the same war, unlike British HQs in Calcutta, Delhi and Kandy, which saw campaigns in northern and central Burma as diversions from the amphibious operations which were to reconquer the colonies of southeast Asia. For his part, Slim was very conscious that he was at the cutting edge of an alliance which was under considerable strain, and he always made a point of affording Stilwell every assistance possible. Slim was very aware that Stilwell could always play his 'China card', which would allow him to syphen off American transport aircraft to support the armies of Chiang Kai Shek. To a very large extent Slim and Stilwell's relationship was the product of a happy coincidence of interest, but it is also clear they liked each other. Slim found Stilwell's violent anglophobia amusing rather than offensive, and he half-suspected Stilwell put much of it on for the benefit of the Chinese.

Slim had much greater problems with his own superior headquarters, HQ Eastern Army in 1942 and 1943, and HQ ALFSEA in 1944–5. Slim's three political crises (the first after the retreat from Burma, the second after the First Arakan, and the third after the recapture of Rangoon) involved cabals of senior British army officers attempting to engineer his removal. General Noel Irwin, an officer of the Essex Regiment, was the genius behind efforts to ensure that Slim received the blame for the loss of Burma and for the disaster of the First Arakan. The ostensible reason behind Oliver Leese's attempt to sack Slim two years later was that he was a tired and sick man, though in truth Leese was trying to create space for all his London District friends who would shortly be arriving from Europe. This effort received support from Irwin, and from a now-embittered Scoones. Slim saw off all three attempts by maintaining links with Auchinleck, C-in-C India, and by cultivating (in a sometimes quite shameless fashion) Lord Louis Mountbatten, the supremo of the new

SEAC. It is often not appreciated that Slim's brilliant Meiktila–Mandalay operation, and the subsequent dash for Rangoon, was fought against the background of intense internecine strife between HQ Fourteenth Army and HQ ALFSEA, with Slim moving further and further into Burma to escape from his army group commander. On 17 March, for example, with the fall of Mandalay imminent, Leese flew to Monywa to set up a tactical HQ next to Fourteenth Army HQ, only to discover that Slim had already flown south to Meiktila. In *Defeat into Victory* Slim projected an image of himself as a simple fighting soldier, naive in the politics of high command, an image which continues to be accepted. His protestations to the contrary, it is clear that Slim was an extremely skilled political soldier; so skilled, indeed, that he was rarely surprised by his enemies.

There were times when Slim failed, but failure is a relative term. It is fairer to put the question not in terms of success or failure, but in terms of what he could have done better. The first area is that of logistics, but not in the way that most people expect. Slim's own experiences and his HQ system made him peculiarly susceptible to the anxieties of his logisticians, to the extent that he delayed the counterattack in Second Arakan and delayed the flight of reinforcement into Imphal, in both cases because logisticians doubted their ability to sustain additional front-line forces. The result was an unbalancing of his forces, and the possibility of a strategic defeat. In Meiktila–Mandalay he brushed his logisticians' objections to one side and succeeded, but only because of near superhuman efforts by the transport squadrons.

This leads naturally to the second area in which there could have been an improvement. Co-location of air and ground headquarters seemed an excellent idea, but it led inevitably to the higher echelons of the air force being cut out of the command chain. The general opinion was that this led to greater efficiency, but it also removed one of the important functions of higher headquarters, which is the protection of their assets from abuse. Because the airmen and soldiers of Fourteenth Army had become close friends, it proved very difficult for the airmen to resist the ever-increasing calls of the Army. As a result aircraft were flown to destruction, accidents were frequent, and casualties were heavy. Baldwin and Old could have appealed to Park and Stratameyer, but they were emotionally incapable of doing so.

Air transport was not the only element which was virtually destroyed. Slim's anxiety to remain on the best possible terms with Stilwell led him virtually to hand over the Chindits to Stilwell after Wingate's death, which force Stilwell proceeded to destroy in frontal attacks on Myitkina. It is difficult to avoid the conclusion that Slim's apparent lack of concern sprang, at least in part, from his conviction that Special Forces of this sort were useless.

For all the creative brilliance of Fourteenth Army HQ there was one area in which it was chronically weak, and that was in operational intelligence. In contrast to the tens of thousands of fluent speakers of German who crammed the intelligence units of 21st Army Group, as late as 1944 there were only about 200 intelligence personnel fully fluent in Japanese. The volume of radio traffic could be ascertained, but it was usually anybody's guess as to what the Japanese might be saying. Slim saw the creation of a strategic reconnaissance force as a solution, and after the war became a vociferous advocate for the re-establishment of the Special Air Service (SAS).

Most of these criticisms were made by Slim himself in his own account of the Burma campaign, *Defeat into Victory*, probably the most self-revealing analysis ever written of the experience of high command. *Defeat into Victory* is rightly regarded as one of the finest works on military history produced in the twentieth century. But Slim was not aiming merely to provide an historical record: this work was designed as a guide to high command for future generations, and hence an element of fictionality is involved in the self-portraiture. Slim's confession of his many weaknesses is balanced by his claims to certain military virtues, some of which he did not in fact possess. He portrayed himself as a simple fighting soldier, uninterested in the political machinations of superior headquarters, when in fact he was one of the toughest political in-fighters the British military system has ever produced. As one Fourteenth Army staff officer admiringly recorded 'He always won.' He claimed he refused to cultivate a Slim 'gang', when in fact he supported (and was supported by) one of the most tightly-knit rings to emerge during the Second World War. And he wrote convincingly of the need to confer the greatest possible independence upon subordinate commanders, when in reality he controlled their activities in a manner not too dissimilar from that of Montgomery and the corps and divisional commanders of Eighth Army.

The most severe criticism that can ultimately be levelled at Slim is that he did not always practise what he preached. *Defeat into Victory* upheld an abstract ideal of high command, an ideal to which its author always aspired, even if in reality (as the evidence amply proves) he sometimes fell short. If his reputation were to rest solely on his handling of the retreat in 1942 he would be remembered as a twentieth-century Sir John Moore. If, conversely, his reputation were to rest on the retreat and Second Arakan and Imphal–Kohima he would now be remembered as a calm and tenacious general, excellent in positional attritional warfare; a commander who would certainly have been able to fight the same sort of battle Wellington fought at Waterloo or Montgomery fought at Alam Halfa. But one must also consider the Meiktila–Mandalay operation (Operation Extended Capital), and this places Slim in an altogether different category.

It is true that at the beginning of 1945 Fourteenth Army enjoyed many advantages. It was at last operating in the flat broad plains of central Burma, possessed total superiority in air and armour, and was facing an enemy which had been reduced to the technology of 1915; the Japanese either used rail communication or they marched. Operation Extended Capital was launched in very favourable circumstances, but a number of things could have gone terribly wrong. Let us for a moment play the ever popular counterfactual game and place Mountbatten's headquarters, which was then planning Operation Zipper, in charge of Extended Capital. Staff work at Kandy left much to be desired, and an unavoidable consequence of poor staff work would have been a breakdown in the logistic chain. It would not have taken very much to have brought the mechanised columns to a grinding halt in the midst of still resolute Japanese infantry; even with lavish air support it is likely that some of the British columns would have been defeated in detail. Compartmentalisation was also rife at Kandy, with different segments of the headquarters hoarding information as squirrels hoard nuts: such an environment would have inhibited the production of accurate and timely operational intelligence. It is more than likely that a headquarters so organised would have directed assaults across the Irrawaddy on to Japanese strongpoints rather than those areas held by the hapless Indian National Army, so that the campaign would have been characterised by a series of small-scale Dieppes along the southern banks of the mile-wide river. It is also possible that such a headquarters, unable to read the developing battle clearly, would have decided that Mandalay rather than Meiktila was the centre of gravity, and thereby condemned Fourteenth Army to months of bitter attrition, fought on terms very much favourable to the Japanese. There was, in short, nothing inevitable about the triumph of Fourteenth Army. That none of these things happened was in large part due to the generalship of William Slim, and the creative, co-operative culture he had fostered within the headquarters of Fourteenth Army. Slim, then, can be taken as the very model of a modern manoeuvrist general; there is none better.

Notes

1. See the biographies by Ronald Lewin, *Slim: The Standardbearer* (London: 1976) and Lieutenant-General Sir Geoffrey Evans, *Slim as Military Commander* (London: 1969).
2. John Connell, *Auchinleck* (London: 1959) p. 196.
3. It is noticeable that Slim receives no mention in Alexander's autobiography; John North (ed.), *The Alexander Memoirs 1940–45* (London: 1972).
4. Louis Allen, *Burma: The Longest War 1941–45* (London: 1984) pp.94–7.
5. Rowland Ryder, *Oliver Leese* (London: 1987) especially pp.243, 247, 251.
6. Reprinted as 'Higher Command in War', *Military Review*, Vol. LXX, No. 5 (May 1990), pp.10–21.
7. See George MacDonald Fraser, *Quartered Safe Out Here* (London: 1992) pp.35–7. This quotation summarises Slim's leadership qualities from the point of view of a young British infantryman.
8. Ronald Lewin, *Montgomery as Military Commander* (London: 1971) p.267.
9. Michael Howard, 'Leadership in the British Army in the Second World War: Some Personal Observations', in G.D. Sheffield (ed.), *Leadership and Command: The Anglo-American Military Experience since 1861* (London: 1997) pp.117–27.
10. John Keegan, *The Mask of Command* (London: 1987).
11. Sir William Slim, *Unofficial History* (London: 1959).
12. Views on Wingate are strongly polarised. For assessments that favour Wingate and are critical of Slim, see John W. Gordon, 'Wingate', in John Keegan (ed.), *Churchill's Generals* (London: 1991) and David Rooney, 'Command and Leadership in the Chindit Campaigns', in Sheffield, *Leadership and Command*.
13. Michael Calvert, *Prisoners of Hope* (London: 1952) p.29.
14. See Slim, 'Higher Command', p.10.
15. Philip Ziegler, *Mountbatten* (London: 1985) pp.278–80.
16. Brian Bond (ed.), *Chief of Staff: The Diaries of Lieutenant-General Sir Henry Pownall*, Vol. II (London: 1974) pp.127–8.
17. Ryder, *Oliver Leese*, p.203.
18. Slim, *Defeat into Victory* (London: 1962 edn) p.183.
19. Slim, *Defeat into Victory*, pp.450–1.

7
The Art of Manoeuvre at the Operational Level of War: Lieutenant-General W.J. Slim and Fourteenth Army, 1944–45

*Robert Lyman**

> Slim was not a great captain of war by any means. At a time when warfare was changing very rapidly, he was responsible for no great innovations in tactical method or strategic thought. Nor, unlike Wavell, was he quick to pick on any new means for outwitting the enemy. For example, he never liked to use special forces... His deployment of troops was sound but rarely brilliant.[1]

Michael Calvert's assessment of Slim's performance at the head of the victorious Fourteenth Army could scarcely be more tendentious, not the least because it accords with no other critical evaluation of Slim's military achievements in Burma. Calvert, a protégé of Wingate in the two Chindit expeditions of 1943 and 1944, no doubt had his own axe to grind. Duncan Anderson, by contrast, places Slim 'in the same class as Guderian, Manstein and Patton as an offensive commander'.[2] But even Calvert was prepared to accede one accolade to Slim, describing the capture of Meiktila in 1945 as bearing 'the mark of genius'.[3] Calvert was right about this if nothing else: through dint of Fourteenth Army's remarkable defeat of the Japanese in Burma in 1945 it can be argued that Slim did indeed reach the epitome of military virtue.

The British Army is concerned – now more than at any previous time in its history – to define the conceptual component of fighting power, and in so doing it has largely rejected the attritional approach to warfighting adopted by Montgomery and the postwar British Army.[4] Yet in adopting this approach the British Army has paradoxically tended to retain Montgomery of Alamein as its inspiration, and has not sought to develop as models for future practice those commanders in the Second World War who adopted the 'manoeuvrist' approach to their conduct of war. The paramount example, and by far the most successful commander of this type, was 'Bill' Slim.

This chapter will argue that although very much more a practitioner of war than a military theorist, Slim's experience of command in war provides a particularly apposite model for the modern British Army. In Burma between 1944 and 1945 he taught, practised and fought a style of warfighting to which the British Army now aspires. Slim was not uncomfortable with ideas and doctrine, however. As any reader of *Defeat into Victory* must acknowledge, Slim was 'a subtle, articulate and clever man'.[5] To his peers before the war, despite the vagaries of peacetime promotion, he was already a man apart. Archibald Nye, a fellow instructor at the Staff College at Camberley with Slim in the 1930s, 'rated him as probably the best all round officer of his rank in the Imperial Army...The point about him was that he had an outstandingly clear mind, a very keen intellect and moved in a careful, logical way towards his problems.'[6] But Slim's intellectual energies as Fourteenth Army commander were expended not on cerebral activity for its own sake or solely for the purposes of military doctrine, but on devising clear and simple strategies for defeating the Japanese.

Modern British military doctrine is built on the 'manoeuvrist approach' to warfighting. Although Slim would not have recognised the term, his exercise of command in Fourteenth Army indicates clearly that he espoused all of its fundamental characteristics. 'Manoeuvre' is defined as 'the means of concentrating force to achieve surprise, psychological shock, physical momentum and moral dominance... [A]t the operational level, manoeuvre involves more than just movement; it requires an attitude of mind which seeks to do nothing less than unhinge the entire basis of the enemy's operational plan.'[7] The 'manoeuvrist approach', therefore, is designed to be 'an approach to operations in which shattering the enemy's overall cohesion and will to fight is paramount. It calls for an attitude of mind in which doing the unexpected, using initiative and seeking originality is combined with a ruthless determination to succeed.'[8] It is, moreover, the antithesis to a strategy of attrition which, as Thomas asserts, is characterised:

> by a direct confrontation with the enemy mass, in an attempt to erode his strength to the point where he no longer has the physical wherewithal to continue the contest ... Manoeuvre warfare, in contrast, is an

expression of the 'indirect approach' and has connotations of cunning, subtlety and military sophistication. It is aimed at undermining the enemy's mental strengths and, in particular, his will to win.

Thomas concludes: '[E]ven if it is difficult to define manoeuvre warfare precisely, it is easier to identify what it is not. It is certainly not an unthinking approach that seeks to pit strength against strength in a fair fight. In essence it involves fighting "clever" and within the accepted rules of warfare – fighting "dirty"!'[9]

In October 1943, seventeen months after the British withdrawal from Burma, Lieutenant-General William Slim was appointed to command the newly raised Fourteenth Army, whose responsibility it was to confront and defeat the Japanese in Burma.[10] The omens for British success in Burma, however, were not good and Slim's appointment did not appear to offer any radical solution to the problem of how to restore British fortunes in the Far East. Slim had, to that date, won no victories, was relatively unknown outside the rather insular circles of the Indian Army, had been dismissed as second-rate by some of his military superiors and had in fact been party to successive British defeats in the field since the retreat from Burma in early 1942.[11] What is more, he now commanded an army that had been comprehensively and regularly beaten in two years of bitter experience at the hands of the Japanese. On the face of it, and to the uninformed observer, Mountbatten's appointment of Slim to command the renamed Eastern Army could hardly have seemed more ominous.

However, it was a decisive move that would very quickly provide a handsome return for Mountbatten's investment. Within five months Slim had halted and destroyed a Japanese army of 100,000 that had invaded India to destroy Slim's army on the Imphal Plain. By the end of 1944 his forces were on the offensive and were crossing the Chindwin, and by March 1945 the formidable 250,000 strong Japanese defence of the Irrawaddy shore was crumbling as the consequence of an operation described by General Kimura as the 'masterstroke of allied strategy'.[12] By May 1945 Slim was the proud possessor of a hastily vacated Rangoon, a city whose loss in early 1942, together with Singapore, epitomised every failure in British prewar south-east Asian strategy. In so doing Slim had not only defeated a formidable opponent but had overcome the most extraordinary of physical obstacles. It is for these reasons that Mountbatten believed him to be 'the finest general the Second World War produced'.[13]

It is the contention of this chapter that Slim exemplified the manoeuvrist approach at the operational level of war perhaps more clearly than any other successful army commander in the British Army during the Second World War.[14] Modern British military doctrine provides a number of characteristics of manoeuvre warfare together with a list of command style and leadership skills required of a manoeuvrist commander. These were met, in whole or in substantial part, by Slim's command of Fourteenth Army in Burma. This chapter will examine Slim's credentials as a manoeuvrist commander on the basis of his performance in the campaigns of 1944 and 1945. He will be judged against the characteristics of manoeuvre warfare provided by *Army Doctrine Publication (ADP) Operations* and the requirements of a manoeuvrist commander as laid down in *British Military Doctrine (BMD)*.[15]

The joint environment

The first characteristic of manoeuvre warfare listed by *BMD* is that it is *joint*; that is, it combines the resources of all elements of combat power – air, sea and land as appropriate – in the planning and conduct of operations.[16] The maritime dimension necessarily played only a minor part in the conduct of operations in eastern India and Burma between 1942 and 1945. However, there were several occasions, not least when Slim commanded XV Corps between June 1942 and May 1943, when he successfully integrated maritime operations into his concept of operations for both the defence of the north-east Indian coastline and in planning for offensive operations in Arakan.

In the overall context of the Burma campaign, however, it was the air dimension that was of critical importance. Part of Calvert's criticism of Slim was that 'though he could have achieved nothing... without air supply, he was slow to put his whole trust in it'.[17] This criticism, however, is wholly gratuitous. No significant account of the campaign, including *Defeat into Victory* itself, fails to recognise the centrality to Slim's plan of command of the air. A truer judgement, perhaps, of Slim's appreciation of air power is provided by Slim's own air commander, Air Marshal Sir John Baldwin, who commented that 'Slim was quicker to grasp the potentialities and value of air support in the jungles of Burma than most Air Force officers. Particularly did he understand what the air required and was always ready to understand their difficulties and limitations.'[18] The potential worth of air supply was not a new concept for Slim. During the inter-war years, following his time as a student at the Indian Army Staff College at Quetta, Slim 'was credited with initiating early attempts at air supply on the North West Frontier'.[19]

Arguably the most decisive element in the whole air power equation was the successful employment by the allies of air transport to overcome the enormous problems posed by the poor ground lines of communication in India and Burma. Despite limited payloads, atrocious terrain and weather conditions, the effect of Japanese interdiction and limited range, transport aircraft provided Fourteenth Army in Assam, then Arakan and subsequently in Burma with the means to continue fighting when the physical constraints of terrain prevented re-supply by land. In fact without air supply victory could not have been achieved in Burma. Whilst in 1942 the Japanese held overwhelming command of the air, this situation had entirely reversed by early 1944.[20]

The long battles for Imphal and Kohima in 1944 demonstrate how essential the aerial dimension of warfare was to Slim's plans. From 18 April to 30 June 1944, some 12,550 reinforcements and 18,800 tons of supplies were delivered to Imphal and about 13,000 sick and wounded and some 43,000 non-combatants were evacuated. The success of the airlift was made possible only by allied air superiority, which enabled transport aircraft to be used with relative safety close to the enemy.

Slim described air transport to be Fourteenth Army's distinctive contribution 'towards a new kind of warfare'.[21] This alone gives the lie to Calvert's charge. Slim was also entirely dependent upon air supply for both the conduct of the Chindit operations in 1944 and for Operation Extended Capital, Fourteenth Army's remarkably successful crossing of the Irrawaddy River and the surprise seizure of Meiktila in March 1945. 'The second Chindit expedition in March 1944, when we landed some thirty thousand men and five thousand animals far behind the enemy's lines and maintained them for months, was the largest airborne operation of the war' wrote Slim. 'The decisive stroke at Meiktila and the advance on Rangoon were examples of a new technique that combined mechanised and air-transported brigades in the same divisions. To us, all this was as normal as moving or maintaining troops by railway or road.' Throughout the entire campaign, he wrote:

> [The Fourteenth Army] had proved right in our reliance on the air forces ... first to gain control of the air, and then to supply, transport, and support us. The campaign had been an air one, as well as a land one. Without the victory of the air forces there would have been no victory for the army.[22]

There was no doubt that 'Ours was a joint land and air war; its result, as much a victory for the air forces as for the army.'[23]

Strength against weakness

The second characteristic of manoeuvre listed by *BMD* is that manoeuvre aims to apply strength, in the form of combat power, against weakness, rather than against strength.[24] As Thomas asserts, manoeuvre warfare 'espouses above all the need to attack the will and cohesion of the enemy, by all means available. Wherever possible this should be achieved by exploiting weaknesses, rather than confronting strength and thus defeating the enemy in the most efficient manner and on the most favourable terms.'[25] Rather than attacking the enemy's strength *directly*, manoeuvre warfare seeks to attack an enemy's weaknesses. Thomas argues helpfully that manoeuvre warfare is best regarded as a collection of activities (such as attacking weakness, getting inside the enemy's decision cycle, and so forth) 'which seek to "loosen the bonds" of the enemy cohesion... a collection of ideas which, if taken together, amount to a manifestation of the indirect approach'.[26]

Operation Extended Capital exemplified the concept of the indirect approach at the operational level of war. The foundations for Slim's successful defeat of the Japanese can be found in his experience of operations against the Japanese during the retreat in 1942 as well as during the ill-fated Arakan offensive later that year. In the latter operation Wavell tasked elements of Slim's XV Corps, under the direct command of Lieutenant-General Noel Irwin, the Army commander, to recapture the Arakan Peninsula, particularly Akyab with its strategic airfields. The operation began in December 1942 but very quickly came to a standstill. The first of a series of setbacks for the British occurred at Donbaik, where part of a Japanese battalion, protected in mutually supporting bunkers, held off for 50 days, 'attack after attack by massed battalions of the 14th Indian Division'. Japanese defensive strength lay in the tenacity of their defence and their ability to dig virtually impregnable bunkers. Allen describes the latter as 'basically a pill-box using natural materials' which was able to:

> hold up to twenty men... The revetment is built of logs and earth up to five feet thick, and the roof is secure from bombing and shelling. Many bunkers survived even direct hits from bombs and shells, and were so sited as to give crossfire from one bunker to another... It was defences of this kind which brought [the] offensive to a halt, not once but time after time.[27]

The Japanese position had the sea on one side and the jungle-clad hills of the Mayu peninsula on the other, and it resisted all that

14th Indian Division could throw against it. Both Irwin and the divisional commander, Major-General Wilfred Lloyd, believed that a solution could be found by massing infantry for an assault on a narrow frontage, a technique which Slim considered disastrous when he visited the forward brigades in March 1943. Lloyd assured Slim that there was 'no other way' of attacking Donbaik. Slim argued that he believed Lloyd 'was making the error that most of us had made in 1942 in considering any jungle impenetrable and that it was worth making a great effort to get a brigade... along the spine of the ridge'.[28] Lloyd and his brigadiers disagreed, and in any case Slim had no operational control over them. The final attack on Donbaik took place on 18 March 1943 but ended disastrously. Slim wrote:

> 6 Brigade made a desperate attempt to break through the strengthened Japanese defences. Advancing again, straight in the open, over the dead of previous assaults, they got in among and even on top of the bunkers, but they could not break in... they were caught by the merciless Japanese counterbarrage and bloodily driven back... Donbaik remained impregnable.[29]

Many factors combined to bring about British failure in the Arakan. Wavell (the Commander-in-Chief India), Irwin and Slim listed low morale, limited resources, the high incidence of disease and the low standard of training and preparation evident in many units engaged in the operation. A principal reason was the fact that poorly-trained and inexperienced troops were thrown piecemeal against seasoned Japanese veterans, and that all units had displayed a lack of tactical flair or vision.[30] But perhaps the most fundamental failure was the lack of tactical flair and vision displayed by commanders at all levels, including Irwin and Lloyd. The fundamental lesson, learnt the hard way by Burma Corps during the retreat of 1942, and spelt out clearly by Slim, was that 'there should rarely be frontal attacks and never frontal attacks on narrow fronts. Attacks should follow hooks and come in from flank or rear, while pressure holds the enemy in front.'[31] The 'impenetrable jungle' had led British commanders, as it had during the retreat, to play into the hands of a well-entrenched enemy commanding extensive fields of fire. Slim had written of Burma Corps after the withdrawal: 'Tactically we had been completely outclassed. The Japanese could – and did – do many things that we could not.'[32] It was Slim's conduct of Operation Extended Capital that was finally to prove that, at the operational level, the British in Burma had learnt the fundamental lesson that strength, when applied against weakness, provided by far the greatest return on the investment of scarce military resources to achieve a desired objective.

Attacking the enemy, not ground

The third characteristic of manoeuvre is that 'the emphasis is on the defeat and disruption of the enemy rather than attempting to hold or take ground for its own sake'.[33] Throughout the campaign in India and Burma Slim's constant theme was the 'fundamental aim of destroying the enemy at the expense of all else'.[34] The focus of his effort was always 'on the enemy and not ground'.[35] Slim commented in this respect, regarding the battle for central Burma, that 'It was not Mandalay or Meiktila that we were after but the Japanese army, and that thought had to be firmly implanted in the mind of every man of the 14 Army.'[36] During the ill-fated Arakan operations in 1942 and 1943 both Wavell and Irwin's obsession with holding ground – the elongated Mayu Peninsula – led to 14th Indian Division becoming hopelessly stretched along an extended line of communication, in difficult country, ripe for the inevitable Japanese outflanking and encirclement.

Destroying the enemy's will

The fourth characteristic of manoeuvre is that it 'aims to defeat the enemy by destroying his will and desire to continue by seizing the initiative and applying constant and unacceptable pressure at the times and places that the enemy least expects'.[37] Operation Capital and, after it, Operation Extended Capital, were focused on persuading Kimura that he was faced by insurmountable odds precisely where he was most vulnerable. Slim's intent was to *persuade* his enemy that the battle was lost rather than *prove* it to him through the physical destruction of his army. It should be noted, nevertheless, that Slim recognised the necessity to *defeat* Kimura in battle: this required the physical destruction of the enemy. Slim did not confront Kimura with the bulk of his combat power in the teeth of the Japanese defence along the Irrawaddy to the north of Mandalay; rather, Slim's feint in the north and his bold attack in the south to seize Meiktila surprised and dislocated the enemy – at every level of command – so that the Japanese were forced to admit that the battle could not be won.

'It may necessitate all the phases of war'

The fifth characteristic of manoeuvre is that:

> it will invariably include elements of movement, application of firepower and positional defence. There will almost always be a requirement to fix the enemy, to deny him access to routes and objectives, and to secure vital ground and key points. The manoeuvrist should not be afraid to take up a defensive posture provided always that he never sees it as an end in itself, but for example as a preliminary to resuming the offensive or to regain balance.[38]

It follows therefore that a range of divergent methods may be legitimately employed in the pursuit of the mental dislocation of the enemy, which itself lies at the heart of 'manoeuvre' at the operational level of war. As Thomas asserts '[m]anoeuvre warfare does not imply warfare by movement alone. Firepower is integral to the concept and a degree of attrition is essential to its successful prosecution.'[39] Indeed, the use of attritional *means* to achieve manoeuvrist *ends* is an accepted theme in the literature of manoeuvre warfare.

Writing with the campaign in Asia against the Japanese in mind, Thomas argues that '[e]liminating the enemy's will to fight implies convincing him that resistance is futile, and forcing upon him acceptance of our superiority. The level of physical damage required to achieve this will depend upon the determination and sophistication of the enemy.'[40] The allies discovered that in Asia the application of overwhelming firepower was always necessary to 'knock the fight out of the Japanese'.[41] At Imphal Slim recognised that the mental dislocation of the enemy required first that they be decisively engaged in an attritional battle. This was the *means* which would bring about the enemy's physical destruction, so as to set the conditions for the eventual attack – the *ends* – by Fourteenth Army into Burma.

Momentum and tempo

Finally, 'significant features of manoeuvre are momentum and tempo, which in combination lead to shock action and surprise'.[42] Tempo is defined as the 'rate or rhythm relative to the enemy',[43] the aim of which is:

> to dislocate and unhinge the enemy by overloading his command and control system ... By moving faster mentally and physically than

the enemy we seek to cripple his ability to make meaningful and relevant decisions. The aim is to generate a series of problems for the enemy at a rate exceeding his capacity to solve them, thus getting into his decision cycle.[44]

Slim's achievement in this regard is clear. The pursuit of the Japanese forces retreating after Imphal–Kohima is clear evidence of Slim's ability to dictate the tempo of operations. He constantly acted to prevent the Japanese from organising an effective defensive plan, and in doing so denied the enemy an opportunity to recover. Similarly, of the high tempo of operations conducted by IV Corps in the pursuit to Rangoon following the capture of Meiktila, Lewin wrote:

> 4 Corps moved fast, using *blitzkrieg* techniques... Racing from bound to bound, one division in the lead at a time, the spearheads would seize an airstrip, an airborne battalion would fly in after the engineers had done their work, (airfield engineers were put to travel with the foremost tanks), and then the pattern would repeat, every 50 miles or less. Where well-defended strong points could be by-passed by the advancing armour, they were left for the following infantry to subdue. The emphasis throughout was on unbroken forward movement.[45]

A faster tempo relative to that of the enemy allowed Slim to dislocate the Japanese high command and so dominate the battlefield that the Japanese were unable to break his decision-making cycle. 'No sooner was a plan made to meet a given situation than, due to a fresh move by Slim, it was out-of-date before it could be executed', wrote Evans:

> and a new one had to be hurriedly prepared with a conglomeration of widely scattered units and formations. Because of the kaleidoscopic changes in the situation, breakdowns in communication and the fact that Burma Area Army Headquarters was often out of touch with reality, many of the attacks to restore the position were uncoordinated.[46]

Calmness in crisis

BMD establishes a number of broad characteristics required of a manoeuvrist commander. First, the commander 'must be able to operate successfully within confusion and disorder. Little will be predictable. Decisions will often need to be made on the basis of incomplete information. Much will then depend upon the nerve and instinctive feel of the commander.'[47] The ability of Slim to remain calm and seemingly unperturbed in the face of the most acute crises, and at times when military crises seemed relentless and insurmountable, was astonishing. 'Whatever his private fears', writes Michael Hickey, 'Slim never showed them in public.'[48] 'Rock-like and imperturbable, he never lost his temper', commented a senior staff officer, 'and when looking into the jungle of possibilities, he could disentangle the irrelevancies and select the vital one'.[49]

His calmness in crisis acted to highlight Slim's own extraordinary powers of leadership. He was a natural leader of men who possessed an ability to inspire men to do their utmost for the common cause. To most observers Slim personified his own definition of leadership (discussed below). James Lunt, who shared with Slim the experience of the withdrawal from Burma in 1942, regarded Slim as an equal to Oliver Cromwell. He listed his honesty, humour, 'unstuffiness' and humanity as his crowning characteristics.[50] Field Marshal Sir Claude Auchinleck remarked on Slim's 'quite outstanding determination and inability to admit defeat or the possibility of it: also the exceptional ability to gain and retain the confidence of those under him and with him, without any resort to panache. Success did not inflate him nor misfortune depress him.'[51]

The evidence from the 1942 retreat in this regard is unequivocal. Anderson remarks that Slim's appointment in 1942 acted on Burma Corps following his appointment during the dark days of March 1942 'like a tonic'.[52] But whilst his appointment undoubtedly enabled Burma Corps to extricate itself from Burma, his tired troops, lack of air support and insufficient resources of every kind could not halt the onward rush of the Japanese in 1942. Even Calvert magnanimously agrees that:

> Slim really never had a chance... The Burmese battalions had practically folded up, and could not be relied on. The three British battalions had taken the brunt of the fighting but only a few of the best men remained. The Indian battalions would hold together in defence but could not be trusted to attack after their best officers and NCOs [non-commissioned officers] had been killed. Even Slim's own Gurkhas started to crack under the strain of a 1,000-mile retreat.[53]

But dynamic leadership could at least ensure that the battered remnants of Burma Corps were able to withdraw to the comparative safety of India. Major-General Bruce Scott, a fellow Gurkha and the commander of 1st Burma Division during the Retreat, commented that: 'He immediately imposed his personality to the extent that we felt that someone behind had taken charge of us. Up to then we had been left to our own devices.'[54]

Slim was cheered by the survivors of his battered Corps when the long column reached Imphal. 'To be cheered by troops whom you have led to victory is grand and exhilarating', he wrote. 'To be cheered by the gaunt remnants of those whom you have led only in defeat, withdrawal, and disaster, is infinitely moving – and humbling.'[55] A significant feature of Slim's personal leadership evidenced during the campaign in India and Burma was his repeated emphasis upon the fact that his soldiers were 'the most important weapon in war'. Accordingly he regarded his primary task, when given command of Fourteenth Army in October 1943, to be that of rebuilding the fighting spirit of a defeated army. He defined morale as 'that intangible force which will move a whole group of men to give their last ounce to achieve something, without counting the cost to themselves'. Having a high level of morale will mean 'that every individual in a group will work – or fight – and, if needed, will give his last ounce of effort in its service'.[56]

Originality, verve and the indirect approach

BMD asserts that the commander 'must be able to think quickly and act in an original way, if the enemy are to be surprised and disrupted, before eventually being destroyed. Adopting an indirect approach and achieving rapidity of manoeuvre will nearly always be essential prerequisites for success.'[57] Slim believed implicitly in the veracity of the 'indirect approach': that is, he sought to defeat the Japanese through cunning rather than by the application of combat power against enemy strength through the vehicle of incremental attrition, as has been shown.

In this regard Norman Dixon notes that key ingredients in military incompetence have been a predilection for frontal assaults, often against the enemy's strongest point, a belief in brute force rather than the clever ruse, and a failure to make use of either surprise or deception.[58] In any case the material conditions in which the Fourteenth Army found itself whilst campaigning in Burma militated against any possibility of Slim ever being able to apply combat power against his opponents in anywhere near equal strength. Japanese combat power, whilst singularly less effective in terms of its physical component than the combined forces of South East Asia Command (SEAC) from mid-1944 until the end of the war, was nevertheless endowed in superabundance with moral vigour, such that a deficit of the former rarely made much difference to the latter. That the vast body of Japanese soldiery preferred death in battle to the shame of captivity testifies to the veracity of this fact.

This aside, Slim was not a commander who was temperamentally or professionally disposed towards an attritional, or confrontational, approach to warfighting, an approach he had eschewed from his earliest days of soldiering and which he had regarded with horror when he saw it applied by Irwin and Lloyd in Arakan in early 1943. An anecdote from Slim's early career pays testament to this. A sergeant-major, noticing Slim's perusal one day of the 'Principles of War' listed in a military manual, told him that: 'There's only one principle of war and that's this. Hit the other fellow, as quick as you can, and as hard as you can, where it hurts him most, when he ain't lookin'!'[59] Slim never forgot this simple lesson. Consequently, both deception and surprise were employed as the keynotes of Operation Extended Capital and acted decisively to attack the will of the enemy.

Knowing your enemy

The third requirement of a manoeuvrist commander is that 'he must study the mind and doctrine of an opponent'.[60] Slim's knowledge of the enemy was unparalleled. He fought the Japanese continuously from early 1942, at the start of the 1,000 mile retreat, until final and unequivocal victory had been achieved over three years later. He regarded a full and comprehensive knowledge of the enemy to be a vital prerequisite for any commander 'because battle is largely a struggle between the wills of the commanders'.[61] Despite strictures in this regard Slim's reliance on his knowledge of the enemy led him into complacency in his planning for Operation Capital. General Kimura, who proved to be very different from his predecessor, had replaced General Katamura, upon a knowledge of whom Slim had based his plan. As Slim admits: 'I relied on my knowledge of the Japanese and of the mentality of their high command as I had known it...I thought he would never dare to lose face by giving up territory without a struggle.'[62] Kimura, however, was prepared to move behind the Irrawaddy rather than defend forward of the river, thus forcing Slim to abandon his plan and seek to outflank him by attacking Meiktila rather than Mandalay.

Slim also recognised the fatal propensity so regularly evident in Japanese planning of inflexibly reinforcing failure, even when there was sufficient battlefield evidence to warrant changing a particular plan, and he ruthlessly exploited his knowledge of Japanese habits in this regard to his advantage. Bryan Perrett comments that by 1944:

> when deprived of the tactical initiative the Japanese were poor battle practitioners whose lack of flexibility was aggravated by a meagre communications network and a command system which failed to co-ordinate the activities of its units... once the Japanese had made a plan they stuck to it needlessly, being slaughtered in their bunkers and trenches by the more sophisticated and fully developed British infantry/tank tactics.[63]

It is interesting to see how, by 1944, the tables had been turned. Perrett's description of Japanese tactical and operational inflexibility also summarised many of the problems which bedevilled the British in their earlier encounters with the Japanese. That Fourteenth Army was able to develop the fighting skills necessary to overcome the Japanese was in large part due to Slim's success in training and motivating his army; but that is another story.

Slim's mastery of operational art

The fourth requirement of a manoeuvrist commander is that 'he must understand the operational level of conflict and the associated operational art'.[64] The operational level is the level of war that 'provides the vital connection between the military strategic objectives and the tactical employment of forces on the battlefield through the conception, planning and execution of major operations and campaigns'.[65] The nature of operational art lies in the skill the commander can bring to the allocation of military resources to meet the operational objective.[66] The characteristics of the operational level of war listed in *ADP Operations* include the need for a tangible and definable relationship with the military strategic objectives, the combined and joint nature of operations and finally, control over resources.[67] Slim's appreciation of the absolute necessity of joint operations is clearly evidenced from his use of air power. Additionally, he proved remarkably adept when it came to relations with allies, especially the Chinese and the Americans.

Dixon comments that, unusually for a senior commander, Slim 'was non-ethnocentric and therefore able to achieve the almost impossible... goal of maintaining a good relationship with his Chinese allies, however frustrating they may on occasion have been'.[68] His characteristic was an enormous advantage, for instance, in Slim's relations with the American general, 'Vinegar Joe' Stilwell, who possessed a notorious loathing of 'limeys'. It is noteworthy that Stilwell willingly subordinated himself to Slim but to no other British commander. Certainly it was a characteristic Slim held in common with many of his Indian Army colleagues, accustomed as they were by a lifetime of soldiering in India to living and dealing on a daily basis with a wide variety of races, not least those in the Indian Army itself. All those who knew Slim recall his fondness for his soldiers, particular his beloved Gurkhas.[69] Likewise Lieutenant-General Wheeler, Mountbatten's American deputy following the dismissal of Stilwell in 1944, commented that: 'General Slim inspired all of us with his competence and courage. He was regarded with particular admiration by all the Americans with whom he associated, and was frequently referred to by them as the American ideal of a great combat leader.'[70]

Slim blamed many of the failures of 1942 on the lack of a precise strategic objective. 'As a result', he wrote:

> our plans had to be based on a rather nebulous, short-term idea of holding ground – we were not even sure what ground or for what purpose... [A] realistic assessment of possibilities there and a firm, clear directive would have made a great deal of difference to us and to the way we fought. Burma was not the first, nor was it to be the last, campaign that had been launched on no very clear realisation of its political or military objects.[71]

Bitter experience in 1942 persuaded Slim that a clear strategic aim was essential if the main effort at the operational level was to be focused unambiguously on the task in hand, if the force was to be concentrated at the crucial point and if the most efficient and effective means available were used to achieve the task. Mountbatten as Supreme Commander SEAC provided Slim with the strategic direction he required to plan and conduct his campaign. These were themselves a product of strategic deliberations at the level of the British Joint Chiefs of Staff (in London) and the Allied Combined Chiefs of Staff (in Washington). 'My object', Slim wrote of Operation Capital, 'was to destroy the enemy's main forces in Central Burma. It was not the occupation of any particular place or area; that would follow automatically.'[72]

Slim's command style

At the heart of Slim's success as a commander lay his full intellectual and practical appreciation of the nature of 'manoeuvre' at the operational level of war, the essence of which was not just the physical dislocation of the Japanese Army but its mental dismemberment as well. This reality acts to highlight several distinct characteristics of his command style.

In the first instance Slim was, unlike the majority of British generals in command at army level in the Second World War, an exponent of Mission Command, although of course he would not have recognised it by that name. *BMD* argues that: 'Mission Command derives its strength and value from the intention to tell subordinates what to achieve and *why*, rather than what to do and *how*.'[73] Slim employed Mission Command over his widely dispersed forces, not simply because of geographical constraints but because he believed that his subordinate commanders could best achieve his requirements without him breathing down their necks whilst they were conducting operations. This was a lesson Slim had learned as a young officer.[74] 'Choose your subordinates and then, decentralise to them', he wrote.[75]

This imperative was the result not just of Slim's own character, but of the nature of campaigning in Burma. His troops were forced to fight:

> on a front of seven hundred miles, in four groups, separated by great distances, with no lateral communications between them and beyond tactical support of one another. My corps and divisions were called upon to act with at least as much freedom as armies and corps in other theatres. Commanders at all levels had to act more on their own; they were given greater latitude to work out their own plans to achieve what they knew was the Army Commander's intention. In time they developed to a marked degree a flexibility of mind and a firmness of decision that enabled them to act swiftly to take advantage of sudden information or changing circumstances without reference to their superiors. They were encouraged, as Stopford put it when congratulating Rees's 19th Division which had seized a chance to slip across the Irrawaddy and at the same time make a dart at Shwebo, to 'shoot a goal when the referee wasn't looking.' This acting without orders, in anticipation of orders, or without waiting for approval, yet always within the overall intention, must become second nature in any form of warfare where formations do not fight closely *en cadre*, and must go down to the smallest units. It requires in the higher command a corresponding flexibility of mind, confidence in its subordinates, and the power to make its intentions clear right through the force.[76]

'The exercise of initiative with pre-determined parameters established by mission analysis' comments Thomas, 'allows commanders to exploit fleeting opportunities in pursuit of the overall design for battle. The net result is to create conditions facilitating an increase in tempo to such a pitch that the enemy is overwhelmed and unable to respond effectively.' Likewise: 'Commanders possessing a clear understanding of their superior's intent and concept of operations enjoy a degree of immunity against the vicissitudes of combat and are more readily able to overcome the inevitable friction of war.'[77] Slim insisted on writing the intention part of every operation order that was promulgated under his signature. He wrote:

> It is usually the shortest of all paragraphs...but it is always the most important, because it states – or it should – just what the commander intends to achieve. It is the one overriding expression of will by which everything in the order and every action by every commander and soldier in the army must be dominated. It should, therefore, be worded by the commander himself.[78]

This was a procedure Slim had long followed, working out plans with his subordinate commanders but thenceforth leaving the implementation to them, 'remaining at hand...to help or advise and to take responsibility for any changes and decisions that had to be made if plans went awry'.[79] Geoffrey Evans, who had direct experience of Slim's style of command, commented that as a consequence of a long association with Slim through adversity, all his formations:

> had confidence in the Army Commander and themselves; they had been trained to meet any eventuality, to adapt their tactics according to the country...and to make the most of what was given to them; encouraged to use their initiative, they did so without fear. And such was Slim's confidence in them that once plans were made and orders issued, he left them to fight the battle in their own way, making himself and his staff always available to help. Starting with 14 Army Headquarters itself, he created an atmosphere of friendliness and co-operation within the whole Army.[80]

Slim's attitude to the creation and development of HQ staff merits some comment. Evans writes that:

> Unlike some generals who moved up the scale from one command to another, he did not believe in taking the cream of the staff officers with him, a practice which denuded junior formations of their staffs

and, through no fault of their own, turned out those of the next headquarters who had borne the burden of the heat of the day.[81]

Neither did Slim adopt the Chief of Staff system used in the Eighth Army, Evans asserting 'that he could better project his own personality in that way rather than through an intermediate officer'.[82]

Slim's style of command evidenced itself in the manner in which he ran his headquarters planning staff. His planning was consensual, a mixture of staff and command-led processes.[83] Lewin notes that Slim was 'neither Napoleonic nor egocentric in his approach. Disapproving of "soviets" or any hint of "government by committee" he was nevertheless a natural democrat, sparing no pains to elicit from his subordinates a full spectrum of opinions about any important problem.'[84] As Lewin points out, although the 'responsibility, and therefore the credit, for undertaking EXTENDED CAPITAL are Slim's...it would be wrong to maintain that the concept of the operation was uniquely his...the atmosphere at Slim's headquarters was one of collaborative discussion. He and his staff tossed ideas about.' Meiktila was a prime example of such joint thinking. Morris comments regarding this battle that:

> [much] depended on Slim's subordinates at every level, on their enterprise and quick-wittedness, and indeed on the military skills of his British and Indian soldiers. Thanks to them, the Japanese counterattacks failed with heavy loss, and the entire Japanese defence of central Burma collapsed. This, in my view, was the cleverest, boldest and most brilliant single British victory in World War II.[85]

Flexibility

Slim was a master of strategic flexibility. 'The speed and overwhelming success of 14 Army's advance from the Chindwin to Rangoon', writes the Official Historian, 'was largely due to the flexibility in planning, tactics and organisation shown by Slim and his commanders'.[86] Perrett comments that Slim 'had a gift of instinctively recognizing the strategic potential of a situation while it was actually developing, and this places him in the foremost rank of *Blitzkrieg* commanders'.[87] His approach to planning allowed him, only two weeks after the start of Operation Capital, to switch plans to Extended Capital when he became aware that the strategic intent of his first plan – to engage Kimura on the Shwebo plain – had come to nought. The decision to change plans from

Capital to Extended Capital was undoubtedly the crucial move of the campaign which, in the 'brilliance and speed with which Slim appreciated the new situation, changed his plan, and executed the new plan', concludes Sixsmith, 'deserved the praise which Kimura gave it in describing it as the "master stroke"'.[88]

Risk

Operational art requires a commander to apportion scarce resources in the most effective manner to achieve what *ADP Operations* describes as the two principles of war 'which require particular emphasis at the operational level': namely, concentration of force and economy of effort.[89] This obviously entails the acceptance of risk: the 'art' of command at the operational level clearly encompasses the ability to judge the risks confronting the decision accordingly. Slim was not a reckless commander, but one who took calculated risks only after a thorough evaluation of the likely consequences.

The primary examples of risk taking are fourfold. At Imphal Slim risked pulling his troops back to accept battle on the Imphal plain rather than in dispersed positions in the mountains west of the Chindwin. Mistaking the direction and intent of the Japanese attack would have spelt disaster. His first risk was an assumption of enemy intentions. He believed that the Japanese would seek to capture Fourteenth Army's supplies to fuel their 'march on Delhi' and in doing so he judged correctly that they would display overbold and inflexible – yet fanatical – measures. It was safe, therefore, to pull back his formations from their forward positions to defend the Imphal Plain. The second risk he took was in withdrawing 17th Indian Division from Tiddim, back to the Imphal plain, in sufficient time to prevent it being isolated by Japanese encirclement. Slim's third risk was in not defending Kohima against much more than the regiment that he expected. As it turned out this was one risk that nearly had fateful consequences for Fourteenth Army as the Kohima garrison, thinly manned by 1,500 troops, was eventually faced by a division of 15,000. The fourth risk was the decision to survive on air supply. This entailed a significant degree of logistical risk as any number of factors could have come in to play to restrict the ability of Slim to sustain his troops for the duration of the battle.

This highlights a striking aspect of Slim's command of Fourteenth Army, namely his willingness to take considerable, though calculated, logistical risks. He wrote that:

> At the beginning of the war there was the greatest contrast between the Japanese and the British logistical outlook, between what they required to operate and what we thought we required. They launched their troops into the boldest offensives on the slenderest administrative margins; our training was all against this. The British Army [for a hundred years] had tended to stress supply at the expense of mobility.[90]

Evans likewise comments in this regard that British military staff training had tended to place undue emphasis on logistics to the extent that one senior wartime commander instructed Slim: 'Never commit yourself until you have everything you need.'[91] This was, of course, a hallmark of Montgomery's style of warfare and it reflected the failed approach of Irwin and Lloyd in the ill-fated campaign in the Arakan Peninsula two years before.

The Burma campaign was as much a struggle for mastery of logistics as it was a struggle for mastery on the battlefield, and it was about risk as much as it was about adherence to logistical principles. Slim had an implicit understanding of the constraints placed on warfare by the demands of logistics. 'I knew', he wrote at the outset of his command of Fourteenth Army, 'that the campaign in Burma would above all be a supply and transport problem'.[92] Great efforts were made to increase the quantity of supplies to Burma. Railways were extended, roads built and surfaced, sunken ferries re-floated and repaired, barges and rafts built for use on the numerous waterways. These and other measures were so successful that, whereas in November 1943 an average of 2,800 tons a day was moved forward against a target figure of 3,700 tons a day, by September 1944 the tonnages achieved were 6,500 tons a day against a target of 5,900. By March 1945 nearly 9,000 tons a day were being lifted against a target of 6,900. This acted to create an effect described by Morris as 'logistic surprise'.[93] In this regard Lieutenant-General Nye regarded Slim's mastery of logistics to be the most significant measure of his greatness as commander of Fourteenth Army in Burma:

> I would say that Slim's feats in Burma should not be recognised just as something that came about, but they should be judged by what he did with what he had – or to be more accurate – with what he had not. He was always at the bottom of the scale of priorities – he never had enough to do what he had to do and this... is the measure of his greatness.[94]

Conclusion

Slim's military genius is incontestable. The measure of a great commander lies in the degree to which he can affect the diverse influences that impinge on military effectiveness so as to create a synergistic result. Being a master of strategy, of logistics, of technical proficiency and so on are important in themselves, but by themselves they remain insufficient. Military command requires someone who can, through dint of personality and inspirational leadership, weld all of the components of fighting power together so that an *extraordinary* result transpires.

What marks Slim out from the crowd was much more than just his winning of a succession of extraordinary battles. His strength lay in his ability to produce a decisive effect from scratch; to mould thousands of disparate individuals together into a single team with a single goal; to persuade a defeated army that it had the potential to turn the tables on their enemies; to master the complexities of terrain, climate and administrative deficiency so that self-help, resourcefulness and ingenuity became as much prized as fighting skill. In these individual areas, and more, Slim proved the master. But his genius for war was the consequence of his ability to bring together all of these elements to create an extraordinary result, the visible sign of which was the greatest defeat suffered by the Japanese on land during the Second World War.

It is strange that neither of the two greatest twentieth-century British theorists of warfare, Major-General J.F.C. Fuller or Sir Basil Liddell Hart, made very much of Fourteenth Army's achievements. Liddell Hart's description of the reconquest of Burma in his *History of the Second World War* is factual but cursory. This is somewhat surprising given his otherwise spirited advocacy of the 'indirect approach'. Interestingly, in the bibliography appended to this book, published in 1970, there is no mention of *Defeat into Victory*, published in 1956.[95]

The key factor in Slim's military success was his espousal of the principles of what we today call 'manoeuvre warfare'. Undoubtedly, victory in Burma in 1945 was achieved by an army that applied, with absolute consistency and devastating effect, a manoeuvrist approach to warfighting. It was a victory not just for the moral over the physical but for the application of warfighting procedures and doctrine which stressed pre-eminently the need to hit the enemy where he was weakest and then, by the careful, selective and cunning use of force, remove his will to win. The masterpiece of Allied strategy, as Kimura so rightly acclaimed, was the product of the calculated orchestration of a dynamic, skilful and victorious army; Slim was the maestro who conducted it all. Slim's experience of command in war provides an almost perfect model for the study of manoeuvre warfare and warrants, at the very least, its renewed attention today.

*Quotations from G. Evans, *Slim US Military Commander* and W. Slim, *Defeat into Victory*, appear by kind permission of Salamander Books and Viscount Slim respectively.

Notes

1. Michael Calvert, *Slim* (London: 1973) pp.157, 159.
2. D. Anderson, 'Slim', in J. Keegan (ed.), *Churchill's Generals* (London: 1991) p.319.
3. Calvert, *Slim*, p.159.
4. For a brief resume of Montgomery's postwar legacy see J. Kiszely, *The British Army and Approaches to Warfare since 1945* (Camberley: 1997) pp.7–9.
5. A.J. Barker, *The March on Delhi* (London: 1963) p.49.
6. Later Lieutenant-General Sir Archibald Nye. Quoted in G. Evans, *Slim as Military Commander* (London: 1969) p.27.
7. *Army Doctrine Publication (ADP)*, Vol. 1, *Operations* (London: 1994) pp.3–17. Hereafter *ADP* Vol. 1.
8. *Design for Military Operations – The British Military Doctrine* (London: 1996) pp.4–21. Hereafter *BMD*.
9. I.N.A. Thomas, 'Manoeuvre Warfare – Its Place in British Military Doctrine', *British Army Review (BAR)* 110 (August 1995), p.75. This is an extremely good short treatment of the subject.
10. The Fourteenth Army was actually predominantly an Indian army. In 1943 only 15 per cent of the divisions were British, while 15 per cent were West African and 70 per cent Indian. By 1945 this had changed to 17 per cent British, 25 per cent West African and 58 per cent Indian.
11. M. Hickey, *The Unforgettable Army: Slim's XIVth Army in Burma* (Tunbridge Wells: 1992) p.227.
12. Quoted in E.K.G. Sixsmith, *British Generalship in the Twentieth Century* (London: 1970) p.290.
13. Quoted in Evans, *Slim*, pp.214–15. See also Philip Zeigler, *Mountbatten* (London: 1985) p.295.
14. It should be noted, however, that even though Slim did not command anything larger than an 'Army', Fourteenth Army was nevertheless the largest Army put together by the United Kingdom during the Second World War.
15. *BMD*, pp.4–25.
16. *BMD*, pp.4–22.
17. Calvert, *Slim*, p.159.
18. Baldwin commanded the 3rd Tactical Air Force between 1943 and 1945. Quoted in Evans, *Slim*, p.134.
19. I.L. Grant, *Burma: The Turning Point* (Chichester: 1993) p.32.
20. Slim, *Defeat into Victory* (London: 1956) pp.7, 211.
21. Ibid., p.544.
22. Ibid., p.368.

23 Ibid., p.546.
24 *BMD*, p.4–22.
25 Thomas, 'Manoeuvre Warfare', p.75.
26 Ibid., p.76.
27 Louis Allen, *Burma: The Longest War* (London: 1984) p.98.
28 Slim, *Defeat into Victory*, p.154.
29 Ibid.
30 See Allen, *Burma*, pp.113–15 and Frank Owen, *The Campaign in Burma* (London: 1946) p.46.
31 Slim, *Defeat into Victory*, p.142. See also D. Fraser, *And We Shall Shock Them* (London: 1983) p.295.
32 Slim, *Defeat into Victory*, p.119.
33 *BMD*, pp.4–23.
34 Slim, *Defeat into Victory*, p.213.
35 Colonel A.R. Morris, 'Manoeuvre Warfare: Can the British Army Cope?', *BAR*, Vol. 105 (December 1993), p.8.
36 Slim, *Defeat into Victory*, pp.466–7.
37 *BMD*, pp.4–23.
38 Ibid.
39 Thomas, 'Manoeuvre Warfare', p.79.
40 Ibid.
41 Ibid.
42 *BMD*, pp.4-2–3.
43 *ADP*, Vol. 1, pp.3–17.
44 Thomas, 'Manoeuvre Warfare', p.77.
45 Ronald Lewin, *Slim: The Standard Bearer* (London: 1976) p.233. See, for example, Allen, *Burma* pp.433–4. Commenting on this particular attack, Slim remarked that 'The Japanese had had no experience of these massed armoured attacks and seemed quite incapable of dealing with them. The position was rapidly overrun. Its considerable garrison was hunted into the open, and there was a good killing'. Slim, *Defeat into Victory*, pp.441–2. In the ability to provide the shock action necessary for Slim to dominate the battlefield Louis Allen argued that it was the possession of armour that gave Slim a decisive advantage: Louis Allen, 'The Campaigns in Asia and the Pacific', in John Gooch (ed.), *Decisive Campaigns of the Second World War* (London: 1990) p.168. See also Slim, *Defeat into Victory*, p.445.
46 Evans, *Slim*, p.202.
47 *BMD*, pp.4–25.
48 Hickey, *Unforgettable Army*, p.216.
49 Quoted in Evans, *Slim*, p.84.
50 J. Lunt, *'A Hell of a Licking': The Retreat from Burma 1941–2* (London: 1986) pp.197–8.
51 Quoted in Evans, *Slim*, p.152.
52 Anderson, 'Slim', p.308.
53 Calvert, *Slim*, pp.44–5.
54 Quoted in Evans, *Slim*, p.67. See also G.M. Fraser, *Quartered Safe Out Here* (London: 1992) pp.35–6 and Hickey, *Unforgettable Army*, pp.216–17.
55 Slim, *Defeat into Victory*, pp.114, 182. For the retreat from Burma in 1942 see ibid., p.30. See also Sir John Smyth, *The Valiant* (London: 1970) p.98;

T. Carew, *The Longest Retreat: The Burma Campaign 1942* (London: 1969) pp.67–71, 111; J. Cross, *Jungle Warfare: Experiences and Encounters* (London: 1989) p.48; T. Mains, *The Retreat From Burma* (London: 1973) p.94. For the Arakan debacle in late 1942 and early 1943 see Slim, *Defeat into Victory*, pp.161–2 (for Slim's remedies for the crisis in morale, see pp.179–83, 186–92).

56 Slim, *Defeat into Victory*, pp.182.
57 *BMD*, pp.4–26.
58 Norman Dixon, *On the Psychology of Military Incompetence* (London: 1976) pp.152–3.
59 Quoted in Slim, *Defeat into Victory*, p.551.
60 *BMD*, pp.4–26.
61 Slim, 'Higher Command in War' *Military Review*, Vol. LXX, No. 5 (May 1990), p.14.
62 Slim, *Defeat into Victory*, pp.379, 390–2. See also Slim, 'Higher Command in War', *Military Review*, Vol. LXX, No. 5 (May 1990), pp.10–21.
63 Bryan Perrett, *A History of Blitzkrieg* (London: 1983) p.232.
64 *BMD*, pp.4–26.
65 Quoted in A.S.H. Irwin, *The Levels of War, Operational Art and Campaign Planning* (Camberley: 1993) p.7.
66 *BMD*, pp.4–11.
67 *ADP*, Vol. 1, pp.3–8.
68 Dixon, *On the Psychology*, p.342.
69 See Evans, *Slim*, p.24.
70 Ibid., p.107.
71 Slim, *Defeat into Victory*, pp.535–6.
72 W. Slim, *Campaign of the 14 Army* (Melbourne: 1950) p.8.
73 *BMD*, pp.4–17. See also *ADP*, Vol. 2, *Command* (London: 1995) pp.2-4–5.
74 See W. Slim, *Unofficial History* (London: 1959) p.156.
75 Slim, 'Higher Command in War', p.13.
76 Slim, *Defeat into Victory*, pp.541–2.
77 Thomas, 'Manoeuvre Warfare', p.77.
78 Slim, *Defeat into Victory*, pp.210–11. See also Slim, 'Higher Command in War', p.18.
79 Evans, *Slim*, p.52. On at least one occasion, however, this backfired on Slim. Before Imphal he left the decision to withdraw 17th Indian Division from Tiddim to Scoones, the Corps commander. Scoones in turn left the decision to the divisional commander. However, not having full visibility of the whole front the divisional commander made the decision to withdraw too late, and almost lost the division to Japanese encirclement.
80 Ibid., p.215.
81 Ibid., p.106.
82 Ibid., p.116. See also Slim, 'Higher Command in War', p.19.
83 For a description of this activity in his HQ see Slim, *Defeat into Victory*, pp.209–11.
84 Lewin, *Slim*, p.194.
85 Morris, 'Manoeuvre Warfare', p.26.
86 S. Woodburn-Kirby, *The War Against Japan*, Vol. IV, *The Reconquest of Burma* (London: 1965) p.428.

87 Perrett, *Blitzkrieg*, p.233.
88 Sixsmith, *British Generalship*, p.290.
89 *ADP*, Vol. 1, pp.3–6.
90 Slim, *Defeat into Victory*, p.539.
91 Evans, *Slim*, p.27.
92 Slim, *Defeat into Victory*, pp.169–76.
93 Morris, 'Manoeuvre Warfare', p.26.
94 Quoted in Evans, *Slim*, p.212.
95 B.H. Liddell Hart, *History of the Second World War* (London: 1973 edn) pp.667–8.

8
Lessons Not Learned: The Struggle between the Royal Air Force and Army for the Tactical Control of Aircraft, and the Post-mortem on the Defeat of the British Expeditionary Force in France in 1940

David Hall

'Who should control aircraft on the battlefield'? This was a fundamental question that exercised the Army and the Royal Air Force (RAF) in the aftermath of the disastrous campaign in France and the Low Countries in 1940. It involved a clash of strategic cultures that turned on the issue of command and control of close air support, and revealed how far from true 'jointery' the British services were at the beginning of the Second World War.

Britain's first air war – the Great War 1914–18 – was, for the most part, an army co-operation war.[1] First the Royal Flying Corps (RFC), and from 1 April 1918 onwards the bulk of the RAF, served as ancillary units to the Army. As such, Britain's air forces were subordinate to the Army's military campaigns which, on the Western Front, aimed to win the war by defeating the German armies opposite in the field. Accordingly, British aircraft were deployed by their Army commanders as a mere tactical adjunct to the principal fighting arms of the ground forces. Most senior army officers did not concern themselves with any application of air power beyond the immediate ground battle zone. Neither did they seek out their air counterparts for advice on how best to integrate air operations into the ground battle plan. In fact it was in part the Army's introspective approach to the employment of aircraft which moved the government to establish a separate air service in the last year of the war.[2]

By creating the RAF, and giving it a mandate for a wider, more strategic application of air power, Lloyd George's War Cabinet also brought out into the open the growing differences of opinion that divided the air enthusiasts and the more traditionally grounded tacticians in the Army over the proper employment of aircraft in war. The soldiers claimed that aeroplanes were 'tactical instruments'. Aircraft, just like artillery and tanks, provided essential ancillary support for the infantry and the cavalry, the arms that won battles by occupying enemy territory. Four years of relatively successful combat experience with aircraft operating in this role seemed to indicate that the Army's concept of tactical employment was sound. The airmen, not surprisingly, rejected this 'narrow view', contending that 'air power' offered a new way of approaching the strategic and operational challenges of war. Air forces, they asserted, were employed to best advantage when they were concentrated against targets above and beyond those traditionally selected by army commanders. Through a system of central command and control, air commanders would be able to employ every aircraft available to them when and where they were required most, whether it was in establishing and maintaining air superiority, flying reconnaissance, attacking ground targets, or a simultaneous combination of these basic tasks. Most important, in the eyes of the airmen and other air-minded officers and theorists, was the belief that aircraft were neither flying artillery pieces nor just 'another weapon' in the Army's arsenal, condemned as all too often they were in the 1914–18 war to some inapposite, ancillary and subordinate support role. Aircraft offered enlightened commanders both operational and strategic reach.[3]

The main issues of contention that divided Britain's airmen and soldiers were those of command and control. Who should control aircraft in a land battle and how and for what purpose should they be deployed? Answers to these apparently simple questions, answers that both airmen and soldiers could live with, were not quick in coming. There were fundamental differences between the two services over doctrine and their respective concepts of operations which led to a long and bitter dispute during the years between the wars and at least the first half of the Second World War, if not beyond.[4] The ignominious defeat of the British Expeditionary Force (BEF) in France in May–June 1940 exacerbated a problem that had never been dealt with adequately, and it resulted in a renewed call from the War Office for the establishment of an independent Army Air Arm.[5]

inter war years

The long and troubled history of army–air co-operation in Britain from the end of the First World War and throughout most of the Second World War has recently become a subject of some interest to historians. It embraces a wide spectrum of subject matter in which conflicting strategic priorities, domestic politics, international crises and events, economic interests and realities, technologies and service cultures all play significant parts. The inter-war years were particularly difficult years for the Army and the Royal Air Force, as they were for the Royal Navy, because of the lack of coherent political direction the Armed Forces received for their specific as well as collective responsibilities. The three services were also hurt by the bitter inter-service rivalries that developed out of their fierce competition for small and seemingly ever dwindling resources. Acrimony and division were compounded further by the lack of a common approach within the services to the planning and conduct of war at the strategic level. Throughout the inter-war years the three services were effectively left to their own devices to find their respective roles and to determine how they would conduct their business. Whilst the RAF concentrated on how to defend Great Britain from air attack and the Royal Navy concerned itself with the task of securing open seas (both strategic tasks in nature), the Army focused on the tactical practicalities of defending the Empire. None of the services, either individually or in any combination, possessed the doctrine, force structure, or operational level of command necessary to provide them with the vital link between the strategic direction of war and its tactical execution.[6] During the 20 years of difficult peace between the wars the services rarely consulted with each other and they had very little experience of working together. It is hardly surprising, then, that in the spring of 1940, in the unforgiving arena of battle, the Army and the RAF struggled to find an agreed, never mind an effective, joint land–air response to the German *Blitzkrieg*.

It is not the intention of this brief chapter to synthesise the extant literature on the development of Anglo–American battlefield interdiction and close air support during the Second World War. Readers who are interested in this subject should refer to the published works of B.F. Cooling, Ian Gooderson, Richard Hallion, Dan Mortensen, Richard Muller and Vincent Orange.[7] This list is not, and is not meant to be, exhaustive; it is, however, representative of a growing cadre of scholars who recently have turned their attention to the historical study of tactical air power.

The aim of this chapter is to examine the General Staff's immediate response to the Army's defeat in France and its proposed solution to reverse the Army's prospects in future campaigns against the *Wehrmacht*. That the Army undertook an examination of the recent fighting in France is not a surprise, defeat or otherwise, but what is surprising is the premise that the War Office adopted for its starting point a post-mortem of a battle lost. Even before after-action reports were submitted for examination and debate, most of the generals and senior Army officers – whether they had fought in France or toiled in the War Office – were convinced that the Army's organisation and its tactical conceptions as practised were sound. They proudly stated that no frontal attack against the BEF had succeeded in breaking through. Moreover, throughout the Army, there was widespread belief that the BEF's withdrawal to (and evacuation from) Dunkirk was the natural consequence of the unwillingness of Belgian and French armies to fight and the failure of the 'Royal Absent Force' to provide essential close air support. Convinced that defeat in France was not their fault, the Army blithely ignored questions concerning its own methods and operational procedures, and comforted itself with the mistaken belief that 'the next time' would be different. New and better equipment on a greater scale, and, of greater importance, returning to army commanders in the field their prerogative to command air forces in support of a land battle, would make it so.[8]

The Army presented its hastily derived position on what was required to reverse the fortunes of the war whilst the BEF's successful evacuation from Dunkirk was at its very height. On Saturday, 1 June, the Commander-in-Chief of the British Expeditionary Force, General the Viscount Gort, attended the morning session of the War Cabinet. After receiving the Cabinet's warm congratulations for saving the Army from certain destruction, the General was invited to give his assessment of the recent fighting. Gort told the War Cabinet that the BEF had been let down by its allies, namely the Belgians and the French, and that the RAF had left the Army exposed to the murderous combination of German dive-bombers and tanks which had had, throughout the campaign, a deleterious effect on the morale and fighting ability of his troops. Gort criticised the RAF for its failure to provide the proper type of air support and for the woefully insufficient number of aircraft it deployed to France for the battle. The Chief of the Imperial General Staff (CIGS), General Sir John Dill, echoed Gort's concerns. Dill also informed his War Cabinet colleagues that the War Office was already undertaking a review of the recent fighting in great earnest.[9]

Gort's official despatch, which was published on 25 July, re-stated all the main points he had raised earlier before the War Cabinet. It was a short and remarkably composed document considering that its author had just presided over one of the worst beatings ever suffered by a British Army. Gort emphasised the superior fighting power of an enemy army lavishly equipped with air and armoured forces. He noted, too (with, it seems, unjustifiable surprise), the accelerated pace of operations brought on by the partnership of offensive air power and modern mechanised ground forces.[10] None of this was new. In the run-up to the war, British officers had been regular guests at German Army manoeuvres.[11] In fact, as late as August 1939, two officers attended a major two-week exercise in central Germany. From 5 to 18 August, Captains Stratton and Hogg observed a series of large divisional exercises that included attacks by massed formations of tanks supported by large numbers of aircraft. Evaluating these exercises for the War Office, Stratton and Hogg stated in their report that the Germans took unacceptable risks, and that the basis of all their tactics was 'speed and more speed, repeated ad nauseam'. Whilst they praised the fitness and professionalism of German officers and other ranks, they were also contemptuous of German offensive methods. In their concluding remarks Stratton and Hogg dismissed German procedures, writing that they were 'somewhat rigid and disclosed no new ideas'.[12]

Gort may have been incognisant of German methods before the Battle for France but, in July 1940, he recommended that the Army receive something on the lines of the German Air Force before it fought its next battle.[13] His colleagues at the War Office agreed. Lieutenant-Colonel (later Field Marshal) F.W. Festing, and his staff of two in MO7 (the War Office department responsible for Army/Air co-operation), strongly advanced Gort's argument. MO7, despite its remarkably small size, and the fact that it had only just been established in January 1940, demanded a new air policy that provided army commanders in the field with fully adequate air forces under their direct and immediate command. What Festing wanted was balanced army air forces, comprising fighters, reconnaissance and specialised bomber aircraft, sub-allotted to ground commanders at Corps and Divisional levels.[14]

Before the war Festing was one of a number of officers at the War Office who were responsible for evaluating reports written by officers who had attended German manoeuvres; he initialled as read the report written by Stratton and Hogg. It is also clear that he misunderstood German operational procedures for air and land warfare. The Luftwaffe did not sub-allot its aircraft to army commanders in the field: German aircraft were concentrated for attacks on specific targets and they were directed by a centralised command. For the German offensive in the West in 1940, virtually the whole of the Luftwaffe was committed to an integrated air–land battle plan. Each service, however, pursued relatively independent objectives, which, when taken together, converged on a common goal. Initial air action was aimed at establishing air supremacy. Once a favourable air situation had been established the Luftwaffe gradually shifted its main effort to a series of pre-planned air support objectives for the ground forces. It was only after Allied resistance had more or less collapsed that the Luftwaffe released squadrons on roving commissions in search of opportunistic targets. This was not the penny-packet system of air support employed by the French Air Force in 1940, or the one that Festing and his colleague at the War Office advocated for the Army.[15]

Festing was not the only Army officer to have misread the Luftwaffe's method of operations and to call for the creation of an independent Army Air Arm. Similar uninformed advice also came from recently defeated British Army commanders. Lieutenant-General Claude Auchinleck, in his despatch on the lessons learned from recent operations in Norway, wrote that 'the predominant factor' was air power. 'The enemy', Auchinleck stated, 'had complete initiative in the air, and used it first and foremost, to support his troops'.[16] The general's sentiments were repeated by others in the BEF who had just returned from France, demoralised and defeated. Brigadier Greenslade, Deputy Quartermaster General at BEF Headquarters, re-stated Auchinleck's principal lesson and added: 'it is impractical to attempt to fight without there being adequate air forces under the operational control of the Army'.[17]

A third general, Lieutenant-General Alan Brooke, drawing on his recent experience in France with II Corps, claimed that 'pre-war conceptions of air–army co-operation were at fault'. Brooke advocated an immediate and thorough overhaul of the existing system. He believed that troops in the field required both a fighter umbrella for defence and dive-bombers for close offensive support, all under the military commander's direct control.[18]

The traditional air force belief in unified air power was under attack. This air force concept, however, was not the problem. Lack of aircraft rather than the RAF system of control of British Air Forces in France (BAFF) was the reason why the Army did not receive sufficient air support. Recent war experience, noted Air Marshal Sir Arthur Barratt, Air Officer Commanding-in-Chief, BAFF, in his despatch, confirmed that success on the ground depended on superiority in the air: 'No carefully balanced force of reconnaissance, bomber and fighter squadrons parcelled out in penny-packets to each Division and Corps could ensure the success of a land campaign.' Effective air support was dependent on a high degree of air superiority. 'To win it', noted Barratt, 'required an air force superior in strength to the enemy's air force immediately opposite; not, as the army was inclined to believe, vast numbers of close support bombers tethered to the ground forces'.[19]

The General Staff was not convinced. In mid-June 1940, General Sir John Dill, CIGS, established a committee to examine the lessons to be learnt from the recent fighting in France. Dill appointed General Sir William Bartholomew to chair the committee.[20] It was a bad decision.

In selecting Bartholomew neither Dill nor the War Office could have chosen a more unsuitable senior officer for such an important task. Bartholomew's 'wire-pulling' and his distaste for combined service solutions to defence problems soured inter-service relations so completely in the 1930s that the War Office was forced to post him to India in order to get him far away from Whitehall.[21] His undisguised hatred of the RAF also thwarted his prospects of ever becoming CIGS.[22] Approaching retirement at the end of 1940, and serving out his commission as ADC General to the King, Bartholomew was to have one last opportunity to champion sectional interests in the War Office and to reveal the obsolete nature of his military thinking.

Only Army officers served on Bartholomew's committee, and all but one of the 40 senior officers who had returned from France and appeared before the Committee were soldiers.[23] Not surprisingly, Bartholomew's report exonerated the Army's organisation and its tactical methods, and blamed its retreat and evacuation from Dunkirk on the RAF. The air force, stated the report, failed to provide adequate air support for the army at all stages of the land campaign in France. The Committee also claimed that the Luftwaffe's *raison d'être* was to fulfil the needs of the Wehrmacht, and it portrayed German air operations as being subordinate to the objectives of the ground forces. Building on their false assessment of the Luftwaffe's role in the battle for France, the Bartholomew Committee concluded that the British Army needed an air support system comparable to that of Germans, where the air force was compelled to co-operate with the army in pursuit of the latter's operational tasks. In order to achieve this, the Committee stated that the Army required its own specialised aircraft under its own direct command and control. Just as Festing and his two assistants in MO7 had advocated earlier in June 1940, the Bartholomew Committee, at the end of the month, recommended that the Army receive its own independent air force.[24]

The Air Staff acknowledged that improvements in the organisation and provision of air support for the field force were required, but the creation of a separate army air arm was not the answer. Based on their own analysis of the recent campaign, the Air Staff was convinced that the Army had failed to recognise the new approach to war that had been taken by the German armed forces: one of lightning thrusts and sudden rushes designed to overwhelm the enemy's forces through dislocation rather than wholesale destruction. In the Battle for France, the Air Staff found confirmation for their belief in the general application of air power. Strategic air operations, first to win air superiority and followed by measures to isolate the battlefield, were of equal if not greater importance than ground support missions in achieving the Wehrmacht's stunning victory.[25] The Deputy Chief of the Air Staff (DCAS), Air Vice-Marshal Sholto Douglas, made this point more clearly than anyone: 'We appear to have forgotten more completely than I would have believed possible one of the plainest lessons of the last war. During the brief periods where the Germans enjoyed air superiority we found ourselves unable to carry out normal Army Co-operation work.' To overcome these difficulties, Douglas concluded, 'we need to build more and better fighters and regain air superiority over the battlefield'.[26] Moreover, the analysis of the Chiefs of Staff of German air operations in Poland and France – undertaken at Churchill's request for both himself and the War Cabinet – reached conclusions that were very similar to those of the Air Staff.[27]

The Air Staff were correct in holding to their belief that air superiority over the battlefield would enable aircraft, including those not necessarily designed for a battlefield role, to provide all of the army's offensive air support needs. Only at the expense of a powerful striking force for all strategic purposes, cautioned the airmen, could a specialised army support air force, entirely under military control, be provided.[28] The soldiers disagreed.[29] This fundamental difference in perception between the Army and the RAF over their respective approaches to fighting a combined air and land battle was an obstacle that was not to be overcome quickly. In addition to the struggle between the Army and the RAF to reach an agreed position on the function of air forces when in support of a land battle, the Army also had to find new operational procedures in order to obtain the best results from its own organic combat power. The Army's weakness, in terms of doctrine and tactics, would be exposed again in other theatres, particularly in North Africa. In fact, throughout the first half of the war, and perhaps even longer, the Army did not know how to fight and win a modern war.[30] Effective co-operation depends entirely on how well all of the parties involved work together. 'The system fails if one party to it collapses', which is what one historian,

John Terraine, criticised the Army for doing all 'too frequently in the face of the Afrika Korps'.[31]

As intractable as the problems seemed to be between the Army and the RAF during the summer of 1940, they did not preclude genuine attempts by the two services to break the impasse and institute effective reforms. Between July and October 1940, the Air Staff gave serious attention to the problem of how best to meet the Army's air requirements. Memoranda were written and discussed, conferences were held with the Army, and a number of exercises and trials were mounted.[32] Perhaps the most important of these exercises was the joint army–air experiment in Northern Ireland directed by Group Captain A.H. Wann and Lieutenant-Colonel John Woodall. From 5 September to 28 October 1940, Wann and Woodall conducted a series of signals exercises and command and control trials that led to the formation of a rudimentary joint (army/air) battle headquarters equipped with direct communication links to forward troops and both forward and rear airfields.[33] By the end of the year both the Army and the RAF would celebrate three notable achievements: the creation of a Combined Central Operations Room at GHQ Home Forces, the adoption of Close Support Bomber Controls following extensive experiments and trials in Northern Ireland and, on 1 December, the formation of Army Co-operation Command. There was reason to be optimistic about the future.[34]

Air Marshal Sholto Douglas offered an encouraging view on the subject: 'Army co-operation? There's nothing in it. All you need is willingness to co-operate and good signals.'[35] In the end it took a little more than this to produce the well-honed procedures that gave Anglo–American armies the finest tactical air power enjoyed by any army during the war. The process had, however, begun. During the summer of 1941, more signals and command and control exercises on the Wann–Woodall design were conducted in Egypt and, along with the battlefield experience obtained in the Western Desert, much progress was made on how best to provide the army with flexible, timely and overwhelming air support both in offensive and defensive operations.[36] To a large degree, the issues of command and control of Close Air Support were resolved. The successful co-operation achieved by the Western Desert Air Force and the Eighth Army in 1942, and the formation of the Second Tactical Air Force in the spring of 1943, attest to the accuracy and prudence of Air Marshal Douglas's vision, as well as the laborious work of the many airmen and soldiers who overcame numerous conceptual, political, procedural and technical difficulties in their search for an effective army air support system. Perhaps then, the title of this chapter is somewhat of a misnomer. The lessons of the command and control of Close Air Support were learned. On the other hand, there is no escaping the fact that during the Second World War Britain's most senior soldiers were very slow and reluctant learners.

Notes

1. Sir John Slessor, *Air Power and Armies* (Oxford: 1936) p.1.
2. For a synopsis of Britain's air effort in the First World War see Public Record Office (PRO) AIR 8/13 Cmd. Paper 100: Synopsis of British Air Effort During the War (1919); Sykes Papers, RAF Museum, RAF Hendon, MFC 77/13/62; Sir Walter Raleigh and H.A. Jones, *The War in the Air*, 6 vols, (Oxford: 1922–37); and Malcolm Cooper, *The Birth of Independent Air Power* (London: 1986). For the early disagreements between soldiers and airmen over the optimum role of aircraft in support of a land battle and the creation of the Royal Air Force, see Trenchard Papers, RAF Museum, RAF Hendon, MFC 76/1/357, Lecture I: 'Policy 1917–1923'; Malcolm Cooper, *The Birth of Independent Air Power*, pp.27–41 and 97–107; Sir Maurice Dean, *The Royal Air Force and Two World Wars* (London: 1979) pp.21–3; Sir Charles Webster and Noble Frankland, *The Strategic Air Offensive Against Germany 1919–1945*, Vol. 1 (London: 1961) pp.36–7; Shelford Bidwell and Dominick Graham, *Fire-Power. British Weapons and Theories of War 1904–1945* (London: 1982) pp.20–1; and Sir Walter Raleigh and H.A. Jones, *The War in the Air*, Appendices pp.8–14 for the full text of General Jan Christian Smuts's final report on the need to create an independent air force in the aftermath of German bombing raids on London, entitled: 'The Second Report of the Prime Minister's Committee on the Air Organisation and Home Defence against Air Raids, 17 August 1917'.
3. The RAF's first official attempt to codify the lessons of the 1914–18 War in the form of an air doctrine began in 1922 with the publication of RAF Operations Manual CD 22 (sometimes referred to as Air Publication (AP) 882, and later re-issued with revisions in 1928 as the RAF War Manual Part I – Operations, AP 1300). See PRO AIR 5/299. See also Trenchard Papers, RAF Museum, RAF Hendon, MFC 76/1/357, Lectures VII and VIII: 'Principles of War' and 'Air Strategy'; and Slessor, *Air Powers and Armies*, pp.165–99.
4. Two of the leading participants in this debate were Air Marshal Sir Hugh Trenchard and Field Marshal Sir Henry Wilson. For a detailed account of their respective arguments see Derek J.P. Waldie, 'Relations Between the Army and the Royal Air Force 1918–1939', PhD Thesis, King's College, University of London, 1980, pp.7–33. See also Air Marshal Sir Hugh Trenchard, 'Aspects of Service Aviation', *The Army Quarterly*, Vol. 2, No. 3 (April 1922), pp.10–21; Sir John Slessor, *The Central Blue* (London: 1956) chs II and III; and Sir Maurice Dean, *The Royal Air Force and Two World Wars*, p.34. Detailed scholarly accounts of the deep and unrelenting bitterness towards the RAF, from both the Army and the Royal Navy, can be read in John Ferris, *The Evolution of British Strategic Policy 1919–1926* (London: 1989); Malcolm Smith, *British Air Strategy between the Wars* (Oxford: 1984); Brian Bond, *British Military Policy between the Two World Wars* (Oxford: 1980); and Geoffrey Till, *Air Power and the Royal Navy* (London: 1979).

5 War Office efforts to obtain a separate Army Air Arm prior to the BEF's defeat in France can be followed in the War Cabinet Minutes and Memoranda and the Land Forces Committee's Minutes and Memoranda during the autumn of 1939. For the main arguments of the two services in this debate see: PRO CAB 66/3 WP(39)110, 111, 112 (2–3 November 1939) Memoranda by the Lord Privy Seal, the Secretary of State for War and the Secretary of State for Air on Air Requirements of the Army. See also CAB 92/111 LF(39)17, 18 and 19 (17–21 October 1939) Land Forces Committee Minutes and Memoranda. Scholarly analysis of this debate can be read in D.I. Hall, 'The Birth of the Tactical Air Force: British Theory and Practice of Air Support in the West, 1939–1943', DPhil Thesis, University of Oxford, 1996, chs II and III.

6 Norman H. Gibbs, *Grand Strategy*, Vol. I (London: 1976); Bidwell and Graham, *Fire Power*, pp.1–4, and *passim*; Harold Winton, *To Change an Army. General Sir John Burnett-Stuart and British Armoured Doctrine, 1927–1938* (London: 1988) pp.1–2; and Mungo Melvin, 'The Land/Air Interface', Draft Paper (Bracknell: JSCSC, 2000) p.6, note 17.

7 B.F. Cooling (ed.), *Case Studies in the Development of Close Air Support* (Washington, DC: 1990); Ian Gooderson, *Air Power at the Battlefront: Allied Close Air Support in Europe 1943–45* (London: 1998); Richard Hallion, *Strike from the Sky: The History of Battlefield Air Attack, 1911–1945* (Washington, DC: 1989); Daniel R. Mortensen (ed.), *Air Power and Ground Armies. Essays on the Evolution of Anglo-American Air Doctrine 1940–1943* (Maxwell, AL: 1998); Daniel R. Mortensen, *A Pattern for Joint Operations: World War II Close Air Support North Africa* (Washington, DC: 1987); Richard Muller, 'Close Air Support: The German, British, and American experiences, 1918–1941' in Williamson Murray and Allan R. Millet (eds), *Military Innovation in the Interwar Period* (Cambridge: 1996) pp.144–90; and Vincent Orange, *Coningham* (London: 1990). Additional sources of interest to those readers who seek a more comprehensive analysis of this subject include: RAF Historical Society (ed.), *The End of the Beginning. Symposium Proceedings on Land/Air Co-operation in the Mediterranean War 1940–43* (Bracknell Paper No. 3, 20 March 1992); C.E. Carrington, 'Army/Air Co-operation, 1939–1943', *Journal of the Royal United Services Institute*, Vol. 115 (December 1970); Air Marshal Sir Arthur Coningham, 'The Development of Tactical Air Forces', *Journal of the Royal United Services Institute*, Vol. 91 (1946); Michael Bechthold, 'The Development of an Unbeatable Combination: US Close Air Support in Normandy', *Canadian Military History*, Vol. 8, No. 1 (Winter 1999); Christopher Evans, 'The Fighter Bomber in the Normandy Campaign: The Role of 83 Group', *Canadian Military History*, Vol. 8, No. 1 (Winter 1999); W.A. Jacobs, 'Air Support for the British Army, 1939–1943', *Military Affairs* (December 1982); and Robert Vogel, 'Tactical Air Power in Normandy: Some Thoughts on the Interdiction Plan', *Canadian Military History*, Vol. 3, No. 1 (Spring 1994).

8 PRO CAB 106/246 'Despatch from the Commander-in-Chief, BEF, General the Viscount Gort', 25 July 1940; PRO CAB 106/220 The Bartholomew Committee Final Report: 'Lessons to be Learnt from Operations in Flanders', June 1940; PRO WO 106/1754 'Memorandum on the Co-operation of Air Forces with the BEF during the period 10 to 31 May 1940', 18 June 1940; PRO AIR 20/4447 'Direct Support of the BEF in France', Memorandum by Colonel F.W. Festing, War Office (MO7), June 1940; and Report of the RAF Committee to Investigate War Experiences 1939–40, 22 July 1940.

9 PRO CAB 65/7 WM 151(40)14; and CAB 65/13 WM 151(40)14 Confidential Annex, 1 June 1940.
10 PRO CAB 106/246 General Gort's Despatch, 25 July 1940.
11 At a luncheon party held by Colonel General von Fritsch, in honour of the foreign guests who attended the German autumn manoeuvres in 1937, Field Marshal Sir Cyril Deverell asked General Guderian for his honest opinion on operations involving concentrations of tanks. Deverell did not think mass formations of tanks would be effective in battle. He thought the concentration he saw in the exercises was merely to amuse Hitler and Mussolini. See Field Marshal Heinz Guderian, *Panzer Leader* (London: 1952) p.46; and Field Marshal Sir Edmund Ironside, *The Ironside Diaries 1937–1940*, ed. J. Mcleod and B. Kelly (London: 1962) pp.26–32.
12 Camberley Staff College Library, 'Report of Attachment of German Army, 1939', by Captain W.H. Stratton and Captain D.W.B.T. Hogg, September 1939.
13 PRO CAB 65/7 WM 151(40)14 and CAB 65/13 WM 151(40)14 Confidential Annex, 1 June 1940; and WO 106/1596 and WO 106/1754 'Air Policy', June–July 1940.
14 PRO WO 277/34 Army Air Support, pp.8 and 18; and WO 106/1763 Various notes and letters initiated by Lt-Col. F.W. Festing on the new arrangements required to meet the Army's air support needs.
15 General Paul Deichmann, *German Air Force Operations in Support of the Army*, USAF Historical Studies No. 163 (New York: 1968) pp.155–7; Williamson Murray, *German Military Effectiveness* (Baltimore, MD: 1992) pp.99–100, 115–19; and James Corum, *The Luftwaffe. Creation of the Operational Air War, 1918–1940* (Lawrence, KS: 1997) pp.276–80. See also Camberley Staff College Library, 'Notes on "Siegfried Taktik 37" and French concepts on offensive operations and war', by Lt-Col. Armand Mermet (French Army), September 1939.
16 PRO WO 233/60 'Report on Operations in Northern Norway from 13 May 1940 to 8 June 1940 by Lieutenant-General C.L.E. Auchinleck', June 1940.
17 PRO WO 197/111 'Report on the Operations of the BEF by Brigadier Greenslade, DQMF, BEF', 17 June 1940.
18 PRO WO 106/1708 'A Few Lessons to be Drawn from the Fighting of 2nd Corps, 10–30 May 1940'; and Alanbrooke Papers, 12/x/6 'Air Co-operation', Liddell Hart Centre for Military Archives, King's College London.
19 PRO AIR 35/354 'Battle of France: BAFF, Despatch by AOC-in-C Air Vice Marshal Sir Arthur Barratt', July 1940.
20 PRO CAB 65/7 WM 157(40)2, 7 June 1940.
21 B.H. Liddell Hart, *The Memoirs of Captain Liddell Hart*, Vol. II (London: 1965) pp.155 and 313–14; and Brian Bond (ed.), *Chief of Staff: The Diaries of Lieutenant-General Sir Henry Pownall, 1933–1940*, Vol. I (London: 1972) pp.21–2 and 46.
22 Liddell Hart, *Memoirs*, Vol. II, p.71.
23 In addition to General Bartholomew, the members of the Committee included Major-General C.C. Malden (Director of Military Training), Major-General N.M.S. Irving, Brigadier D.G. Watson and Brigadier W.C. Holden. The secretariat included Colonel R. Gurney, Major C.W.S. Burton and Captain R.W.M. de Winton. A full list of names of the officers who gave evidence to the Committee is appended to the final report.

24 PRO CAB 106/220 Bartholomew Committee Final Report, June 1940.
25 PRO AIR 41/21 AHB Narrative: 'The Campaign in France and the Low Countries, September 1939–June 1940', pp.465–6 and 480.
26 Air Vice-Marshal Sholto Douglas as cited in Group Captain E.B. Haslam, 'Services Required from the RAF for the Field Forces' (Air Historical Branch, RAF, 1976) p.10.
27 PRO CAB 66/8 WP(40)212 Weekly Resume (No. 24) of the Naval, Military and Air Situation, 13–20 June 1940, Appendix IV; and COS(40)483 German Air Operations in France, 21 June 1940.
28 Slessor, *Air Power and Armies*, p.10; and Lord Tedder, *With Prejudice* (London: 1966) pp.170, 175–6, 187–90, 443–4.
29 Successive CIGSs from Gort through to Alanbrooke all made formal requests for the establishment of a large independent army air arm. At its most absurd, in the spring of 1942, the War Office asked for some 111 squadrons of specialised close air support aircraft and a further 207 squadrons of transport aircraft to meet the Army's airborne troop and air lift requirements. At the RAF standard of 12 aircraft per squadron (initial establishment) the War Office's request amounted to some 3,816 aircraft, which exceeded the first-line strength of the entire RAF. See John Terraine, *The Right of the Line* (London: 1985) p.121; and J.M.R. Butler, *Grand Strategy*, Vol. III, Part II (London: 1957) pp.529–44.
30 PRO WO 259/64 Criticism in the Press of the Army (February–April 1942); Frank Owen, 'The Destiny of the British Army', *The Evening Standard* (24–6 March 1942); Tedder, *With Prejudice*, pp.307, 312, 314 and 318–27; Dominick Graham, *Against Odds. Reflections on the Experiences of the British Army, 1914–1945* (London: 1999); and David Fraser, *And We Shall Shock Them* (London: 1983).
31 John Terraine, 'Introduction', in C.E. Carrington, *Soldier at Bomber Command* (London: 1987) p.x.
32 PRO AIR 2/5224 Close Support Aircraft: Policy; AIR 2/7336 Army Air Requirements; AIR 20/2787 VCAS Correspondence; AIR 20/2809 Army Air Requirements; AIR 20/3706 Army Co-operation Requirements; WO 106/5160 Notes on future Army Operations...and the use of Air Power; and PREM 4/14/9 Army–RAF Co-operation.
33 Wann–Woodall Report. See PRO AIR 39/140 Close Support by Bombers and Fighter Aircraft.
34 PRO AIR 20/2811 and AIR 20/4301 Formation of Army Co-operation Command; and C.E. Carrington, 'Army–Air Co-operation, 1939–1943' *Journal of the Royal United Services Institute* (December 1970).
35 Air Marshal Sir Sholto Douglas as quoted in Carrington, *Soldier at Bomber Command*.
36 The Air Ministry, Air Publication 3235, *The Second World War 1939–1945. The Royal Air Force, Air Support* (London: 1955) pp.54–60.

9
Sir Arthur Harris: Different Perspectives
Christina Goulter

It is not the intention of this chapter to regurgitate the usual debates over Harris's conduct of the bomber offensive.[1] Like most historians of the air war, the author has suffered for many years with 'Harris fatigue', and felt that there was little new to say about the man. However, a number of unexplored 'rabbit holes' presented themselves in the course of recent research into the Commonwealth contribution to the air war, and a re-examination of Harris as a leader is warranted. It is worth considering the wider leadership issues raised by Harris's early career and tenure during the war, first as Air Officer Commanding No. 5 Group, Bomber Command, then as Deputy Chief of Air Staff, rather than focusing purely on his time as AOC-in-C of Bomber Command.

Harris has been described by a recent biographer as 'the last of the RAF's [Royal Air Force's] great captains and certainly its greatest operational commander in the Second World War'.[2] This is quite a statement, for it all depends on how we define 'greatness'. The Second World War was well stocked with 'great commanders' (many would point to Wavell, Slim, Sir Keith Park and Rommel, to name just a few), and Harris's light did not shine appreciably brighter than most of these. As the good Clausewitz observed, greatness comprises a number of elements, and we see some, but by no means all, of these attributes exhibited by Harris.[3]

Clausewitz wrote that the great commander requires first and foremost courage; not only the obvious physical courage in the face of personal danger, but the courage to accept responsibility and the courage of one's convictions.[4] Clausewitz spoke of the courage which is required to pursue a plan, even in the darkest hours, and how determination is necessary to lessen the agonies of doubt.[5] So, using these criteria, some would say that Harris scores particularly well. However, this strength of character, which Clausewitz says is the main feature of a good commander, can easily degenerate into obstinacy and dogmatism, and it is this obstinacy and dogmatism which prevent Harris from being called a truly great commander. These features of Harris's character came perilously close to derailing British strategy at a number of points in the war, especially after 1942. The pressures of high command also betrayed some less than attractive opinions, which will be discussed later. However, if we return to the period before Harris took over as AOC-in-C of Bomber Command, we see much to admire in Harris.

Certainly no one can accuse Harris of lacking constancy of purpose. He had been a staunch advocate of bombing since the early 1920s, and demonstrated an unshakeable faith that this was the proper role for air power. The formative experience for Harris was his involvement in the Empire policing role, particularly after he took command of No. 45 Squadron in Iraq in 1922. Like others involved in Empire policing, he came to view this experience as sufficient evidence of the bomber's invincibility and of the efficacy of bombing. What he and the others preferred to forget was that there was a world of difference between these operations and a full-scale bombing offensive against an industrialised nation such as Germany. Aircraft were effective in a policing role for a variety of reasons, not least of which was the fact that the various rebellious peoples in the Middle East and on the North-West Frontier had little prior exposure to aircraft, and were therefore easily intimidated; the targets were typically undefended villages; and attempts at anti-aircraft defence were rudimentary, usually no more than small arms fire. Sir John Slessor was to comment about those who had been involved in the Empire policing experience: 'Our belief in the bomber was a matter of faith.'[6] It was faith without good works, and it raises the question of the intellectual honesty of those concerned, including Harris.

Having said this, Harris's time with No. 45 Squadron was the point from which we see him having a keen appreciation of the operational problems facing bomber crews. Showing imaginative flair, Harris set about converting his transport aircraft into bombers, and was personally responsible for designing the crude bombing equipment used by the unit. Not content with bombing only by day, Harris went on to develop night operations. He understood that success in night bombing depended on good navigation and the means to mark the targets; these were the same operational problems that plagued Bomber Command between 1940 and 1942.[7]

Harris's interest in operational problems was seen again when he took over command of No. 5 Group just after the war broke out. He instituted a comprehensive training programme, which laid the foundations for the Operational Training Unit (OTU). The OTU was a fundamentally important addition to the RAF's training establishment, and was shown to decrease aircrew fatalities in both Bomber and Coastal Commands when introduced across the board. Prior to the inception of OTUs, Bomber and Coastal Command aircrews would go directly from training on non-operational types of aircraft into combat. The first flight an aircrew had in its operational aircraft was usually a full combat mission. Harris also made recommendations to improve synthetic training, as it was called then. Within days of taking over command of No. 5 Group, Harris also made a study of his aircrews, aircraft and equipment, and wrote lengthy memoranda to the AOC-in-C of Bomber Command, Sir Edgar Ludlow-Hewitt, detailing the various faults of the Handley Page Hampden, his main operational aircraft, including its lack of defensive armament and its draughty cockpit.[8]

This was not mere micro-management on Harris's part. It is important to emphasise these initiatives, as it demonstrates that Harris was acutely aware of the operational realities facing those aircrews he sent into battle. It has passed into popular mythology that Harris cared little for the men at the grass-roots level, and the fact that he rarely visited stations while he was AOC-in-C of Bomber Command may be seen by some as evidence of his callousness. This would be an unfair accusation. Clausewitz observed: 'War is the realm of physical exertion and suffering. These will destroy us unless we can make ourselves indifferent to them.'[9] Doubtless Harris adopted the same psychological mechanisms for coping with the war as his aircrews did. Harris's concern for his aircrews' welfare went beyond the provision of improved equipment and training. He was also openly critical of those operations he felt to be foolhardy and wasteful of aircrew lives. While AOC of No. 5 Group, he was a vociferous critic of the so-called 'nickelling' operations, the dropping of propaganda leaflets over Germany and Italy.

Both Harris and Ludlow-Hewitt believed that the Bomber Command of 1939–40 was not able to undertake the strategic bomber offensive envisaged. Harris was fully supportive of Ludlow-Hewitt's efforts to improve training standards by ploughing back into training many of the squadrons from the front line. Harris commented that in doing so Ludlow-Hewitt had saved Bomber Command, preventing the 'dog from eating its tail'.[10] However, because Ludlow-Hewitt had the courage to do this, and reported frankly on the condition of his Command, he was labelled a doom-monger by many of the Air Staff. He was moved on, becoming Inspector General of the Royal Air Force. Harris had made almost all the same criticisms and recommendations as Ludlow-Hewitt, but, benefiting from the change-over in Chief of Air Staff (CAS) in October from Cyril Newall to Charles Portal, Harris went on to be appointed Deputy Chief of Air Staff in November 1940. It is worth considering how Harris would have fared had he been AOC-in-C of Bomber Command when war broke out. Ludlow-Hewitt, like Bowhill of Coastal Command who received the same poor treatment, had the misfortune of being at the head of a Command at the start of the war, when the gulf between prewar plans and wartime realities was the greatest.[11] This is an important point about command at the start of wars, when operational readiness, more often than not, falls far short of expectation, and senior commanders are unfairly blamed for the poor performance of their charges.

The post of Deputy Chief of Air Staff required the incumbent to take an interest in all aspects of the Royal Air Force but, not surprisingly, during Harris's six-month tenure Bomber Command received priority. Harris focused on four principal areas: aircrew training; the development of more powerful explosives; the development of aids to navigation and bomb-aiming; and the introduction of four-engined bombers, which would increase the weight of attack on Germany. In this respect, Harris was instrumental in securing for Bomber Command the means to conduct effective operations later in the war when he became AOC-in-C. However, this has to be balanced against the neglect which was suffered by the other operational commands at this time. As far as Fighter Command was concerned, he railed against the findings of Sir Thomas Inskip, prewar Minister for Co-ordination of Defence, who was responsible for increasing fighter production during the late 1930s. Such an increase, Harris suggested, robbed the aircraft industry of materials which should have gone into bomber production. He was quick to point out that a lack of pilots was the limiting factor during the Battle of Britain, and not a lack of fighters. Of Army Co-operation Command, created in December 1940, he agreed with the former CAS Newall's view that it represented a 'gross misuse of the RAF'. Harris was not the only Air Staff member to subscribe to this view, but he did not spend any time considering the Command's requirements. Therefore, all the important lessons learned in the Battle for France were allowed to languish, and had to be painfully relearned in the Western Desert during 1941–2. Harris's views on Coastal Command, meanwhile, are the stuff of legend. Coastal Command, he said, was an 'obstacle to victory'. This opinion dated back to at least 1937 when, as Deputy Director of Plans, he regarded the purchase of aircraft for shipping protection work as a 'dangerous subtraction' from the RAF's ability to wage an offensive war. Because of their range and endurance, bombing aircraft were being demanded by the Admiralty for anti-submarine patrol work, and by the middle of 1941 these demands were particularly insistent as Allied shipping losses reached record levels (in April 1941, the Allies lost 195 vessels, as compared with the previous April's figure of 58). Harris's argument against giving Coastal Command any long-range aircraft was that submarine hunting in the Atlantic was the proverbial 'needle in haystack' operation, and he believed that to hit submarine production at source, in the German industrial cities, was far more efficacious. What this argument overlooked was that his approach would not deal with the immediate U-boat threat posed in the Atlantic, which was claiming a growing number of ships each month. By the beginning of 1941 U-boats were sinking more ships than were being built, and projections for the rest of the year showed Britain to be in danger of starvation. Harris's argument also overlooked the fact that sinking U-boats was not the only measurement of efficacy in the Battle of the Atlantic; to keep U-boats submerged prevented them from firing their torpedoes, and this is what air patrols did very successfully.[12]

A Directive from Churchill in March 1941 gave priority to the Battle of the Atlantic. Nevertheless, Harris's anti-Coastal Command rhetoric continued unabated. It reached new heights when, in May 1941, he was sent to Washington as head of the British Air Staff Mission. His job was to secure as much aid as he could from the Americans under the recently signed Lend-Lease Act, and he was incensed when B-24 Liberators and B-17 Fortresses were destined for trade defence and not service in Bomber Command. As we know, provision of these aircraft was responsible for closing the 'Atlantic Gap' in 1942 and, in conjunction with the widespread fitting of air to surface vessel (ASV) radar in Coastal Command's aircraft and improved depth charges, U-boat losses to aircraft attack grew throughout the year (from 30 per cent of total claims to nearly 50 per cent). Harris was unmoved by this success, and continued to begrudge any Very Long Range (VLR) aircraft given to Coastal Command, particularly after he became AOC-in-C of Bomber Command in February 1942. Even when there was a serious reversal in Allied fortunes in the Battle of the Atlantic in the spring of 1943, Harris remained adamant that the best way to defeat the U-boats was to attack German war production as a whole. His focus was on building up his part of the Combined Bomber Offensive.[13]

The hallmark of the great senior commander is the ability to grasp the big strategic picture, and Harris certainly failed in this respect. When we talk about his flawed strategic judgement, we usually think of the debates which occurred in the autumn of 1944 when he questioned the wisdom of giving priority to attacks on oil and communications targets, even though he had been directed to do so. However, his greatest lapse in judgement occurred in relation to the Battle of the Atlantic. It would be won or lost in that theatre, and without an Allied victory, the Combined Bomber Offensive was not going to happen, and neither was re-invasion of the Continent. Furthermore, what Harris failed to appreciate was that the Battle of the Atlantic was similar to gaining air superiority; it was an ongoing battle, in which the Allies had to be constantly engaged.

There can be little doubt, however, that Harris served the interests of Bomber Command to the best of his ability, and was primarily responsible for putting in place those factors which made Bomber Command a decisive weapon. He was probably the right man at the right time when he took over as head of Bomber Command in February 1942. By the force of his convictions, he inspired confidence not only in his aircrews at a time when they were suffering devastating losses (regularly over the 6 per cent monthly level the Air Ministry considered the maximum sustainable, which meant that an individual had less than a 30 per cent chance of survival), but he also gave a very necessary fillip to the nation's morale at a point in the war when Britain had suffered more defeats than victories (especially in the Mediterranean, North Africa and the Far East). Bomber Command remained the only means of hitting Germany directly, and Harris promised to hit Germany as hard as he could. He was utterly convinced that a concentration of force over a selected range of industrial cities would break German morale and fatally damage the enemy's war-making capacity. This is why he was so resentful of the Admiralty's attempts to have more VLR aircraft sent to Coastal Command. He argued that only a concentration of force would work, and this is what he strove for during the rest of his time as AOC-in-C. The dogged pursuit of this objective was seen first in the famous '1,000 bomber raid' on Cologne at the end of May 1942, when Harris trawled through all the operational commands in order to achieve 1,000 aircraft in total.[14]

Harris is generally regarded as the author of area bombing, but the Directive which sanctioned this strategy was already in place by some weeks when Harris took over Bomber Command. The area versus precision bombing debates which occurred in the late summer and autumn of 1944 are an overly well ploughed field, and so discussion here will be limited; suffice it to say that the author is not one of those who considers the area campaign to have been a waste of resources. As Richard Overy has amply demonstrated, the area campaign played a decisive role: first, by placing a ceiling on German industrial production, preventing increases being any larger than they were; and second, by diverting potential front-line resources to defence of the Reich. However, as numerous postwar studies have also demonstrated, oil and communications were critical vulnerabilities for the Germans, and Bomber Command could have started to attack these targets at a much earlier point in the war (1943 and not 1944).[15]

Rather than discuss the area versus precision debate *per se*, it is interesting to consider why Harris should have had such a deep aversion to precision attack. It cannot be explained purely in doctrinal terms. It can be explained, in part, by his distrust of civilian advisers. Harris, while not alone in expressing this view, was firmly of the opinion that the only people qualified to advise on any matters to do with strategic bombing were of the 'light blue' persuasion. When the Ministry of Economic Warfare was created in 1939 it had a very sound pedigree, being formed around the inter-war Industrial Intelligence Centre. However, it was viewed by most of the Air Staff as a body merely for the collation of intelligence on the enemy economy, so as soon as the Ministry of Economic Warfare (MEW) offered an opinion on targeting priorities, many, including Harris, took exception. Liaison between the Air Staff and the MEW was almost non-existent during the first year of the war. If the Air Ministry Plans and Operations departments consulted the MEW at all in the first part of the war, it was usually when a department wanted to confirm its own ideas. The Air Staff and Harris were particularly dogmatic over the question of the enemy's aircraft and related industries. There were a number of occasions on which the MEW cautioned against certain operations, but Harris pressed on regardless. One such was the ill-fated attack on a diesel engine factory at Augsburg in April 1942. The MEW warned that even if this one plant were to be completely destroyed, it would have little appreciable impact on the supply of engines. Harris went ahead and ordered a daylight attack, and the result was the loss of 60 per cent of the force despatched; and subsequent Battle Damage Assessment proved that the factory did not stop production, and any shortfalls were compensated for by production at five other factories in Germany and the Occupied Countries. Similarly, the MEW gave a very cautious estimate of the probable effects of the attacks on the Ruhr dams. It believed that the economic impact of the attacks, even if wholly successful, would be marginal. Again, subsequent analysis showed the MEW to have been correct. (It can be argued, of course, that this operation was important for British morale.) But Harris believed, erroneously, that the MEW had been advocating the dams raid 'for years', and was scathing about the MEW's analysts when the impact of the operation was shown to be small.[16]

However, MEW–Harris relations passed the point of no return at the end of 1943, when the MEW placed pressure on the Air Ministry to have Bomber Command join the US Eighth Air Force in its attacks on ball-bearing production. The MEW believed that the ball-bearing industry was the most serious bottleneck then existing in the German industrial economy, and identified one plant in Schweinfurt as the producer of 52 per cent of the total German production. Although the Americans had suffered crippling losses in their first attack on Schweinfurt on 17 August 1943, the MEW called for immediate night-time attacks by Bomber Command. The Air Ministry's Directorate of Bombing Operations concurred. Harris, however, rejected the proposal outright, and claimed that Schweinfurt was not necessarily a major producer of ball-bearings, and that the MEW had given insufficient consideration to the question of ball-bearing stocks. He was wrong about the relative contribution made by Schweinfurt, but was correct over the issue of stocks. The MEW was not entirely to blame for this miscalculation as the Germans themselves were not aware of the scale of stocks throughout German industry as a whole; but, when the anticipated fall in enemy industrial production failed to materialise, Harris felt vindicated in his view of the MEW analysts as 'panacea mongers'. Harris warned Portal that in future he would not consider any target systems put forward by the MEW. This had serious consequences for British strategy in the second half of 1944, when plans were being made for the resumption of a full-scale air offensive after the break imposed by D-Day support operations. There appeared for consideration a number of target systems, regarded scathingly by Harris as yet another collection of 'panaceas', but which, this time, were key weaknesses in Germany's war effort, including oil and communications.

Harris's view of the MEW was typical of the man. Intolerant of mistakes, once he had made up his mind about an individual, an organisation or a plan of action, he was usually unshakeable. As has been shown elsewhere, MEW analyses were usually very accurate, and the only time Harris had real cause to complain about their analysis was over the ball-bearing issue; but even without this, he would have had an instinctive distrust of their advice because they were civilians. The official historians make the comment also that Harris 'made a habit of seeing only one side of a question and then of exaggerating it. He had a tendency to confuse advice with interference, criticism with sabotage and evidence with propaganda.'[17]

The pressures of command also betrayed some less than palatable opinions of other nationalities, even if we acknowledge the 1940s context in which these opinions were set. In January 1943, a debate brewed which would have had a disastrous impact on relations between Britain and the Dominions and other Allies had it been publicised. Harris wrote to Portal, expressing his concern over the large number of Dominion and foreign aircrew in his Command. On first reading, his letter seemed to be another one of Harris's complaints about the Canadians establishing their own Group in Bomber Command. However, his criticisms went well beyond this issue. The letter is worth quoting:

> I cannot help wondering if the potentially serious effects of the ever increasing tendency to alienise and Dominionise the RAF are fully apparent. Out of the 63 squadrons now on my books, no less than 20 are already foreign or Dominion ... I cannot imagine the Admiralty getting themselves into a position wherein half the Grand Fleet, if we had one, would be composed of colonials and foreigners ... The bomber force, which might be described as the Grand Air Fleet of this country, is surely entitled to man its own aircraft with its own personnel ... I feel very uncertain as to the reactions of the British public when it becomes apparent to what extent the British character of what, after all, is the Royal Air Force, has been debauched by what is now happening.[18]

The letter was circulated among the Air Staff, who dismissed it outright, and many were to comment at length about the benefits of having Dominion aircrew in Bomber Command. Portal said that for Bomber Command to have one-third of its squadrons manned by Dominion or Allied personnel was not excessive.[19]

That Harris should have been exercising himself over this issue at this point in the war seems extraordinary. Harris was, after all, something of a colonial himself, having lived in Rhodesia before the First World War. In his memoir, *Bomber Offensive*, he was also scathing about the quality of non-British aircrew, saying that 'the British, being in general better educated and more amenable to discipline, are apt to be quicker in the uptake during the complicated training which has to be given before troops can handle modern machines of war'.[20] What does this reveal about Harris's character? While most senior British commanders spoke of the Allies all being 'in it together', Harris drew sharp lines of demarcation.

The intriguing aspect is that Harris had always said that the only thing to matter was the success of the bomber offensive, however this was brought about. This was the same mindset which allowed him to disregard other theatres of war, other strategies, and other facets of the war effort. It was the same mindset which allowed him to debate with Portal over Directives issued to him in October 1944, requiring him to devote the main bombing effort to oil and communications.

Many historians have suggested that, in the face of Harris's insubordination, Portal should have relieved Harris of his command. However, this overlooks a number of considerations. Quite apart from the friendship between the two men and high professional regard Portal had for Harris, it would have been extremely difficult for Portal to relieve someone of Harris's stature at that point in the war. This was at the peak of the Combined Bomber Offensive when, at last, Battle Damage Assessment (BDA) and intelligence showed the bomber offensive to be working. To have relieved Harris would have dented Bomber Command's morale when, for the first time in the war, it was relatively good. Such a move would also have been a blow to the nation's morale, at a point in the war when the enemy was far from beaten, launching the Ardennes offensive in December and assaulting Britain with V-weapons. German propaganda would also have made much of Harris's departure from Bomber Command. We only have to look at the mileage the Germans got out of Patton's stalled career after the famous slapping incidents in Sicily. Harris was too important to let go, and Portal understood this.[21]

To sum up Harris's strengths, they would be his level of understanding of what his business (bombing) was all about, and particularly his frank approach to operational problems. His weaknesses, which were more numerous, were his dogmatism, obstinacy and associated lack of diplomacy as exhibited within his own service, with other services, and other nationalities. It is ironic that society and military hierarchies, in general, tend to be more tolerant of dogmatic senior commanders such as Harris during unlimited wars, where national survival is at stake, when one would have thought flexibility and broad strategic vision would be key. But this is because single-mindedness and determination are more likely to be needed in wars of this type, particularly during the dark days, and this, some would say, is when Harris was at his best. But we are unlikely to see Harris-style figures in our military in the near future, not only because of creeping political correctness, but also because of the limited, low-intensity type of warfare in which we will be engaged. In the heavily Joint, and probably Combined, environment of the future, good intra- and inter-service, and inter-state, relations will be of paramount importance, and the Harrises and Pattons of this world are unlikely to be found in prominent positions.

Notes

1. See, for example, S. Cox's introduction in A. Harris, *Despatch* (London: 1995) esp. pp.xxi–xxiv.
2. H. Probert, *High Commanders of the Royal Air Force* (London: 1991) p.30. Probert has written a biography of Harris (*Bomber Harris: His Life and Times*, London: 2001).
3. C. von Clausewitz, *On War* (Princeton, NJ: 1976) p.100.
4. Ibid., p.101.
5. Ibid., pp.101–3.
6. J. Slessor, *The Central Blue: Recollections and Reflections* (London: 1956) p.204.
7. D. Saward, *Bomber Harris* (London: Cassell, 1984) p.29.
8. Ibid., ch. 8. See also C. Goulter, *A Forgotten Offensive: Royal Air Force Coastal Command's Anti-Shipping Campaign, 1940–1945* (London: Frank Cass, 1995) pp.136–8.
9. Clausewitz, *On War*, p.101. See also Probert, *High Commanders*, pp.28–9; Saward, *Bomber Harris*, pp.75–6.
10. Saward, *Bomber Harris*, p.77.
11. Goulter, *A Forgotten Offensive*, pp.127–8.
12. Saward, *Bomber Harris*, ch. 10; J. Terraine, *The Right of the Line* (London: 1985) pp.64, 426; J. Terraine, *Business in Great Waters: The U-boat Wars, 1916–1945* (London: 1989) Appendix D, 'Shipping and U-boat Losses, 1939–45'; Goulter, *A Forgotten Offensive*, pp.76–7.
13. Terraine, *Right of the Line*, p.427f, esp. 428.
14. C. Webster and N. Frankland, *The Strategic Air Offensive Against Germany, 1939–45* (London: HMSO, 1961) Vol. II, pp.104, 110, 123; Vol. III, p.80; A. Harris, *Bomber Offensive* (London: 1990) pp.110–12, 122, 267.
15. R. Overy, *The Air War, 1939–1945* (London: 1980) pp.122–3; Air Historical Branch (RAF), Ministry of Defence, Reports of the British Bombing Survey Unit; United States Strategic Bombing Survey, Overall Report (Europe).
16. Air Historical Branch (RAF), 'Bomber Command Quarterly Review', April–June 1942; ORS Bomber Command Report, 5 May 1942; United States Strategic Bombing Survey Report 164, 'M.A.N. Werke, Augsburg'; Report 93, 'Maschinenfabrik Augsburg-Nurnberg, A.G. Augsburg, Germany'; Webster and Frankland, *Strategic Air Offensive*, Vol. I, pp.441–4, 463, 464 fn; Vol. II, pp.168–78, 288, 292.
17. Webster and Frankland, *Strategic Air Offensive*, Vol. III, p.80. See also Vol. II, pp.25, 39–40, 39 fn, 62–5, 269, 270–2; USSBS Report 53, 'The German Friction Bearings Industry', p.18; Goulter, *A Forgotten Offensive*, pp.269–70, 276–7, 291–2; 'The Ministry of Economic Warfare and British Air Strategy'.
18. Public Record Office AIR 20/3096, Harris to Portal, 10 January 1943.
19. Ibid., Minute to AMP, AMT from Portal, dd. 12 January 1943. See also Memo to CAS from AMP, dd. January 1943, and related correspondence.
20. Harris, *Bomber Offensive*, p.64.
21. See discussion in Cox, introduction in Harris, *Despatch*; Webster and Frankland, *Strategic Air Offensive*, Vol. III, pp.75–94.

Part III
The Contemporary Scene

10
The Realities of Multi-national Command: An Informal Commentary

General Sir Mike Jackson

For navies and air forces multi-national command is neither new nor difficult, and has been done for a long, time. But for the soldier, and I am going to discuss this issue as a soldier,[1] multi-national command is an aspiration; on land life gets a little bit more complicated. The command purists would argue that however many nations are involved, multi-nationality requires the cake to be sliced into equal parts, a part for each nation contributing. Furthermore, the Commander with the allocating knife will be assisted by at least one Deputy Commander, probably many more, and a Chief of Staff and a Deputy Chief of Staff of this and a Deputy Chief of Staff of that. All of these posts, of course, will be shared out on a national basis, and regularly rotated every two or three years. As in musical chairs, the music will begin and they will all move round and the whole Command team will change: different people from different backgrounds will come and do different jobs. That is the purist approach. One or two organisations of which I have had recent experience go even further. They do not have just one Deputy Commander, but as many Deputy Commanders as there are nations contributing, and they take it in turns to be the 'real' Deputy Commander, so there is, as it were, a sub-set to the musical chairs. It is all jolly important because we have to keep the flags flying.

There is, on the other hand, a more pragmatic approach, of which I will develop my thoughts in a moment. The Allied Command Europe Rapid Reaction Corps was invented in the immediate aftermath of the Cold War, actually on a very farseeing basis by the North Atlantic Treaty Organisation (NATO), which did look quite carefully at what might be required. NATO decided that there was going to be a need for a deployable three-star Headquarters which would actually be able to go quite a long way from its barracks, not 30 kilometres down the road and into the nearest wood. A strategically deployable Headquarters was needed. It was put out to contract on a 'framework nation' basis. It was thought that the way to create this Headquarters would be to have a lead nation, or framework nation, and it was the UK which volunteered to have a go at this; so far as I know, we were the only people who did so. That said, fourteen nations are involved and politically that is excellent, but with it comes the military problem of friction. Without doubt, the single most efficient way of delivering military capability is for a single nation to do whatever needs to be done. A single nation has a common training system, doctrine, culture, and language and faces the least friction. But in today's world this will not run. The trick is to get the right balance between political desirability and military feasibility. If the equation eventually comes out such that the political advantage offered by multi-nationality is greater than the military friction it inevitably brings with it, then all is well, but we have to make sure that it is not the other way about. It is a dialectic: political desirability is the thesis, military friction the antithesis and the synthesis is to be certain that the political advantage outweighs the military disadvantage. 'The Realities of Multi-national Command' are about this kind of military friction.

The level of intensity

The first thing I think you need to look at is what is being demanded of you as a Multi-national Commander within whatever operational environment it may be; what is to be the level of intensity, and how hard is the fight to be? Are you going to be engaged in warfighting or in something more benign, and where are you on the spectrum of conflict? The Commander needs to be very hard nosed about the degree to which he accepts multi-nationality as a political advantage, while at the same time remaining able to deliver a military outcome in what could be a very demanding situation.

Then there is the question of the forces with which you, the multi-national Commander, are going to have to do this operation. The probability these days is that we are likely to be looking at non-Article V operations, which of course makes it a matter of national choice as to what the nations are willing to contribute. The resultant force generation process is extraordinary and it is interesting to see how the nations approach this, how willing they are without the absolute disciplining effect of Article V. How willing are they to become involved? What risk, nationally, are they prepared to take? Their answers are hedged around in terms of size of commitment and in terms of constraints. These constraints may be what sort and how many people they will send, who they will work with, or under, who they want, where they will go and where they will not. This is not a criticism, just the reality. Nations take sovereign decisions on these matters, which need to be stitched together. The Operational Commander will not find this easy and will probably not get quite the force structure he wanted. It is complicated even further if you have some ethnic problems in the area in which you will be operating. Some of those ethnic problems will be recognised by national constraints, but some will be hidden and left for you to discover.

First, Command and Control; command styles do vary enormously. Mission Command is certainly what the British Army talks about and the Americans and Germans have their versions of this too. Frankly, in my experience, not enough courage is shown actually to implement 'Mission Command' in its true philosophy and some countries, particularly those who are recently only emerging from their 50 years in the Warsaw Pact, have real difficulty with even knowing what Mission Command means. They are much more comfortable with very direct orders, in great detail.

Language is another problem. There is no doubt that any serious military force will have to operate in English. That is not much fun if you are not a native English speaker, but I fear it is the reality and some national contingents are better at coping with this fact of military life than others.

Standardisation is a well-worn cry that has been around for a long time, but progress is glacial. Despite the many NATO committees that meet and study the matter and all the papers that are produced, it is frankly very hard to make a great lot of progress while sovereign states have national industrial and economic concerns of which they need to be aware.

Force Protection is a phrase much bandied around these days, but it can be a source of friction. Different nations come at force protection in different ways, partly through their own military way of doing things and their own military experience and partly through national political considerations. Despite all this, it would be interesting to see how the mortality rates in, say, Bosnia compare to those of normal peacetime operations, and how, or whether, they vary from one national contingent to another. The results of such a survey might be very surprising. I would also like to see the contrast between each of those and the overall average for the force in Bosnia put against the average mortality of soldiers in barracks in peacetime life. I think one might be rather surprised by the results, despite the fact that so much political capital is expended on this question of force protection.

My last sort of friction is intelligence. Again, intelligence is guarded very jealously nationally, and very understandably so. Sources and access differ, and so do national approaches to the balance to be struck between technical and human intelligence, in specific regard to what you are doing.

How do you minimise friction?

First, to the command arrangements, because more often than not it seems to me if they are not right the whole thing is a disaster: command arrangements are the first thing you need to get absolutely right. We have many different types of command; full command, operational command, operational control, tactical command, and so on. The political capital which is invested in terms such as operational command will take a lot of overturning. All too easily such disputes can degenerate into a new command lexicon of 'Op Can' (the 'will do' approach), 'Op Can't', 'Op Won't' and 'Op Yours'. These diverse terms have outlived their usefulness and it is high time we re-addressed them. But if you as the Operational Commander have not got the necessary unity of command, you must go for unity of effort and that is a matter of leadership and personal relationships. It may sound banal, but I have come to understand just how important such relationships are in the multi-national environment. This approach requires a very lavish use of Liaison Officers; they are unsung heroes in many cases. The Mission Command approach helps too, though some cultures have difficulty in understanding exactly how it works. It can help in that you can tell a national Commander what he is to do, by when and with what; what you do not do is tell him how to do it. I think you have to leave that to him not only from the point of view of our own military doctrine, but also in international terms; he is best left doing it the way he knows best and is most confident about.

Training and exercises

It is self-evident that the more a potential multi-national force can train together, and can exercise together, the less the friction it will face; just by personnel getting to know each other, the better will be the understanding of the scope of the problem. The framework nation has a very important role to play in producing the synthesis between multi-nationality in its purest sense and the minimisation of military friction.

Political guidance

Political guidance can be really helpful if you get it. Sometimes you do not and it is, I think, very indicative of the difficulty of doing all of this that my predecessor, General Mike Walker, on going to Bosnia, had in effect to write his own campaign plan. He was 'merely' the land component Commander, but the doctrinally pure will know perfectly well that a component Commander (even though it was a land dominant campaign) has no business to be writing a campaign plan. This is the responsibility of the theatre Commander reacting to the strategic guidance and the political direction given to him at the strategic level. We did not get it right that time.

Peace support operations

The extent to which it is wise to push multi-nationality down the command chain has to depend on the intensity of the operation. While in war it is unwise to go below the divisional level, in peace support operations we may be able to go much lower, perhaps even to the Baltic platoons we see in the Stabilisation Force in Bosnia and Herzegovina (SFOR). There is no hard and fast rule.

Political leaders will also be wary of releasing control over logistics, perhaps particularly in the medical area. As a national Minister of Defence, are you willingly going to take the political risk of having your soldiers meet their end through lack of proper medical care, in theory provided by somebody else, when you could have done it yourself? You could be dead in the water as a politician for not having provided, from national sources, medical cover for your own soldiers. And so straight away the ideal of multi-nationality frankly conflicts with the politics of the sovereign state. This is very likely to limit the scope for role specialisation within NATO outside Article V situations. It is not that we do not trust each other; it is rather the other way round. This is seen as a national responsibility and if you are going to field people for an operation (whether it be on the ground, in aircraft or in ships) you at the end of the day will have to make sure it all works. That may not be necessarily the most rational answer, but I think it is a real world answer. Frankly I do not see much desire to go down the road of specialisation other than sticking together for a particular operation when deals may be struck. The nations will not want to give up their own field hospitals.

The bottom line is that there are a number of potential mine fields out there, and every national commander has his national 'red card' which he will pull out when he does not like something, wave it in your face and say 'Sorry, General, I'm not doing it.' The Operational Commander will have to do his level best to work out what the red card issues are and how they may be best avoided. They are much less likely to be encountered in Article V national survival situations than in less intense circumstances when the pursuit of political advantage makes national governments more anxious to take their own view. This is often shown by their separate Rules of Engagement which are a means of political direction at the national level. They are quite diverse and limiting because no government can overturn its own domestic and constitutional situation.

Despite all this, when the ACE Rapid Reaction Corps (ARRC) went to Bosnia, we were all utterly clear that this was a watershed; this was the first major ground operation that NATO had embarked upon and it had to work. The unity of effort (not necessarily the unity of legal approach) was there, without doubt, and many people broke their own rules because they were as concerned as anybody else to make sure it all worked. It is this unity of purpose that derives from a common view that we are all here to do a job of work and to succeed which makes the difference; it is less a question of mechanisms than of relationships. It is often up to the individual commanders to get on with it. So do not exaggerate what I have been saying here; I have laid out to you some of the problems, but equally multi-national command does work although it takes effort. Even just to keep the machine ticking over requires more fuel going into the carburettor than it would on a purely national basis.

It is important not to overemphasise the difficulties: for example, take Kosovo. Had there been a military involvement on the ground, which there has not yet so far been, there is no single country that would have taken it on, not one. The biggest drive towards multi-nationality in fact is the willingness of the sovereign states to accept that if they do not hang together, they will surely hang separately. Only the United States can go it alone, but even they will rarely choose to. That sort of operation can only be conducted with a collective multi-national force, whether that be a NATO operation, or an ad hoc coalition of the willing; it can only be done on a multi-national basis. But for those who have not had to make it work, there are too many rose-tinted spectacles around and what I have tried to do is take them off and tell you that you have to be honest about the problems.

In the old days of the Central Region we all had a great north/south layer cake of forces, and frankly we went up national command tubes and there was not a lot of cross-border multi-national activity. Today is utterly different and if you cannot 'task organise' for the mission you have you will probably fail, but task organisation means people not living in little national islands; they have to come together. Things really are different now.

Note

1 This chapter is based on an informal after-dinner speech given by General Sir Mike Jackson at the conference on which this book is based.

11
Reinventing Command in United Nations Peace Support Operations: Beyond Brahimi

Stuart Gordon[1]

Despite all the disillusion and cynicism over the UN's peacekeeping performance in the past 10 years, there seems no alternative but to take whatever practical measures are possible to reform and revitalise the organization. There may be more efficient and streamlined vehicles on the road, but the UN is the only one in which everyone consents to travel.[2]

Managing peacekeeping: the UN's three-dimensional crisis

The management, command and control of peacekeeping missions throughout the post-Cold War expansion of UN peacekeeping activities has plagued the UN Secretariat. These problems have been exhaustively documented[3] and the latest set of reform proposals, the Brahimi report, neatly summarises them as 'problems in strategic direction, decision making, rapid deployment, operational planning and support and the use of modern information technology.'[4] In effect these difficulties contributed to a crisis in three dimensions: strategic, organisational and conceptual. The strategic crisis itself had several layers. Peacekeeping mandates were frequently overambitious, lacked clear strategic direction or were inappropriate for the circumstances. The second element of the UN's crisis then became apparent: a lack of resources generally, and specifically within the Department of Peacekeeping Operations (DPKO),[5] as well as cumbersome procedures for deploying troops and securing mission critical equipment. These problems ensured that operations were often slow to begin once formally agreed by the Security Council. Once under way they were frequently underfinanced, sometimes lacked sufficient troops and encountered a host of difficulties in sustaining both personnel and operations. Operationally, UN commanders also faced interference from governments contributing troops, difficulties reconciling the agendas of a multiplicity of third party organisations and actors (all with differing mandates and sources of accountability), and not least the variable quality and cultures of troops under command. All of these factors contributed to UN peacekeeping missions exhibiting a rather ad hoc feel, demonstrating the attributes of a temporary activity rather than a core function of the UN.[6]

The crisis in the management and sustainment of peacekeeping missions coincided with a broader 'conceptual' crisis that challenged the credibility and relevance of the tool itself. The application of peacekeeping in circumstances where the belligerents' commitments to cease-fires were questionable or where they resented the nature of the UN mandate brought into question its utility. This problem was compounded by the multiplicity of forms in which 'peacekeeping' operations manifested themselves.[7]

By 1995 this three-dimensional crisis had manifested itself in terms of a lack of trust in the capacity of the UN to manage large-scale missions in volatile environments. This was reflected in a reduction in the expectations heaped upon the UN system. In some ways this was a pity; and it coincided with a raft of measures, often initiated by the Secretariat, designed to overhaul the capacity of the UN to manage its own operations. Empirically, the contraction was seen in what transpired to be a somewhat short-lived reduction in the pace of authorisation of new peacekeeping missions and the renewed reliance upon traditional principles of consent plus a tangible commitment to a sustainable peace or cease-fire. Nevertheless, largely as a consequence of missions in Sierra Leone, East Timor and the Democratic Republic of Congo (DRC) the numbers of troops deployed in active missions began to climb once more. Furthermore, several of the conceptual difficulties re-emerged, largely as a consequence of operational difficulties encountered by the UN Assistance Mission in Sierra Leone (UNAMSIL).[8]

Problematising command: the perennial problems

To begin to understand the reasons why the UN confronted this three-dimensional crisis it is worth dwelling on the normative attributes of a military organisation capable of setting and realising objectives. For such an organisation to work effectively it requires the clear definition of political objectives and their effective and realistic translation into military objectives. The military structure needs to be integrated both vertically and horizontally in order that it can sustain unity of purpose as well as effective and rapid decision making (which is itself transmitted to and acted upon by all elements within the organisation). In essence this can be reduced to two clear prerequisites for effective command and control: first, clearly defined, achievable and complimentary political and military objectives; second, both vertical and horizontal integration throughout the intervening organisation. Palin puts this into slightly more practical terms, arguing that:

> At the highest level, the political authorities determine the political objectives, set the politico-military guidelines for the operation and superintend its strategic direction. Within the theatre, the appointed force commander and his staff plan, direct and conduct the operation within those guidelines. In between, a superior military headquarters commands the overall operation, sets the operational concept, deals with the strategic issues, acts as the interface between the political authorities and the theatre commander, and co-ordinates the supply of reinforcements and logistic support.[9]

Achieving this ideal is likely to prove very difficult for the UN, arguably far more so for a global institution than most other military structures found in a national or even alliance context. UN missions are based upon the engagement of multiple institutions, multi-nationality within mission command structures and multi-functionality within and across organisations. These represent both limitations and strengths.

Multi-nationality and the presence of multiple institutions (each with differing objectives in terms of institutional interests) tends to lead to a far greater degree of politicisation of command arrangements in the UN's overarching mission headquarters. This process can occur at a variety of levels, beginning with the form of 'institutional architecture' employed in the theatre. For instance, the international force deployed in Kosovo in 1999 was, at US insistence, not 'commanded' by the UN or subject to any form of dual key arrangement; instead, it was subsumed under the 'auspices' of the UN with the latter legitimising NATO's presence both through an authorising Security Council Resolution and its presence as the organisation responsible for the civil elements of post-conflict peacebuilding. Whilst this arrangement resulted largely from the experience of the two organisations in managing the provision of air power in Bosnia from 1993, it also represented a broader attempt by NATO to avoid being considered a 'Regional Organisation' of the UN system as defined by Chapter VIII of the UN Charter. As such the institutional architecture represented a means for underlining and preserving NATO's institutional and decision-making autonomy.

Involvement in multi-national formations may also prove to be domestically significant for governments, representing a means of raising an international profile and engaging with processes relating to the management of international security. This itself leads to the politicisation of command arrangements. For example, Russian participation in the Kosovo Force (KFOR) was a means of gaining a role within a process thus far completely dominated by NATO. Exclusion from this was potentially damaging both for Russia's foreign policy profile and domestically, representing an abandonment of a regional ally. Nevertheless, the resulting requirement to participate alongside the erstwhile adversary, NATO, translated itself into a series of profound and controversial debates within the Russian political and military elites over the precise command relationships between Russian troops and NATO commanders deployed in Kosovo.[10] For NATO, Russian involvement also presented difficulties. Russia initially pressed for its own brigade area of operations in the north of the province, contiguous with Serbia and largely occupied by what was left of the Kosovo Serb population. The geography of this arrangement was likely to generate operational difficulties for KFOR, placing the Russians in the role of 'Serb protector' on an organisational boundary that may have become a confrontation line between Serb and Kosovar Albanian paramilitaries.

Strategic politicisation is mirrored at the operational level by troop-contributing governments continuing the process of politicking for national advantage. The allocation of command appointments is routinely viewed as part of the currency for national advancement rather than a collective effort to enhance operational efficiency. This is true even within long established headquarters but is far more obvious in new or rapidly adapting headquarters of the type routinely established by the UN. Such a process may have an extremely detrimental effect on the cohesion and unity of command within a mission and may lead to burgeoning bureaucracy as appointments are created on the grounds of satisfying national *amour-propre* rather than operational effectiveness.[11]

Officers deployed within such divided headquarters may also import elements of their governments foreign policy agendas, thereby distorting the decision-making agenda. Within established structures, this happens to a reduced degree, reflecting the development of a corporate institutional identity but also the formalisation and acceptance of national mechanisms for the provision of politico-military advice.

Within new and developing structures, the norms underpinning such arrangements are in a process of flux. Often, as was the case with the United Nations Protection Force (UNPROFOR) in Bosnia-Herzegovina and the United Nations Operations in Somalia (UNOSOM I and II), missions are so comparatively ephemeral that the lines of political command and control cannot be formalised and regularised prior to the mission's completion or termination.

Formations subordinated to a multi-national headquarters may also remain responsible to national Ministries of Defence (MoDs) in addition to the UN military command. They may restrict the employment of their own troops either through 'policy instruments' such as geographically limiting their employment or operational 'force protection measures' designed to limit the risks to their own troops. Alternatively, they may exercise influence through scrutinising and rejecting taskings made by the nominally superior multi-national headquarters.

Unity of command may also be undermined by the disparate nature of the forces under command. Marked variations in national cultures, military ethos, conceptions of military professionalism, varying qualities of troops and equipment, and unfamiliarity within the military formation all serve to undermine the unity of effort. The absence of trust in the effectiveness of the UN command structures also increases the degree to which troop-contributing governments will want to monitor and become involved in operational priority setting, thereby increasing the degree of politicisation of the command arrangements. This process can be reinforced by environmental factors. For example, where the volatility of the environment increases and trust in the capacity of the UN operational headquarters is low, the level of command authority delegated by troop-contributing governments to UN theatre commanders may also be reduced. The potential impact upon the unity of command is obvious as is the potential for such action to encourage other troop-contributing nations to respond in a similar way, further weakening the control of UN commanders over their assigned forces. Where trust is extremely low, this may encourage the complete by-passing of UN military structures through what could be described as 'coalitions of the willing'[12] or of 'unilateral responses within multilateral frameworks'.[13] The command and control structures effectively become victims of their own lesser failures.

Mandate formulation and vertical co-ordination

Whilst the politicisation of command structures presents UN Force Commanders with an array of difficulties, perhaps the greatest problems are those resulting from the nature of Security Council mandates. These have several layers of difficulties, beginning with the difficulties encountered in obtaining consensus in the Security Council. The gradual breakdown of the immediate post-Cold War consensus on the Security Council has ensured that many decisions have reflected the lowest common denominator of what members will accept. Particularly, as in the case of Bosnia-Herzegovina, this has been translated into a limited humanitarian mandate which became increasingly difficult to sustain in the face of Bosnian Serb obstructionism and Bosnian Presidency politicking.[14] The difficulties caused by the tendency for Security Council decisions to reduce to the lowest common denominator is also compounded by the absence of a formal and automatic link between its decisions and the requirement for resources.[15] This problem is accentuated by the declining openness of debate within the Security Council and a reduction in the degree to which member states are accountable for both decisions and the resource implications generated by them.[16]

Even if the Security Council is able to formulate resolutions, translating these into operational mandates is a process plagued with difficulties. The vagueness of Security Council decisions places a far greater burden upon the Secretariat to translate political decisions into operational instructions. The paucity of operational experience of many UN civilian and military staff and the lack of resources was frequently exposed by the difficulties encountered in the increasingly complex missions of the 1990s. At the very least the Secretariat was confronted with the reality that 'expeditionary' operations are a highly specialised and complex form of military activity and are not best supported by an ad hoc, multi-national, often inexperienced, headquarters.

The process of translating resolutions into mandates is one of interpretation and deduction, a potentially highly politicisable and controversial process and one not suited to the style of decision making often employed within the Secretariat. In their defence, DPKO officials frequently, and not unjustly, claim that they are not imbued with sufficient authority or legitimacy to make the types of strategic decisions which serve to convert broad-based political agreements in the Security Council into realistic operational mandates. The process is also made more fraught by the frequent absence of a Force Commander at the point when the DPKO is translating Security Council resolutions into a mandate. Force Commanders and Special Representatives of the Secretary-General (SRSGs) are frequently appointed as the mandate formulation process is nearing completion. Consequently, the process of selling the plan to troop-contributing nations or even limiting the aspirations of the Security Council may be hindered by the lack of effective support (or, in some cases, even their presence) from those ultimately charged with ownership and implementation of the plan.

For the UN Secretariat to overcome such difficulties SRSGs and Force Commanders would need to be appointed early in the process. In addition, there would need to be a completely new relationship forged between the Secretariat as a whole and the members of the Security Council and the troop-contributing nations. Without this the DPKO is ill placed to translate Security Council decisions into an effective operational mandate and is also poorly structured to serve as an operational headquarters. The result is that the UN theatre headquarters is forced to participate to a greater degree in the transformation of Security Council resolutions into operational mandates; It is often ill equipped to perform this process and, given the way it is itself heavily politicised, problematical. Reducing the level at which operational mandates are framed also enables other agendas to interfere with mandate interpretation, in particular force protection measures introduced at this level (primarily by casualty-averse Western governments).[17]

The post-Cold War reform of peacekeeping management

A variety of measures have been established to deal with the institutional shortcomings of the UN's management of Peace Support Operations (PSOs), yet these have not represented the type of root and branch changes necessary to improve the capacity of the UN to effectively manage its missions. Nevertheless, there have been improvements. At the strategic level Annan's 1997 reform process created co-ordination mechanisms which served to improve the chances of effective interdepartmental co-ordination but, less positively, also raised the possibilities that such delegation increased the layers of bureaucracy within the system. The creation of multiple layers of management between the Security Council and the field, and the continuing decentralisation of responsibility through an increasingly disaggregated system, raised as many dangers for the effective management of operations as it did possibilities for improved operational and strategic co-ordination.[18]

Nevertheless the creation of a Planning Division in the DPKO and the Secretary-General's Task Forces on UN operations (established in 1994) provided a framework for co-ordination with the other departments and specialised agencies. Other efforts at improving co-ordination have attempted to delineate responsibilities more clearly in order to provide a clearer division of labour. For example, the March 1994 report of the Secretary-General entitled 'Improving the Capacity of the United Nations for Peacekeeping' sought to delineate the responsibilities of the Department of Political Affairs (DPA), the DPKO, the (erstwhile) Department of Humanitarian Affairs (DHA) and the Department of Administration and Management (DAM). Consequently, the DPA is described as the 'political arm' of the Secretary-General whilst the DPKO is his 'operational arm for the day to day management of peacekeeping operations'. The responsibilities of DHA were described as 'co-ordination and humanitarian operations'. However, these distinctions have proved difficult to sustain within a field operation and have resulted in significant duplication.

The DPKO has also received much specific attention. It has nearly doubled in size since 1994 and now comprises two major sub-departments: the Office of Planning and Support, and that of 'Operations'. The latter was itself divided into several functional units including a Situation Centre, a Policy and Analysis Unit, Training Unit, Civilian Police Units and, perhaps most importantly, a Mission Planning Service. Both Boutros-Ghali and Kofi Annan have also strengthened the Executive Office of the Secretary-General, intending this as an institutional co-ordination mechanism. Such responses clearly make sense yet they introduce another layer between the Secretary-General and the relevant departments and potentially represent obfuscating rather than co-ordinating mechanisms. Whilst Annan's reforms have attempted a greater degree of sophistication than those in the past, they have not addressed the root causes of co-ordination difficulties: namely, institutional overlap, duplication, turf wars and increasing layers of management.

Despite this, there have been significant enhancements to military deployability, particularly in two areas: the DPKO's mission-planning capability and the mechanisms for troop-contributing governments to release forces. On the first of these, the Mission Planning Service has increasingly been involved in the planning of operations. Whilst its creation has enhanced the speed and effectiveness of the planning process, the tendency to appoint SRSGs and Force Commanders late in the process of preparing a mission obviously continues to preclude their involvement. Such a failing is compounded by the difficulties realised by the failure of the mission planners to routinely deploy with the mission itself.[19] This tends to create a lack of ownership of plans that may contribute to a lack of realism. If the operational headquarters is to be spared interpreting both Security Council resolutions *and* DPKO mission-planning instructions, there is an obvious requirement for a seamless link to the field.

The 1995 Canadian proposal for the creation of a high readiness standby brigade may, had it been successful, have gone some way towards addressing this issue. It suggested the creation of a 'Rapidly Deployable Mission Headquarters' (RDMHQ) comprising some 60 staff drawn both from the Secretariat and member states and deployed, once activated by a UN Security Council resolution, in order to establish the mission in theatre. This idea proved to be very popular within the DPKO and a 'skeletal' staff was created by Boutros-Ghali. There was a widespread expectation, bordering upon certainty amongst several senior members of the Mission Planning Service, that it would be fully implemented in 1997. However, the absence of political will in the General Assembly significantly hindered its implementation.

The realism of DPKO mission planning has, in the past, also been negatively affected by the lack of experience of its military and civilian staff. Field commanders have often complained of the lack of 'operationality' or task focus emanating from New York. In part this was a consequence of the culture of the UN's civil service but also reflected an organisation in crisis as a result of the number, complexity and scale of missions it confronted. Consequently, many governments, but particularly NATO governments, provided 'Gratis Military Officers' (GMOs) to the DPKO. At their strongest the GMOs represented over 80 per cent of the staff of the DPKO.[20] Whilst they injected a considerable sense of urgency and realism into the work of the DPKO and certainly enabled it to cope better with the expansion of its workload, they represented an enormously contentious issue. The Non-Aligned Movement (NAM) in the General Assembly argued that they undermined the principle of equitable geographical distribution of posts. Some authors[21] argued that, for several members of the NAM, their position on the issue reflected their unhappiness at the loss of lucrative and prestigious political patronage opportunities rather than concern for the negative impact of their actions on the effectiveness of the UN. To some extent this missed the more important point. The dispute was between those who were unwilling or unable to provide such forces and those who did. For the majority of the former, GMOs were viewed as a means by which UN debtor nations gained influence through securing influential appointments within the DPKO and through exerting leverage by withholding funds. For such states the appropriate means through which the DPKO should have been reformed was to formalise the GMOs, making their funding part of the regular budget and making DPKO appointments subject to the same requirement for universal and equitable representation that governs the recruitment of all other UN permanent staff.

The result of this dispute was ultimately the suspension of the GMO system through General Assembly resolution 51/243. The last of the GMOs finally left UN headquarters in early 1999.

The creation of the GMOs was viewed by several troop-contributing nations as a means of 'hard wiring' the DPKO with a core of effective and experienced staff.[22] This also reflected developments that occurred in the deployed headquarters, particularly in Former Yugoslavia from 1992. Troop-contributing nations, particularly from Western European and North American states, increasingly attempted to transpose either national preformed command structures (as occurred, for example, in UNPROFOR's Sector Sarajevo and Sector South West from 1994 to 1995) or, where this was not possible, to generate a headquarters structure 'hard wired' with officers in whom the real decision-making authority was vested, regardless of the official organograms and conventions of rank that normally applied. Sometimes lower-ranking individuals were authorised, in pressing circumstances, to by-pass nominal superiors from other nations. This was a process different from the injection of national agendas into a headquarters, although it is reasonable to presume that the boundary lines between the two types of activity were often blurred. As a process it was described as 'hard wiring' by those who performed it and 'hijacking' by those who could not.

The other major reform area has been in the speed with which troops can be deployed. The ideal contained in Article 43(1) of the UN Charter is for member governments to 'undertake to make available to the Security Council...armed forces, assistance and facilities...necessary for the purpose of maintaining international peace and security'.[23] The Cold War precluded agreement on the modalities of implementation and, despite several calls for the reinvigoration of this process (the last most significant was Boutros-Ghali's call in *An Agenda for Peace*), there is little chance that they will be heeded. Hence post-Cold War reform measures have tended to address the issue of the speed with which troops can be deployed on loan from member governments rather than making available an 'unconditional' pool of troops.

This process effectively began in 1990 with a request from the Secretary-General for member states to identify the resources they might make available to the UN for peacekeeping missions. This request was further elaborated upon in *An Agenda for Peace* which called for enhancements to databases recording mission critical assets such as strategic lift and, as a response to the overstretch of the organisation, a more equitable sharing of the burden between the UN and regional bodies as described in Chapter VIII of the charter. The process of enhancing the

Secretariat's capabilities continued in February 1993 with the creation of the 'United Nations Standby Forces Planning Team', a small team designed to further the development of a system of standby resources.[24] This evolved into the 'Standby Arrangements Management Unit' (14 April 1994) which now manages what amounts to a database of troop-contributing governments' resources that could *potentially*, on a case by case basis, be provided for peacekeeping operations mandated under Chapter VI of the Charter. Whilst it could be argued that the system amounts to little more than a record of conditional pledges to provide troops within specific response times, it is a positive development in the sense that it enhances the speed of the mission-planning process both within national capitals (of troop-contributing nations) and within the DPKO.[25] It also contributes to identifying strategic lift, logistics, training and equipment shortfalls in national defence planning processes, thereby potentially speeding up the process of identifying troops, the mechanisms for their deployment and sustaining them. In addition it enables the creation of 'niche contributions', a potentially worrisome development allowing the more militarily sophisticated states to increase their role in 'force facilitation' (through participation in less risky activities such as logistics and strategic lift support) rather than fuller participation. Paradoxically, a mechanism designed to enhance the UN's response capability may facilitate a form of covert disengagement by some.

Nevertheless, there is a range of benefits that potentially outweighs this risk. By enabling the DPKO to transfer data on force composition into the DPKO's budgetary mechanisms it may contribute to speeding up the process of mission costing and reimbursing troop-contributing states, thus possibly increasing the numbers of governments willing to contribute forces to a specific mission and certainly contributing to reducing the administrative delays incurred.

The Secretariat has also begun a process of encouraging the development of sub-regionally based, brigade sized, force packages. These are envisaged as being used within sub-regions close to their planned points of embarkation.[26] As such they offer a means of harnessing the political will of states to solve regional security issues and also benefit from the impact that shortened lines of communication will have upon deployment times, and costs. Arguably, the first of these to be established is the multi-national Standby Forces High Readiness Brigade (SHIRBRIG), which was declared operationally ready in January 2000.[27] Implicitly the DPKO envisage several of these packages committed to operating regionally, rather than a limited number capable of operating globally.[28] Consequently, SHIRBRIG represents a model for emulation rather than a complete solution in its own right. Nevertheless, the increasingly broad and geographically diverse membership of the SHIRBRIG Steering Committee (including Canada and Argentina)[29] suggests that, in order to overcome broad resistance to the concept of a reaction brigade, a much broader political platform of support is necessary, thereby raising the potential that the brigades develop a global rather than regional orientation. These proposals are already viewed by some states as potentially providing a Western and 'exclusivist duplication' of the UNSAS (United Nations Standby Arrangements System) system.[30] Whilst its proponents claim that it augments the UNSAS arrangements, it does provide both benefits and dangers. Perhaps the largest of these is the potential for more creative forms of disengagement by some Western states.[31] Early deployments by such brigades, even if augmenting UNSAS, offers governments a means of avoiding having to deploy 'unilaterally' with a UN mission; in effect an all-or-nothing approach, enabling states reluctant to deploy to disengage from crises by hiding behind 'multilateralism'. Alternatively, it may provide a means for contributing to the high profile and often safe part of the mission when the parties' commitment to a cease-fire may be at its peak. This may leave the militarily less accomplished states with the difficulty of being deployed as the cease-fire becomes more fragile and where the deterrent capability of a more capable force may have done far more to deter such a breakdown.

Nevertheless, the brigade package idea does create a process of regional participation in multi-lateral intervention, a new process that could be described as 'commitment security'. Participation potentially becomes enmeshed in broader multi-lateral regional political processes, thereby potentially serving to enmesh blocs of state in what could be described as an ethic of participation. In simple terms it may bind them into the process of reacting by increasing the costs for their regional diplomacy of not doing so.[32] At the very least, it raises the potential for momentum behind the idea of intervention that may pervade foreign and defence planning thinking.[33] This process has already been seen with the deployment of several SHIRBRIG contributors (Canada, Denmark, and the Netherlands) as part of the UN Mission in Ethiopia and Eritrea (UNMEE).[34] The process of deployment was facilitated by the SHIRBRIG planning headquarters and the Force Commander of UNMEE was the serving Brigade Commander of SHIRBRIG. Whilst Dutch participation can be explained in terms of exorcising the ghosts of Srebrenica and legitimising a relatively newly reformulated defence policy,[35] it is conceivable that Denmark and Canada, already contributing to peacekeeping missions in the Balkans, may well have been more reluctant to shoulder the burden of operations in Africa were it not for the multi-lateral co-operation engendered through SHIRBRIG. The SHIRBRIG mechanism also provides other benefits in terms of reducing the impact of national vetoes on deployments. Its structure contains a large degree of overcapacity and duplication that may serve to offset the impact of national vetoes and make deployment more likely.

The UN Secretariat's support for the SHIRBRIG concept is, in part, an implicit recognition that the most effective unit of deployment is a brigade and that multi-nationality poses such demands at this level that the 'coherence' of the formation needs to be established *prior* to a deployment rather than during its critical initial stages. As such SHIRBRIG offers a model for increasing not only the speed of deployment but also the cohesion of the force, as well as neatly ensuring the early appointment of senior commanders at or just below the level of Force Commander.

At the practical level the UNSAS also provides a mechanism that will potentially enhance national capacities for deploying on UN peacekeeping missions and, thereby, in the long run, serving to broaden the base from which troops can be drawn and reducing the rather unhealthy dependence upon Western militaries. However, unlike the force envisaged by the UN founders, the UNSAS has a fragile *conditional* nature that ensures troop provision can never be guaranteed and does not reduce the central problem of troop availability which is the absence of a direct link between a Security Council resolution and the resources necessary in order to achieve it. The absence of the type of obligation placed upon UN member states by Article 43(1) potentially also raises the degree to which politicisation of UN command structures occurs. UNSAS is, in effect, an opt in/opt out process allowing governments to deploy troops with a greater range of conditions and strings attached. This will have obvious effects on the unity of command of the mission as a whole.[36]

The process and context of reform

The slow pace of the UN's post-Cold War reform reflects the fact that it has frequently proved easier to announce than to conduct. Applebaum wrote that, even in 1993, reform:

> [is] a constant topic among the UN's top bureaucrats. Yet from year to year little seems to change. In a bureaucracy which is responsible to everyone and no one, even press scrutiny has had little impact. Individuals who try to reform the system from within risk ostracism and loss of their jobs.[37]

Nevertheless, reforming the UN is far more problematical than effecting changes in a national context partly because of the lack of a clear constituency pushing for reform and partly because of the paucity of consensus on what effective reform means. This problem is compounded by the fact that the UN faces no legislature monitoring its performance, has only limited press scrutiny, does not directly serve any politically enfranchised taxpayers and responds to a constituency of 189 states. In the face of institutional resistance from the myriad of fiefdoms (the specialised agencies and departments), and without consensus (or even trust, in some cases) amongst the member states,[38] a more ambitious reform package is extremely unlikely to succeed. Consequently, managing the process of UN reform, particularly in the area of the UN's security management function, is likely to be an extremely slow process requiring almost constant reinvigoration and with rather limited objectives. The latest reform proposals for enhancing the UN's management of peacekeeping missions are contained in the Brahimi report.

The Brahimi report

On 8 March 2000 Kofi Annan called upon a high-ranking panel headed by former Algerian Foreign Minister, Lakhdar Brahimi, to establish a 'clear set of recommendations on how to do [peacekeeping] better'.[39] In front of the Security Council, Annan spoke of the 'crisis of credibility facing this Council'[40] and called for prompt action, particularly in Africa, in the maintenance of peace and security. He called upon the Security Council to summon the will to act and to develop the ability to act. In effect, he identified two dimensions to the UN's crisis of credibility. The ensuing report, published in August 2000, called for a series of changes to the way in which UN peacekeeping operations are run but also extended its scope to look at other elements of multi-functional responses such as early warning, peacebuilding and judicial reconstruction.

The report was published less than a year after the high-profile reports cataloguing UN failures in Rwanda and Bosnia-Herzegovina.[41] In such a context the Brahimi panel obviously needed to tread a careful line between their report appearing either as a post-mortem of previous failures or as an apologia. In fact, the report appeared to serve a different purpose, maintaining pressure on the Security Council in terms of limiting expectations as to what the UN could be expected to achieve, as well as providing a more positive vehicle for setting forth the reform debate and garnering additional resources beyond documents highlighting the tragedies in the Great Lakes and the Balkans.

The report also served as a means for restoring commitments to the central importance of the UN in the management of peace and stability in the international system. In the aftermath of an apparently increasing tendency to by-pass the Security Council, this renewal of commitments to the *centrality* of the UN was important. The timetable of the report also enabled it to become one of the centrepiece discussions[42] in the commencement of the General Assembly's 'millennium assembly'. Its publication also coincided with the threatened expansion of the coercive elements of the UN mission in Sierra Leone. Possibly there was more than a simple coincidence in the report's general encouragement for the Security Council to show restraint in terms of mandate formulation at a point when the UNAMSIL threatened to evolve uncontrollably into an inappropriately equipped and poorly resourced enforcement operation. The obvious confusion over aims and objectives of this and the nascent UN efforts in the DRC imply that Brahimi raised warnings to the Security Council to stop and reconsider the purpose, resources and limitations of the UN's involvement in each case.

Brahimi's recommendations

The report itself is not revolutionary; it represents the distillation of lessons from a troubled decade in the history of UN peacekeeping. The key to understanding the limitations are encapsulated in Annan's statement that the UN:

> must not promise too much, or raise expectations higher than are justified by the will of the governments to act ... partly it is a question of being clearer about what we are trying to do, what kind of forces we need to do it, what are the conditions in which different kinds of mission are appropriate.[43]

Whilst the report fails to open any new debates it contains a range of challenging proposals. The recommendations largely fall within three broad themes: calls for greater clarity and speed in formulating strategic direction and improving the strength of political support; improvements to the UN's capacity to deploy, manage and resource operations; and more effective conflict prevention and peacebuilding strategies.[44]

Political support

Taking the first of these themes, the report addresses several of the difficulties encountered in formulating effective mandates. Whilst its proposals are generally limited to the reform of management structures, it does call for a recasting of the relationship between the Security Council, the Secretariat and troop-contributing nations. In particular it calls upon the Council to adopt longer-term planning horizons and to demonstrate self-restraint in terms of the tasks required of its troops and the locations to which they are deployed. It also encourages the Secretariat into taking a more robust approach, specifically asking it to 'tell the Security Council what it needs to know, not what it wants to hear, when formulating or changing mission mandates'.[45] In practice this is likely to prove challenging, and in this respect the Secretariat's experience of managing UNPROFOR's mission in Bosnia is salutary: the DPKO frequently lobbied for more effective approaches (and greater resources) towards the implementation of the Safe Areas concept and was just as frequently overruled or ignored by the Security Council.[46] At the root of this difficulty is the lack of accountability of Security Council members for their actions or the resource implications of their decisions.

One of the most interesting proposals is designed to overcome the problem of framing resolutions in the absence of commitments from troop-contributing governments to provide the soldiers and equipment necessary to implement the resulting mandate. The Brahimi panel recommended a more iterative process, calling upon the Security Council, once broad but informal agreement has been reached, to leave its authorising resolution in draft form until the Secretariat has received sufficient commitments of troops and equipment from governments. In effect, the proposal provides a means of strengthening the office of the Secretary-General through an augmentation of his power to influence the terms of a response to a crisis as well as providing obvious benefits in terms of the speed of response and the link between the aspirations of the Security Council and the troops/resources made available. In addition it recommends that the process of framing the mandate itself should include a greater degree of consultation with troop-contributing governments as it is being formulated, or at points where the mandate of the mission is being reformulated, or where significant changes in the operational environment raise security issues. Practically this means including the troop-contributing nations in Secretariat briefings to the Security Council. Whilst this raises the numbers of stakeholders formally included in the management of the operation, and therefore potentially bureaucratises it, most of the stakeholders are already engaged, through informal means, in managing the risks faced by their own troops. The mechanisms employed are usually ad hoc and involve direct contacts between national ministries and their commanders in the field. Brahimi's recommendations raise the possibility that these divisive contacts may be further delegitimised through reducing the obvious need for them.

The Brahimi panel also recommended that more account be taken of the environment in which UN troops are deployed. In particular, it drew attention to the post-Cold War experiences of UN deployments in the context of intra-state conflicts in which 'consent' has frequently been manipulated in ways damaging to the mission. Whilst it stresses that consent, impartiality and the use of force only in self-defence 'should remain the bedrock principles of peacekeeping',[47] it identifies that maintaining equidistance between the parties where one party to the peace agreements is incontrovertibly 'violating its terms' can lead to 'ineffectiveness and in the worst may amount to complicity with evil'.[48] The conclusion is a call for the Security Council to show a greater willingness to distinguish 'victim from aggressor'. Brahimi develops the argument further, calling upon the Security Council to provide UN troops with the wherewithal to defend themselves, specifically calling for missions that are larger (and obviously more expensive), and more robust with credible forces operating with 'robust rules of engagement' and mandates which 'specify an operation's authority to use force'.[49] These missions would be equipped with enhanced intelligence capabilities of the type necessary 'to mount an effective defence against violent challengers'.[50] Practically this means the creation of missions capable of dealing with 'those who renege on commitments or seek to undermine peace accords by violence'. This capability, Brahimi suggests, can also be put at the disposal of preventing violence against civilians. This is reinforced by the suggestion that the mandates should contain a moral component at least insofar as both mandates and peace agreements should be consistent with internationally recognised human rights standards.[51] Such calls can be seen as the offspring of UNAMIR's experience with the Interahamwe the Hutu paramilitary organisation,[52] UNAMSIL's with the Revolutionary United Front and UNPROFOR's with the Bosnian Serb and Croat paramilitaries.

In effect Brahimi suggests that a capacity to deter attacks and obstruction would ensure a greater degree of compliance and avoid the rather rapid unravelling of negotiated agreements as certain combatants exploit the weakness of UN troops. This is a particularly important lesson and reflects the increased likelihood that, in intra-state war, the development of a war economy will generate incentives for some to continue the war. In the context of UN military weakness, these incentives can prove too great to withstand.[53] Whilst creating large and credible military forces raises an enormous array of practical challenges, in some respects it is one of the least contentious 'principles' contained in Brahimi and parallels the convergence of Western military doctrines upon a recognition of the fragile nature of consent and the consequent need for robust 'potential'.[54]

Management of missions

Brahimi also calls for a major overhaul of the DPKO and enhancements to the mechanisms for deploying and sustaining missions. Paralleling the post-Cold War adaptations of many national military crisis management headquarters it called for the early establishment of Integrated Mission Task Forces (IMTF) designed to provide effective mission planning (particularly in the start-up phase) and support. Such teams would comprise seconded staff from all of the relevant departments and would be the generic model used for planning and supporting all missions. Such teams would draw together, in the words of the report itself, 'those responsible for political analysis, military operations, civilian police, electoral assistance, human rights, development, humanitarian assistance, refugees and displaced persons, public information, logistics, finance and recruitment'.[55] Whilst such mechanisms are in principle a fine idea they raise a number of problems. Given the numbers of organisational stakeholders in UN missions (even within the UN itself), IMTFs may prove unwieldy. The Summary of Recommendations makes it clear that Brahimi envisages the IMTF leaders as exercising temporary line authority over seconded personnel 'in accordance with agreements between DPKO, DPA and other contributing departments, programmes, funds and agencies'.[56] However, it is likely to prove difficult to identify and reconcile the precedence of departmental and agency interests complicated by differing sources of accountability, turf fights and struggles for departmental supremacy. Furthermore, defining the exact relationship of the IMTFs with the Executive Committee on Peace and Security (ECPS), a product of Annan's 1997 reforms, is also potentially problematical. Whilst this is a potentially positive adaptation it will not be perceived as such if it obfuscates lines of responsibility and accountability.

The report does not call for the creation of a UN standing army, which has long been resisted by many states; rather more realistically, it calls for enhancements to the UN's speed of reaction and a fostering both of the UNSAS mechanism and the high-readiness brigade concept, and abandoning the call for a dedicated UN-run reaction force. Ambassador Brahimi identified that 'a rapid reaction force is something that exists within a mission'.[57] Brahimi thereby, in diluted form, paralleled Boutros-Ghali's much earlier call for 'enforcement units' within peacekeeping missions but avoided being embroiled in a debate which could have only one conclusion.

Consequently, Brahimi calls upon member states to work together to create several 'coherent, multinational, brigade sized forces and the necessary enabling forces'.[58] These would be available at the start-up phase of an operation, and are specifically envisaged as speeding initial deployments. These would also provide obvious enhancements to the coherence and unity of command within a mission providing they did not become alternative or competing sources of authority. Despite the creation of SHIRBRIG, this remains a remarkably ambitious project, requiring the creation of regional, multi-national, co-operation forums with sufficient strategic lift resources for the type of enhanced missions structures envisaged elsewhere in the report and capable of rapid deployments. Brahimi is equally ambitious in the suggested timelines for deployments, recommending headline goals for cease-fire monitoring operations and civil conflicts of less than 30 days. More difficult missions demanded by complex emergencies or intra-state conflict would require deployments within 90 days. Both of these represent major improvements over the average deployment schedules achieved in the first half of the 1990s and also raise the prospect of the UN missions being able to capitalise and reinforce the early stages of a peace. Brahimi rightly identifies that 'opportunities lost during that period are hard to regain'.[59] Nevertheless, these are ambitious aspirations especially when set in the context that even militarily developed states such as the UK have significant shortfalls in strategic lift capability. Rapid deployment comes at a premium, and the degree to which Brahimi's recommendations are implemented will depend upon the degree to which member states are willing to bear such costs. In the context of generally declining spending on armed forces this is likely to prove challenging.

The speed with which the management team is assembled has also been a major failing of previous missions. To that end Brahimi recommends assembling the leadership much earlier in the planning cycle through the creation of a list of potential SRSGs, Force Commanders and civilian police commissioners, created with due regard to equitable geographic and gender distribution. This should provide a more effective planning cycle but also, when combined with the proposal to change the relationship between troop contributors, should provide a more effective management team which is better placed to sell operational concepts and explain troop requirements. It should also help in the process of drawing more meaningful links between the field and the headquarters, with field officers (civilian, police and military) included in planning at the deployment phase of the operation. The process of appointing the leadership early would also be augmented through the creation of a list of 100 'experienced, well qualified military officers, carefully vetted and accepted by DPKO' who would form another component of UNSAS. These officers would translate the strategic level plans and missions, provided to them through the Force Commander, into what Brahimi describes as 'concrete operational and tactical plans in advance of the deployment of the troop contingents' whilst also augmenting the deployed DPKO mission start-up team. In this sense they mirror the 1995 Canadian idea of an RDMHQ, although they lack the coherence of a preformed headquarters arrangement. Moreover, any apparently 'selective' mobilisation (given the readiness states required, this is quite likely) of predominantly European and North American staff officers is likely to rekindle the ire of certain NAM states, anxious to avoid any repetition of the GMO episode.

These proposed enhancements are paralleled by a range of suggested improvements to mission administration, in particular the range of measures designed to rationalise and streamline operational accounting. The simplest suggestion is that DPKO assume responsibility for both budgeting and procurement, but this is augmented by a more generous and flexible delegation of purchasing authority to field commanders. Previously accounting restrictions placed upon Force Commanders have often served only to encumber the mandate and retard the commander's ability to obtain mission-essential items. As an interim measure Brahimi recommends the creation of as many as five mission 'start-up kits', maintained at the UN logistics base in Brindisi. These would contain vital equipment for missions, such as deployable communications systems.[60] However, this would be created with a view to proposing a broader 'Global Logistics Support Strategy' to the General Assembly encompassing a range of measures from traditional stockpiling of mission-essential equipment through to conditional contracts with the private sector. If such measures could overcome the administrative and rule-based culture which has frequently impeded the rapid setting-up of missions this is all to the good but, given the chequered history of financial probity in some past UN missions, the relaxation of accounting rules is likely to be resisted by some member states.

Perhaps the most contentious administrative proposal is that calling for the Secretary-General to be authorised to allocate funds of up to $50 million from the Peacekeeping Reserve Fund to mission planning in advance of a Security Council resolution authorising the mission itself. Whilst Brahimi recommends oversight from the Advisory Committee on Administrative and Budgetary Questions (ACABQ) this raises practical and theological issues amongst several member states. In particular it raises the danger, voiced privately by officials from several states, that the Secretariat could lead the Security Council into a decision to mandate a mission largely as a consequence of monies already committed rather than any more compelling case. Nevertheless, it is reasonable to expect that Brahimi's recommendation that the Secretariat should identify troop contingents *prior* to the confirmation of a draft Security Council resolution would appear to limit such a possibility. It is still the case, however, to some states such a proposal represents a potentially dramatic, albeit subtle, expansion of the influence wielded by the Secretary-General and affords him a greater role in setting the agenda of the Security Council as well as enhancing the pace of mission deployments. For other states, such as Germany and Austria, the objections to this are rooted in interpretations of their respective constitutions: neither state can volunteer troops until the mandate is formally established through a Security Council resolution.

Intelligence and information

One of the most controversial elements of the Brahimi report is the proposal to strengthen the management of missions through the creation of an Information and Strategic Analysis Secretariat to support the work of the ECPS and the departments represented on it.[61] It is proposed that it would be created through consolidating the DPKO's Situation Centre with the rather fragmented policy and planning offices within DPA. It may also include augmenting the DPKO with additional military and police analysts. In part this recommendation reflects the Security Council's own experience of managing the missions to Somalia. The Council's own report on Somalia highlighted a range of errors which suggest that it lost control of the mission, partly at least as a consequence of inadequate information on, and a false assessment of, the capability of Somali fighters.[62] The Security Council's lacklustre response to impending genocide in Rwanda was also, in part, attributable to a lack of capacity between departments in New York (and also between New York and the field) for distributing publicly available information on the imminence of genocide. In effect, the collation of information was poor and both horizontal and vertical information dissemination were ineffectual.[63] The ECPS Information and Strategic Analysis Secretariat (EISAS) would potentially remedy such deficiencies by enabling a degree a proactive action on the part of the ECPS through ensuring the speedy collation and dissemination of information throughout the New York headquarters.[64] Ideally, it would also produce policy analysis papers and inform and suggest strategic responses to potential, developing and existing crises. Without such a secretariat, Brahimi implicitly suggests, the ECPS would find it difficult to transform itself into 'the decision making body anticipated in the Secretary-General's initial reforms'.

EISAS is one of the most controversial elements of Brahimi, partly because it requires additional resources but more importantly because it raises issues of sovereignty for some states. It is also unclear whether it would remedy all the difficulties in the area of information management. Information flows within the New York Secretariat are regulated as much by political realities as organisational restrictions imposed by the absence of a body such as EISAS. The former New Zealand Ambassador, Colin Keating, for example, argued that the Secretariat portrayed events in Rwanda in late 1993 in terms of a small civil war rather than the beginning of a genocidal orgy of violence. Given the context of events in Somalia, and the conclusions drawn by the UK and US missions as to the degree of overstretch in the Secretariat, it is perhaps unsurprising that the Secretariat would be keen to ensure that the distribution of their information did not fatally undermine the procurement of troop contributions from member states or the passage of mandating resolutions for UNAMIR itself.[65] In the absence of automatic provisions of troops and the fragility of Western will to support Africa this process of information 'management' on the part of the secretariat is likely to continue, although its effects will be felt most keenly by Security Council members with more limited intelligence-gathering and processing capabilities than those of the P5 (permanent five members of the UN Security Council). Nevertheless, EISAS may contribute to the more effective recognition of the type of problem confronting the Secretariat and to the formulation within the Secretariat of a broader range of options that may translate into increasing those available to the Security Council. Nevertheless, it is clear that the provision of information alone will not resolve these issues; rather, it is the combination of the public provision of information and Security Council members feeling accountable and engaged. The Security Council's increasingly secretive deliberations, together with the devolution of authority to structures such as the ECPS, potentially reduce rather than enhance such accountability.

The information management strategy contained in Brahimi is not limited to communication within the Secretariat and to the Security Council; instead, it is extended into the field both through recommendations on enhancing the Extranet information technology link between missions and New York and reconfiguring and improving the internal New York

Intranet. The information strategy is also extended into what could be described as 'mandate support activities' or the development of more effective means for communicating the mandate and its achievement to local populations in areas where UN missions are deployed. In a number of missions, but particularly in Bosnia and Somalia, the UN's activities were distorted by the belligerents to such an extent that it eroded the effective achievement of the mandate. Brahimi addressed the idea of creating an office either within the DPKO or DPI (Department of Public Information) to support the public information messages for particular missions. This reflects the experience of many UN force commanders that the UN Secretariat was ill equipped to deal with 'media operations' and parallels the development of similar capabilities within several Western militaries.[66]

Conflict prevention and peacebuilding

The Brahimi panel also focused on improving the capacity of the UN to manage both conflict prevention[67] and peacebuilding. As a largely political activity the former does not require an enormous range of changes aside from supporting the increasing usage of 'fact finding missions to areas of tension in support of short-term crisis-preventive action'.[68] Where conflict prevention strays into the preventive deployments of troops under UN auspices the changes proposed for UNSAS and rapid deployment in general will lead to enhancements in this area.

The recommended enhancements to the UN's peacebuilding capacities are more substantial but are not new, even within the UN system.[69] Neither is this activity universally supported: it is viewed with a degree of scepticism by several states that view it as an encroachment on the nation-building activities of governments. Yet, particularly for Western Europeans, the increasing focus on the linkage between peacekeeping and peacebuilding is seen as positive and has been paralleled by the development of more 'holistic' and multi-functional approaches to their own peacekeeping doctrine.[70]

Brahimi identifies an additional major change in the way peacebuilding activities can be viewed. Traditionally peacekeeping and peacebuilding activities have largely been viewed as sequential activities. Brahimi observes that several missions have begun in situations where neither side had achieved a decisive military victory, and consequently not all parties to the conflict have been fully committed to a peaceful resolution. In such a context, the UN role has been transformed from underpinning a peace agreement into creating the conditions in which one could be achieved. The implications of this are, according to the Brahimi panel, the interdependence of peacekeeping and peacebuilding strategies. Such a change requires a range of practical enhancements to the capabilities deployed within a UN mission, in particular those relating to the capacities for restoring the rule of law. Consequently, Brahimi recommended that the ECPS present to the Secretary-General a plan for strengthening the permanent capacity of the UN to 'develop strategies and implement programmes'. The Secretary-General added to this process in both the Millennium Report and remarks to the Security Council's Open Meeting on Conflict Prevention in July 2000 where he made an appeal for greater co-ordination and action 'to all who are engaged in conflict prevention and development – the United Nations, the Bretton Woods institutions, Governments and civil society organisations'.[71]

The Brahimi report also identifies a range of more limited and practical measures centred around a 'doctrinal shift in the use of civilian police and related "team approaches" to upholding the rule of law and respect for human rights'.[72] This encompasses a broad programme requiring both doctrinal and institutional adaptations. On the first point Brahimi recommends what amounts to a shift towards developing the capabilities for both more extensive and rapidly deployable supervisory policing capabilities as well as enhancing the capacities for the much more demanding executive policing role. Brahimi also calls for the DPKO to maintain, as part of an augmented and expanded UNSAS, lists of 'civilian police, international judicial experts, penal experts and human rights specialists' in order to strengthen 'rule of law institutions',[73] and the creation of collegial 'rule of law' teams'[74] as well as a generic interim legal code in order to aid in the establishment of the rule of law and a law enforcement capacity[75] in locations where a UN mission is forced to assume temporary executive responsibility (pending the establishment of more enduring forms of authority). In addition it calls upon states potentially providing 'rule of law' experts to appoint a single governmental point of contact for civilian police, reflecting the difficulties of dealing with the fragmented and highly decentralised policing arrangements prevalent in many states. These proposals are obviously designed to facilitate the rapid deployment of the range of 'rule of law' experts and their rapid and early integration into the broader mission.

Implementation

Reaction amongst the member states to the Brahimi report was generally positive.[76] The Security Council meeting of World Leaders prior to the General Assembly Millennium summit made clear their declaratory commitment to the bulk of the reforms articulated in Brahimi.[77] In particular it made a commitment to 'adopting clearly defined, credible, achievable and appropriate mandates', as well as mechanisms for more effectively providing the resources and arrangements for managing missions.[78] Nevertheless, this was not necessarily the forum in which Brahimi would be undermined; rather it is in the General Assembly and its Fifth Committee (Budget and Accounting) that its opponents may be more capable of dismembering it.

The bulk of states viewed Brahimi either with a degree of indifference or as part of the process of reaffirming the central role of the Security Council[79] and providing it with the tools to achieve its mission in the management of international security. In contrast, states such as China, Algeria, India, Pakistan and Cuba saw Brahimi in the context of NATO's intervention in Kosovo, itself viewed as driven by national interests, damaging to the non-intervention norm and its corollary, the sovereignty principle, as well as undermining the centrality of the UN in the management of international security. Thus events in Kosovo in 1999 combined with the legacies of their own experiences under colonialism in order to harden attitudes amongst some members of the NAM against anything that would provide the West with an interventionist capacity or appeared to challenge the sovereignty norm. For these states, Brahimi enhances the 'interventionist' case as well as providing the 'Western dominated' UN with the means to encroach on the sovereignty of weak states. In an unequal world, sovereignty is seen by them as the only guarantee of protection. Consequently, for such states, the proposed creation of EISAS and the recommendations relating to enhancing the UN's peacebuilding capabilities have largely been resisted. The proposed staff enhancements for EISAS in particular have already been halved in the General Assembly's Fifth Committee.

For others, particularly within the Non-Aligned Movement, Brahimi is seen as misguided, drawing attention and potentially funding away from the already declining development budgets as well as reflecting a largely Western agenda. Nevertheless, set against this are equally large numbers of African states that, whilst equally concerned with protecting sovereignty, resent the abandonment of Rwanda during 1994 and are keen to increase the UN's capacity to respond to such crises. For this increasingly large number of African states, Brahimi is seen for what it largely is: a means of building trust in the capacity of the UN to manage the more limited peacekeeping missions with which it was entrusted in the late 1990s. Nevertheless, and despite broad Western support for

Brahimi, deliberations on its implementation have been swept into broader debates on the budget and, in particular, the scale of assessments through which the UN is funded. This issue has several dimensions revolving around EU and US discomfort with the system.[80]

What this points to is a climate in which mutual reductions in financial contributions are more likely than a general increase in budget. Consequently, Brahimi may well begin to represent what, for many states, is an unpalatable choice: the elevation of the reform of peacekeeping above protecting development assistance funding. Nevertheless, Brahimi may well provide benefits, such as adding to the reminders directed towards the membership of the Security Council to be more realistic in the types of missions and resources allocated to the Secretariat. It may also serve to reinforce the overwhelming lesson of the 1990s: that calls for peace enforcement should largely be heeded by others and that peace enforcement, where there is a possibility of sustained combat, remains largely beyond the UN's stock of political, practical and pecuniary capital. As such, Brahimi does help with the process of resolving at least some elements of the UN's three-dimensional crisis. Nevertheless, because of the financial stringencies imposed upon the UN, Brahimi, as an entire package of reforms, is unlikely to succeed in resolving all the management and command difficulties. Yet the positive reforms of the 1990s, and those contained in Brahimi which are implemented, present us with a choice neatly summarised by McLandburgh Wilson: 'Twixt the optimist and pessimist, the difference is droll: The optimist sees the doughnut, But the pessimist sees the hole.' Whilst we undoubtedly face another decade of continuing UN institutional difficulties we are also likely to witness the positive, cumulative effect of reform and the gradual amelioration of the more obvious institutional shortcomings. We can maintain the habits of the 1990s and continue to identify the weaknesses of the UN, or we can choose to view its slowly increasing strengths.

Notes

1 The author is responsible for all of the views expressed in this article. It should not be implied that these represent the views of the Ministry of Defence or the Royal Military Academy Sandhurst.
2 Deaglan de Breadun, *Irish Times*, 23 August 2000.
3 See D.S. Gordon, 'Icarus Rising and Falling', in D.S. Gordon and F.H. Toase (eds), *Aspects of Peacekeeping* (London: Frank Cass, 2001) pp.19–42; W. Durch (ed.), *UN Peacekeeping, American Policy and the Uncivil Wars of the 1990s* (London: Macmillan, 1997) pp.1–35; D.C. Jett, *Why Peacekeeping Fails* (London: Palgrave, 2000).

4   See UN Document A/55/305 and S/2000/809, p.11.
5   For example the Brahimi report identifies that in 2000 DPKO had only 32 officers providing planning and guidance for 27,000 deployed troops. This was mirrored in other areas: nine police officers guiding 8,666 deployed police officers; 15 political desk officers supervising 14 current and two nascent operations: UN Document A/55/305, p.5.
6   It is currently funded from the support account rather than the regular UN budget. Consequently each post is scrutinised and the missions themselves are audited and renewed annually. Both of these represent enormous vulnerabilities and add an additional layer of 'politicisation' to the average UN mission.
7   See R. Connaughton, 'British Peacekeeping Doctrine: A Critique', in Gordon and Toase, *Aspects*; also R. Thornton, 'The Role of Peace Support Operations Doctrine in the British Army', in *International Peacekeeping (IP)*, Vol. 7, No. 2 (Summer 2000), pp.41–62.
8   Particularly the problem of mixing consent based peace implementation mandates with coercive elements. See S. Gordon and J. Higgs, 'Peace at What Price?', in *Jane's Defence Weekly*, 27 September 2000, pp.27–34. See also S. Gordon, *Britain's Ethical Foreign Policy* (London: Centre for Defence Studies, 2001). This problem re-emerged with the UNAMSIL operation. The partial withdrawal of Nigerian 'enforcement' troops and the Revolutionary United Front's belligerency and lack of commitment to the Lomé peace agreement forced the UNAMSIL to begin the piecemeal abandonment of the 'traditional' consent principles or face ignominious defeat or withdrawal.
9   R.H. Palin, 'Multinational Military Forces: Problems and Prospects', *Adelphi Paper (AP)* No. 294 (Oxford: Oxford University Press/IISS, 1995) p.15.
10 The *Wall Street Journal* reported that many in the Russian military establishment were 'deeply uneasy' with Russian troops serving alongside NATO forces. It quotes Russian Col.-Gen. Leonid Ivashov, who once called NATO a 'criminal organisation', as saying that 'we are not quite satisfied with the role of NATO that is being imposed and the diminished role of Russia'. Meanwhile, nationalists in the Duma claimed that 'Chernomyrdin is surrendering Yugoslavia' (Andrew Higgins, *Wall Street Journal*, 4 June 1999).
11 See Gordon, 'Icarus'.
12 For example, the Gulf War coalition.
13 For example, the deployment of French, British and American troops after the Rwandan genocide was in effect a set of parallel national responses within a multi-lateral setting.
14 See the UN's Srebrenica report: UN document A/54/549.
15 See R. Caplan, *Post Mortem on UNPROFOR* (London: Brasseys, 1996). Caplan describes the difficulties faced by DPKO in implementing the ambiguously constructed Security Council Resolution 836 (which created the Safe Areas regime in Bosnia in April 1993) which contained the potential for contradictory enforcement- and consent-based provisions.
16 See L. Melvern, 'The Security Council Behind the Scenes', in *International Affairs*, Vol. 77, No. 1 (2001), p.107. She details the decline in open debate over the past two decades.
17 Force protection measures introduce mechanisms that serve to limit the degree of freedom exercised by operational commanders through legitimising institutional risk aversion.

18 M. Berdal, 'Reforming the UN's Organisational Capacity for Peacekeeping', in *A Crisis of Expectations: UN Peacekeeping in the 1990's*, pp.181–93 and *idem*, 'Whither UN Peacekeeping?', *AP* No. 281 (London: 1993) pp.51–7.
19 See also R. Righter, *Utopia Lost: The United Nations and World Order* (New York: 1995) p.339.
20 See UN Document GA/PK/145, 10 April 1997.
21 See Jett, *Why Peacekeeping Fails*, pp.169–97.
22 Although there is some suggestion that Russia attempted to 'match' the deployment of Western troops into the headquarters.
23 P.A. McCarthy, 'Building a Reliable Rapid-Reaction Capability for the United Nations', in *IP*, Vol. 7, No. 2 (Summer 2000), pp.139–54.
24 This is a well-documented process. See Cdr R.T. Mentzen, 'Annual Update Briefing to Member States on Standby Arrangements', paper presented on 4 November 1998.
25 The process enables the DPKO to link force planning to the budgeting process and even to the generation of the MOU (Memorandum of Understanding) between the UN Secretariat and the troop-contributing state. GA Resolution 50/222 (11 April 1996) required an MOU between DPKO and troop-contributing states to be signed prior to deployment of troops. This process is frequently delayed as a consequence of difficulties encountered in identifying and securing strategic lift resources. Prior submission of what amounts to draft format MOUs allows confirmation at a later date and speeds up the process. Also the completion of a data planning sheet contributes to the early identification of equipment and strategic lift shortfalls by focusing upon generating realistic deployment period information. For a full description of this process see 'UN DPKO Progress Report of the Secretary General on Standby Arrangements for Peacekeeping'.
26 'UN Standby Initiative' briefing document, UNDPI (United Nations Department of Public Information).
27 Whilst this is the first operational brigade the first such proposal was, arguably, that from Canada in September 1995.
28 'UN DPKO Progress Report of the Secretary General on Standby Arrangements for Peacekeeping', p.4.
29 For an excellent analysis of this see McCarthy, 'Building a Reliable Rapid-Reaction Capability', p.143.
30 UN Press release GA/PK/152 31 March 1998. Also quoted in McCarthy, 'Building a Reliable Rapid-Reaction Capability', p.149.
31 Paradoxically it may also serve to reduce disengagement by providing capacities that enable reduced reliance on Western, and particularly US, military capabilities.
32 It is not unreasonable to expect this to occur. For examples see P. Latawski, 'Bilateral and Multilateral Peacekeeping Units in central and eastern Europe', in Gordon and Toase, *Aspects*. This article describes the states of central and eastern Europe as engaging in the creation of peacekeeping battalions as a means of furthering their broader regional agendas and even their aspirations to join the institutions of the Western Europeans.
33 For a development of this idea see Gordon, *Britain's Ethical Foreign Policy*.
34 In June 2000, after two years of fighting in a border dispute, Ethiopia and Eritrea signed a cessation of hostilities agreement following proximity talks

led by Algeria and the Organisation of African Unity. In July, the Security Council set up UNMEE to maintain liaison with the parties and establish the mechanism for verifying the cease-fire. In September, the Council authorised deployment of up to 4,200 military personnel in order to monitor the cessation of hostilities and assist in ensuring observance of security commitments.

35 On 29 January 1999 Dutch Defence Minister, Frank de Grave, announced that in the absence of a credible threat from Russia the new defence policy reoriented the army towards NATO and UN peacekeeping. De Grave was quoted as saying that the Dutch Army 'must in the future contribute to regional conflict management in crisis areas': *Die Welt*, 29 January 1999.

36 Nevertheless the UNSAS should not be seen as a panacea. Just under half of the UN members have signed up to the process but many of these have done little more than express an interest in the mechanism, and there continue to be shortfalls in the numbers of 'support' or 'expeditionary' capabilities; in particular strategic sea and airlift, utility aircraft, road transport and 'multi-role logistics'. It should also be borne in mind that the problems which poleaxed UNPROFOR were far broader and less resolvable than the problem of providing sufficient numbers of well equipped troops: see 'UN DPKO Progress Report of the Secretary General on Standby Arrangements for Peacekeeping'. See also UN Document S/1996/361, 30 March 1999; UN DPKO Srebrenica report; UN Rwanda Report located at www.un.org/News/ossg/rwanda_report.htm.

37 A. Applebaum, 'Is the UN Really Necessary', in *The Spectator*, 31 July 1995.

38 Several of whom used the UN system as an extension of domestic forms of patronage for their own political elites or simply as a means for transferring resources to their own states.

39 Quoted in *UN Wire*, 8 March 2000.

40 UN document SC/6919.

41 It also followed on from a series of meetings of previous and serving SRSGs and Force Commanders at UN headquarters in New York.

42 See UN Document DPI/2108 March 2000.

43 UN News Service 7 March 2000. See also: **http://www.un.org/News/Press/docs/2000/20000307.sgsm7324.doc.html** and **http://www.un.org/News/Press/docs/2000/20000307.brahimibrf.doc.html**

44 See UN Document A/55/305 and S/2000/809, p.1.

45 Ibid.

46 See D.S. Gordon, 'How to Make Safe Areas Unsafe', in Gordon and Toase, *Aspects*, pp.213–31. See also the UN's Srebrenica report.

47 See UN Document A/55/305 and S/2000/809, p.2.

48 Ibid.

49 Ibid., p.2.

50 Ibid., p.3.

51 This is a potentially positive development reflecting the widespread criticism of the 1999 Lomé peace agreement, the implementation of which underpinned UNAMSIL's mandate.

52 Melvern, 'Security Council', p.105.

53 For an excellent analysis of the mechanisms by which war economies develop, see W. Reno, *Corruption and State Politics in Sierra Leone* (Cambridge: 1995) p.19. See also M. Duffield, *Post Modern Conflict. Aid Policy and Humanitarian Conditionality. Discussion Paper for Emergency Aid Department*, Department for International Development (London: 1997).

54 See P.V. Jakobsen, 'The emerging consensus on grey area operations doctrine: Will it last and enhance Operational effectiveness?', in *IP*, Vol. 7, No. 3 (Autumn 2000), pp.36–57.
55 See UN Document A/55/305 and S/2000/809, p.5.
56 Ibid.
57 Brahimi quoted in BBC World News, *BBC Online*, 23 August 2000.
58 See UN Document A/55/305 and S/2000/809, p.4.
59 Ibid.
60 This was part of a broader process of making more flexible the capacity of mission managers to administer their own activities and speed the pace of deployment. It involved an examination of procurement policies and procedures with a view to presenting to the General Assembly proposals for the amendment of existing rules of procedure for mission expenditure. It also contained a proposal to increase the level of delegated financial authority to as much as £1 million for locally available materials or services.
61 This would support the information requirements of the ECPS but would be managed and administered by both the DPKO and DPA. Arguably, this is a recipe for confusion.
62 'Report of the Commission of Inquiry Established Pursuant to Security Council Resolution 885' (1993), 24 February 1994.
63 See Melvern, 'Security Council'.
64 Dissemination would be effected through the New York Intranet and the mission-specific Peace Operations Extranet.
65 Keating, quoted in Melvern, 'Security Council', p.105.
66 The UK developed a 'Media Operations' capability in the early 1990s in response to perceived shortfalls in capabilities highlighted during the early days of UNPROFOR. Prior to this, media handling *within* operations was somewhat directionless and largely aimed at the international and British press rather than the population in theatre. There was an increasing recognition that broader perceptions in the host country needed to be managed.
67 The Secretary-General also called for these in his 'Millennium Summit report', UN Document A/54/2000.
68 See UN Document A/55/305 and S/2000/809, p.2.
69 See M. Pugh, 'Peacebuilding as Developmentalism', unpublished mimeo in possession of author.
70 See UK, *Joint Warfare Publication 3–50*.
71 See UN Document A/55/305 and S/2000/809, summary of recommenda-tions at **http://www.un.org/peace/reports/peace_operations/docs/recommend.htm**
72 Ibid., p.2.
73 Ibid., p.4.
74 See **http://www.un.org/peace/reports/peace_operations/docs/recommend.htm**
75 UN *News Wire*, 23 August 2000.
76 See UN *News Wire*, 24 August for a brief review of member states' reaction. In particular see Canada's Foreign Minster, Lloyd Axworthy (quoted in *Calgary Herald*, 24 August 2000) who was positive about the report's recommendations. See also Richard Holbrooke in the *International Herald Tribune*, 24 August 2001.

77 UN Document SC/6919, *Security Council Holds meeting of World Leaders on Occasion of General Assembly's Summit*. See also UN Document S/2000/845.
78 UN Press release SC/6919 4194th Meeting 7 September 2000.
79 Ibid.
80 Agence France Press, 14 July 2000.

12
Reaching for the End of the Rainbow: Command and the Revolution in Military Affairs

Mungo Melvin and Stuart Peach

Introduction

What is at the end of the rainbow? What is meant by the Revolution in Military Affairs (RMA)? The United States Department of Defense's Office of Net Assessment defines an RMA as 'a major change in the nature of warfare brought about by the innovative application of technologies which, combined with dramatic changes in military doctrine and operational concepts, fundamentally alters the character and conduct of operations'.[1] So much has been written and discussed about the subject in the 1990s, and such are the military-industrial and economic stakes involved, that the RMA may become a self-fulfilling prophecy in the early twenty-first century. But war is an act of policy, to paraphrase Carl von Clausewitz, and not one of technology. Strategy is all about balancing ends, ways and means. The art of high command involves achieving some harmony between these elements and imposing a certain order on the inevitable chaos of war. If technology provides some of the means of conducting war and exercising command, it does not necessarily determine the ends or ways. So to mix a metaphor, are we not running the risk of losing sight of the strategic wood for the technological trees? A study of recent conflicts over the last 10 or 100 years would suggest that technology provides no sleek and clever 'silver bullet'. Like it or not, hard choices over the committal of forces into battle and how they are to be employed will remain for many decades to come. Such questions will continue to challenge commanders at all levels, whether they have a baton, radio, mobile phone or a global positioning system (GPS) in their knapsack.

This chapter will attempt to explore the nature of conflict and of the RMA presently claimed in some quarters. We shall discuss a number of historical antecedents, describe some of the wide range of views on war and technology and offer some personal thoughts on the potential limitations, trends and implications for the exercise of command. Yet we offer no patent solutions; instead, we aim to present a set of indicators and signposts.

Pointers from history

Well before the end of the Cold War, Soviet experts were discussing the impact of modern technology in bringing about a so-called Military-Technical Revolution (MTR) and an associated RMA. For the Soviets, an RMA consisted of 'radical changes in the development of the armed forces and methods of conducting operations that are generated by scientific-technical progress in weaponry and military technology.' According to Soviet accounts, there have been three distinct stages in the development of military affairs: 'aviation, motorization and chemical weapons in the 1920s; nuclear weapons, rocketry, and cybernetics in the 1950s; and microcircuitry, directed energy, and genetic engineering in the 1970s'. In the 1980s, Marshal N.V. Ogarov described the technological changes under way as 'profound and revolutionary, in the full sense of the word'.[2] That the last Soviet stage has yet to be completely fulfilled in the late 1990s is irrelevant. The fact is that the Soviets were theorising about MTR and RMA well before it became a popular subject for Western debate. Indeed, Soviet-Russian predictions on the RMA appeared to be confirmed by their analysis of the Gulf War which concluded that ground forces have a declining role and that air, air defence and naval forces have increasing ones.

Yet the historical roots of RMA are much deeper. 'Revolutions' in warfare have been based typically on rapid advances of technology, including the introduction of steam ships, railways, breech-loading rifles and artillery, aircraft and tanks. By way of illustration, the defeated Anglo–French forces in the Fall of France in 1940 were at the bitter receiving end of German *Blitzkrieg*, which would appear to fit the current United States definition of an RMA. This example of an RMA was based on well-integrated combined arms (including air) operations, manifesting perhaps the epitome of industrial age warfare. We are led to believe by American pundits such as Alvin and Heidi Toffler that the next 'wave of warfare' will be based on the 'information age'.[3] However, dramatic changes in the nature of warfare are not necessarily predicated on technological change alone.

As Tilford has pointed out, the revolution in military affairs that took place during the Napoleonic Wars was *not* based on spectacular technological advances. The technical means of prosecuting war in terms of infantry, cavalry and artillery weaponry had not changed significantly for over a hundred years. What had changed was the size and organisation of armies and the ways in which they were employed on the battlefield. The French political revolution and the rise of Napoleon forced the pace of military change rather than the nascent industrial revolution occurring in Britain. However, that revolution in industrial and technological affairs, which had spread rapidly across Western Europe and America by the middle of the nineteenth century, *did* bring huge advances in weapon ranges, accuracy and lethality. Such was the pace of technological change at sea that whole fleets could become outdated in a decade, but tactics and operational methods on land tended to lag behind developments in armaments. As a result, combat tended to settle down into an extremely costly attritional stalemate as evidenced by the American Civil and the First World Wars. In this respect, the short and decisive campaigns conducted by Prussia against Denmark, Austria and France in the period 1864–71 were exceptional. What is often overlooked, however, is that an RMA did occur towards the end of the First World War in terms of the employment of heavy artillery, aircraft, tanks and the adoption of more innovative infantry tactics.[4]

Views of the RMA

Research into the RMA is particularly well developed and funded in the United States. The European involvement is limited, so our perspective is from the sidelines rather than from the field of play. Only recently have European countries woken up to the heated debates that have been raging in the United States since the Gulf War. A British view, and probably the first publicly aired official position on the RMA, was contained in a supporting essay to the United Kingdom government's 1998 Strategic Defence Review:

> The biggest change in the conduct of future military operations is likely to come not from the weapons alone but from the application of information technology to military command and control. There is a growing body of opinion, particularly in the US, that we are

approaching a 'Revolution in Military Affairs' in which we will see a step change in military capabilities resulting from the synergistic combination of long-range precision weapons with networks of advanced sensors and data processors. Radically improved capabilities in the field of information processing and communications systems will increase situational awareness (knowing where hostile and friendly forces are, and where they are not) by combining information from all available sources and rapidly distributing it to those who need it, thus permitting more effective and efficient use of our forces. Smart long-range precision weapons will enable us to attack targets accurately from [a] distance, thereby reducing our own and civilian casualties.[5]

From a wider Western European perspective, however, it is still difficult to be definitive about the likely trends arising out of the present, largely American-led RMA. Unfortunately, there is little French or German open source material to draw on so this chapter may give a somewhat narrow British view. Yet opinions differ across Europe as to the likely impact and uptake of the RMA. That there will be a 'step-change' in military affairs is disputed, and views vary widely. Four broad schools of thought appear to be emerging involving the RMA and information warfare:

- the RMA has already taken place, manifested in the Gulf War
- the RMA will be developed from the Gulf War experience
- information warfare is the real RMA: 'cyberspace is the fourth dimension'
- information warfare can be applied world-wide into a 'system of systems'

A pragmatic and realistic, but not necessarily accurate view of a future RMA-based armed force, is one based on a 'digital overlay'. This involves an evolutionary, as opposed to a revolutionary, approach, taking existing military structures and linking units together to provide the best possible communications and systems for the sharing of information. In the jargon, this is known as 'battlefield digitisation', and is explained by one leading authority in the following terms:

> It is probably the majority position today to endorse the 'vision', if that is the correct term, of a future that is much like today only more so. The sunk costs in existing systems and approaches, in the context

of recognition of the technical and political uncertainties about future conflict, not to mention plain old conservative habits of mind and some emotional attachments, all can argue for making haste slowly.[6]

This approach will probably prove to be the limited response to the RMA in Western Europe. Yet a more ambitious 'higher-technology' RMA, fuelled by far greater financial resources, rolls on, almost exclusively in the United States. The mainstream American view of the RMA held by its more moderate proponents is encapsulated in the United States Joint Chiefs of Staff endorsed *Joint Vision 2010*. Technology will allow greater emphasis on long-range, precision strikes. Corresponding improvements in information and communication systems will provide commanders with fast and accurate information, improving the quality of their decision making. In combination, the new technologies will allow 'increased stealth, mobility, dispersion, and a higher tempo of operations'. Further, information superiority will be 'crucial and require both offensive and defensive information warfare'.[7]

Possible limitations

Whereas digitisation is the norm in NATO naval and air forces, the implications of even quite modest proposals for digitisation (arguably with GPS the essential prerequisite of the present RMA) of armies have yet to be investigated fully, let alone implemented. It remains to be demonstrated whether conventional yardsticks in land force organisations, such as a maximum of four to five points of command, will hold true. Yet the application of advanced information technology, or any other technology for that matter, when applied to the military will not necessarily reduce the size of command structures. Whilst the overall size of land forces – if not their relevance – is being reduced, static and field headquarters seem to be getting bigger at all levels. With the advent of a rather new orthodoxy of 'near perfect information systems' in the RMA it is easy to forget that the decisive impact of new technology on command and control has been long heralded. A typical 1980s technical text declared:

> The commander in the year 2000 will enjoy an ability to command and control on a battlefield shrunk to spatial and temporal dimensions unprecedented in modern times. Born of a generation that has an almost innate familiarity with computers and information systems, it

will be his knowledge of C3 [Command, Control and Communications] systems and his ability to use them to penetrate the 'fog of war', that will be one of the primary keys to success on the battlefield of the 21st Century.[8]

There are many people who actually believe this has happened. After the Gulf War many claims were made that the 'fog of war' had been lifted and that knowledge had become an 'indispensable factor' (as if it were not before!), but these views now look a trifle suspect. Take, for example, the following claim: 'It was a war where an ounce of silicon in a computer may have had more effect than a ton of depleted uranium',[9] or, as boldly:

> Because of the strategies of deception, maneuver and speed employed by coalition forces in Desert Storm, knowledge came to rival weapons and tactics in importance, giving credence to the notion that an enemy might be brought to his knees principally through destruction and disruption of the means for command and control.[10]

Again, it must be stressed that even a cursory study of the development of technology reveals that each new advance in communications over the ages has promised much but has often failed to deliver all that its proponents have declared. The first extensive use of the Morse telegraph on the battlefield must have excited the Union generals in the American Civil War until the Confederate cavalry specialised in cutting the wires.[11] Likewise, the control of the advancing German armies in the opening stages of the First World War in 1914 was severely hampered by the lack of mobile means of reliable communication once the railway-based telegraph and telephone systems were left behind.[12] This lesson was not lost on a junior German signals officer of the First World War, Heinz Guderian, who later commanded a panzer corps from his mobile radio vehicle (*Funkwagon*) in the Second World War. But even in the First World War the primitive wireless sets of the time were either being intercepted and exploited or being jammed. Carrier pigeons were still in use in the trenches.

Synchronisation of 'combined arms' forces in time and space could not be achieved satisfactorily in mobile warfare until radio technology had been further developed after the First World War. British, and later German, field trials of the 1920s and 1930s demonstrated the need for reliable voice communications between armoured vehicles. The first practicable hand-held radio set on the battlefield during the Second World War (the walkie-talkie) must have appeared an absolute godsend until its batteries went flat and its early miniature valves broke down. The German cipher machines must have appeared code-breaker-proof to their users, but they were not invulnerable as the Ultra story shows. For the thousands involved in deciphering the enigma messages at Bletchley Park, their war was very much an 'information war'. Like it or not, each advance in communications technology can be matched quickly by a countersystem. However, it would be quite wrong in consequence to dismiss the efficacy of information and communications systems in modern war. Montgomery, for example, depended on secure microwave links during the 1944–5 campaign in North-west Europe and strategic and tactical satellite communications came of age respectively during the 1982 Falklands War and the 1990–1 Gulf War.

Yet one cannot avoid the impression that the potential tactical or operational impact of military technical revolutions is often underestimated at the time of their first fielding. The combination of forward commanders, with lots of individual drive and initiative and supported by reliable radio communications, radically increased the tempo of land operations in the Second World War. However, panzer commanders such as Rommel could only lead from the front in France in 1940 or in the Western Desert in 1941–2 because they had the necessary means to do so. But the panzer forces themselves could neither be sustained at the appropriate strength nor their qualitative advantage be maintained for the rest of the War. Faced with the immense resources and strategic depth of the Soviet Union, the *Blitzkrieg*-RMA met its due nemesis on the Eastern Front.

So in considering conflicts of any duration, the quest for decisive technological superiority or information dominance would appear to have been illusory. That said, the employment of atomic weapons on Japan in August 1945 was exceptional and constitutes an RMA. However, overwhelming strategic and industrial resources, coupled with immense tactical precision firepower, provide no guarantees of success in war, as the American experience in Vietnam shows. With hindsight, the 1990/1 Gulf War may prove to be the exception rather than the rule for indicating the nature and conduct of future warfare, and therefore we should be careful about drawing simplistic lessons for other conflicts with quite different strategic conditions and terrain. It remains to be seen whether advances in information and precision (and largely air-delivered) firepower can transform the nature of warfare.[13] Perhaps, as Keaney and Cohen have observed, 'Air power is an unusually seductive form of military strength because, like modern courtship, it appears to offer the pleasures of gratification without the burdens of commitment.'[14]

Spectrum of conflict and the nature of war today

During the Cold War, the terms high- and low-intensity conflict were the 'accepted' wisdom in military doctrine. The terms were widely 'tossed' around in military literature to highlight the distinction between bipolar superpower general war – described as high-intensity conflict – post-colonial, regional or superpower proxy conflict, which was characterised by the term low-intensity conflict. When graphics or diagrams were employed, Cold War 'models' of conflict were generally portrayed in a linear, graduated model. The utility of this style of model reached the end of its shelf life in 1989. Since then, as uncertainty has gripped the contemporary strategic context and the boundaries between war, conflict and crime have blurred and coalesced, the actual types of conflict that have characterised the post-Cold War era have been anything but linear or graduated. Now we see military force being used for anything from humanitarian aid missions to offer relief from environmental catastrophe, through peace enforcement operations which resemble conventional war, to the constant patrols of nuclear deterrent forces to prevent nuclear war.

Ten years on from the Cold War, admirals, generals and air marshals have grappled with the realities of command away from the Cold War comfort zone, whilst academics have struggled to offer a new, universal and definitive taxonomy of conflict. Now, doctrine manuals from the UN to the USA offer a bewildering variety of definitions and types of conflict from humanitarian operations to general nuclear war. Peacekeeping, in particular, has gone through the mangle of terminology from 'Chapter VI 1/2' operations, through 'peace support operations' to 'operations other than war' or, even, 'other' operations. This indiscriminate sprinkling of definitions and terms matters. If we are likely to operate with allies, friends and partners in alliance, combined, multi-national or coalition operations, precision in military language may well be crucial. Even if historians continue to disagree on what the national 'ways' in warfare are, most agree that the blend of national military history, culture, experience and economic strength influences national military doctrines and, by inference, national military definitions.[15]

Many statesmen who prophesied a 'new world order' at the end of the Cold War made valiant attempts to build an agreed conceptual model.[16] In 1992, the then Secretary-General of the UN, Boutros Boutros-Ghali, published *An Agenda for Peace*. He proposed four main concepts: preventative diplomacy, peacemaking, peacekeeping and peacebuilding.[17] Unfortunately, events in Somalia, Bosnia and Rwanda challenged this approach with UN and North Atlantic Treaty Organisation (NATO) forces crossing the so-called 'Mogadishu line' into peace enforcement.[18] Military doctrine writers also accepted the challenge to offer new terminology to describe what was happening and, in the UK, the British Army entered the debate with *Wider Peacekeeping* in 1995.[19] This document was hailed, at the time, as a breakthrough in peacekeeping doctrine and focused on the maintenance of consent and the important hallmarks of impartiality and neutrality. Again, however, the concept was challenged by events.[20] In the USA meanwhile, the term employed was (and is) 'Military Operations Other Than War', commonly abbreviated to MOOTW, a role and mission type which has spawned a number of doctrinally-based documents.[21]

Now, the term Peace Support Operation (PSO) is in general use to describe operations aimed at achieving a long-term political settlement. In PSOs, the deployment of forces can be authorised in a variety of ways with some form of UN Security Council Mandate under Chapter VI (Non-mandatory) of the UN Charter, Chapter VII (Mandatory), or Chapter VIII (Regional Security Organisation). In the complex world of inter-governmental organisations, legitimacy could also be provided by mandates from multi-lateral organisations such as the Organisation for Security and Cooperation in Europe (OSCE), Western European Union (WEU) or NATO. UK joint doctrine defines Peace Support Operations as: 'multi-functional operations conducted impartially in support of an appropriate legal authority, involving military forces and diplomatic and humanitarian agencies'.[22]

Within the spectrum of PSOs, peacekeeping operations are generally mandated under Chapter VI of the UN Charter and involve the deployment of inter-positional forces to monitor and, possibly, to implement or facilitate a cease-fire agreement. The key factor for such operations is consent. Peacekeeping operations require the consent of all major parties or factions involved in a conflict.

If a crisis degenerates into armed conflict or war, the mandate may be changed to authorise the use of force, typically, via a Chapter VII (Mandatory) UN Resolution. The aim of such military operations, known as peace enforcement, is to restore peace and international security. Consent may be lost or uncertain and, therefore, peace enforcement operations are inherently coercive. Recent operations in Iraq and Kosovo have graphically demonstrated that, when they believe it is necessary,

UN Security Council members are prepared to stretch existing mandates or resort to the 'right' of armed intervention for humanitarian purposes.[23] Of course, interpretation of mandates short of 'all necessary means' will vary. The variety of interpretations does matter in this confused contemporary strategic environment. If diversity in types of conflict is the norm, so is diversity in response. Even the USA as the global superpower is reluctant to act unilaterally on all occasions. As a result, reaching some form of consensus on the mandate will begin to shape and to frame the overall framework *before* the military campaign planning process and, thus, the exercise of high command can begin. The political environment and requirement have always shaped our response to conflict; there is nothing new in political limitation or constraint. The challenge will be to train both potential commanders and politicians about the need to understand the impact of such constraints on military planning.

Another major change in the operational environment since the end of the Cold War is the requirement to sustain operations in the long term. Military forces of all types may have to remain in place to monitor the peace and ensure compliance of the parties or former warring factions with the postconflict agreement. Roles and mission types may vary from patrol, surveillance and reconnaissance, to confidence building and infrastructure repair tasks. In such operations, the boundaries between what have been traditionally construed as civilian and military activities have become increasingly blurred. In many ways contemporary military operations have more in common with the 'small wars' and garrisons of nineteenth-century colonialism than the Cold War. Thus, it appears that postconflict activity is now an important (if understudied) activity and represents another challenge for future high commanders.

Moreover, at the dawn of the millennium, the long-term nature of such peace-building activities offers new and, potentially, even more difficult challenges for commanders. Peace building, infrastructure repair and the resettlement of refugees in a stable security environment can take years. This all calls for the employment of engineers and logistic troops on the ground as for any tanker or infantryman. The RMA offers no quick fixes here either. Civilian authorities may lack the will, confidence or experience to take over without external military support, requiring military commanders to act in interwoven civil/military situations. We are rediscovering what it means to run protectorates, despite its connotation of colonialism. Many soldiers and civilians have become adept at the task and do not underestimate the complexities and difficulties of this role.[24] The reality of *long-term* military commitments offers further challenges to those who attempt to offer 'sound bite' labels for the contemporary strategic environment. In fact, the notion of air forces flying patrols over a region to deny activity or enforce no-fly zones for 10 years, or inter-positional ground forces on patrol, year in year out, is hardly expeditionary in nature. By definition, the notion of expeditions implies a swift and expeditious return.[25] Perhaps, therefore, we may need to revisit the 'expeditionary era' label. As some – and particularly those from the maritime community – claim the end of the 'Continental Century', we seem set to commit increasing military effort at sea, on land and in the air in support of operations on the continent of Europe. There is rarely, in any sober analysis, a quick and easy exit strategy of sailing away from the conflict following some form of neo-gunboat diplomacy.

Command in such operations can be challenging. Although routine operations with low military activity may become the operational norm, such operations can intensify unexpectedly, swiftly and dramatically. For example, on a number of occasions coalition aircraft on patrol in the no-fly zones over Iraq have had to respond to surface-to-air missiles or engage Iraqi aircraft. Moreover, for all forces, military equipment wears out in harsh climates as it is used more intensively and for much longer than envisaged during the Cold War. Furthermore, long periods of detached, remote, unaccompanied service can lead to retention problems in all volunteer forces, particularly for those highly-skilled personnel with transferable skills. Although technology can help in reducing the number of deployed forces and operational tempo ebbs and flows, none of these trends can be eradicated completely by technology; they are here to stay. If there is a conclusion to be drawn, it is that we now face a spectrum of conflict that requires a spectrum of response. Further, a continuum of conflict suggests that a circular model could be appropriate to demonstrate the essentially cyclical nature of conflict (see Figure 12.1).

The circular model is completed where it started with peace. The arrows may be reversed, or indeed the 'circle' may be joined at virtually any stage. For example, in Kosovo, the peacekeeping and peace enforcement phases – according to the definitions outlined above – were omitted and, arguably, the NATO-led air 'campaign' against President Milosevic moved the conflict from preventative diplomacy to armed conflict, with an explicit assumption that postconflict activity would continue for some time before the elusive state of peace could be reached. Each segment of the model masks a multitude of roles and mission types with blurred or, on occasion, jagged boundaries. For example, in a deteriorating situation

Figure 12.1 Spectrum of conflict

not yet recognised by the international community as a crisis, nations may elect to deploy into or poise near to a zone of crisis in support of preventative diplomacy. Such operations can be defined as: 'diplomatic action taken in advance of a predictable crisis to prevent or limit violence'.[26] The UK government has recognised the utility of military forces in aiding the process of conflict prevention. The UK Strategic Defence Review, published in 1998, made the role of Defence Diplomacy a formal UK defence task. Defence Diplomacy missions include arms control, non-proliferation and security-building measures, wider military assistance and training. The definition is: 'to provide forces to meet the varied activities undertaken by the Ministry of Defence to dispel hostility, build and maintain trust and assist in the development of democratically accountable Armed Forces'.[27] If a show of force or deterrent posture falters or fails and the operational situation continues to deteriorate, forces may be deployed in a traditional interpositional peacekeeping role.

Friction

In any military operation, often the simplest tasks prove unexpectedly difficult. Many strategists have argued that chaos and uncertainty are the natural states.[28] Clausewitz argued that 'in war it is difficult for normal efforts to achieve even moderate results, friction is the force that makes the apparently easy difficult'.[29] Friction occurs in all types of military operations and it is a key role of commanders to ensure – particularly in coalition operations – that the friction generated does not become a vulnerability or weakness for the enemy to exploit. Navigational errors are made in all environments and missiles can still run off course. Despite advances in technology, as this chapter makes clear, war remains an act of chance and violence. Violence is not casualty free; it injects elements of emotion, human stress, uncertainty and improbability. When human chemistry and proximity to danger are added, even in an RMA era, human emotions shape the conduct of war. As we have already indicated, some doctrine writers and military analysts talk of 'perfect information' for commanders and information dominance.[30] We disagree fundamentally. Whilst technology can enable military operations to be conducted more efficiently with stand-off weapon systems reducing the risk of casualties or collateral damage, risk cannot be eliminated. Commanders still have to lead and act upon their judgement and intuition and exercise moral courage.

An understanding of friction remains fundamental to understanding the realities of warfare. It is, like death and destruction, one its enduring hallmarks. In the same way that an understanding of friction distinguishes the practical engineer from the car stylist, it differentiates the battle-hardened commander or soldier from the armchair historian or hobby wargamer. In an attempt to bridge the gap between theory and reality, modern historiography has produced epic studies as *The Face of Battle, The Mask of Command*[31] and the more recent *Time to Kill*.[32] Van Creveld notes:

> [a] very important source of uncertainty in war derives not from the army's size but from the nature of its human components. War more than any other activity is the domain of anger, fear, pain and death. People who are immersed in these most intense of experiences are likely to be less objective than a man sitting in an office and writing papers.[33]

But we need to go back to Clausewitz if we are to attempt to understand what friction is all about and to derive its contemporary relevance.

Clausewitz defined reality or the 'general atmosphere of war' in a number of ways. In *Vom Kriege* (*On War*) he offered two lists, as shown in Table 12.1.

Barry D. Watts has developed these lists into a new interpretation of Clausewitz's 'unified concept of a general friction'.[34] The view of general friction shown in Table 12.2 (further developed from Watts) is perhaps a more comprehensive summary of the realities or facets of war.

Watts considers whether general friction is a 'structural feature of war or something more transitory'. Simply put, he concludes friction is here to stay and cannot be eradicated because of the human dimension in war. If friction cannot be eliminated, Watts then questions whether 'its magnitude for one adversary or the other can be substantially reduced by technological advances'. In other words, how can we exploit the friction differential between our own and the enemy's forces? So we need 'lubricants' to oil our own mechanisms of command, and sand to clog up those of our opponents. We need to improve our focus and width of vision of the battlefield whilst degrading the enemy commander's view and skewing his perspective. Thus in any study of the future realities of command in general, and in judging the potential of the RMA (and Information Warfare in particular), we should attempt to differentiate between the lubricant and the sand, and assess our vulnerabilities.

Table 12.1 The Clausewitzian concept of friction

Chapter 3, Book One	Chapter 8, Book One
Danger and exertion	Danger and physical exertion
Uncertainty	Intelligence
Chance	Friction

Table 12.2 Facets of war

Classical facets	Modern facets
Danger; physical exertion; chance. Conceptual resistance within one's own forces. Lack of alliance cohesion.	Physical and political limits to the use of military force (restraints and constraints); greater pressure to reduce casualties.
Uncertainties and imperfections in the information on which action in war is based. Unpredictability stemming from interaction with the enemy.	Disconnects between ends, ways and means in war. Uncertainty as to end-states and end-games. Unpredictable and volatile popular opinion and media pressures.

Levels of conflict

Since ancient times, soldiers, statesmen and writers have studied the art of war. In all wars levels of conflict can be identified. Now we describe the strategic, operational and tactical levels of war as if they are enduring truths. In fact, this construct emerged during the twentieth century. In 1926, a Russian (former Tsarist) officer, A.A. Svechin, declared: 'Tactics makes the steps from which operational leaps are assembled: strategy points out the path.'[35] Any understanding of command in any technological era, with or without an RMA, requires an understanding of these levels of war. The fate of entire civilisations has been linked to their military means. The history of warfare continues to influence modern military art with particular influence exercised by the nineteenth-century strategists and thinkers such as Jomini and Clausewitz.[36] If there is a trend in this century, it is that science and technology have continued to drive tactics and the capability of weapons, whilst military art has developed along more enduring lines. Each major military nation has developed military doctrine and produced original thinkers such as Liddell Hart and Fuller in the United Kingdom, Guderian and von Manstein in Germany, de Gaulle in France and Svechin and Tukhachevsky in the Soviet Union. Equally, the naval and air environments have offered theorists such as Mahan and Corbett, and Douhet and Mitchell. Many continue to quote such theorists even if fewer actually read the original texts. No doubt their thinking will continue to exercise modern-day writers and historians.[37] As we ponder the impact of the RMA, it is wise to take a broad perspective of the conduct of war and view technology and RMA as an 'enabler'; the study of military art must not be lost in a mass of tactical and technical detail.

British doctrine recognises four levels of war: grand strategic, strategic, operational and tactical. Even in the description lies a dilemma; the USA as the global superpower does not recognise the term 'grand strategy' but prefers to use 'national' strategy. This distinction is more than semantic since the British view of grand strategy embraces the application of national resources to achieve national (and potentially Allied) policy objectives and involves economic, industrial, political and military components. Military strategy is, therefore, formulated from political direction and guidance and is concerned with military actions, the resources allocated to military operations and the political and legal constraints to be applied. At the operational level, campaigns and major operations are directed, planned and sequenced. The operational level commander is responsible for the overall campaign plan, offering the crucial creative links (or operational leaps, in Svechin's words) between strategy and the employment of forces at the tactical level. The logical deduction, therefore, is that the tactical level is the level at which engagements are planned, forces are deployed and battles are fought. The tactical level is the level at which the environmental component commanders, sea, land, air, special forces and logistics operate but their activities need to be co-ordinated, integrated and synchronised at the operational level.[38]

In reality, the levels of war interact (see Figure 12.2). The degree of interaction will depend on the environment, circumstances and scenario. In certain situations, the operational level can be squeezed to be almost invisible by pressure from the strategic level and interaction with the tactical level. For example, the advent of highly capable digital communications systems enables politicians and military commanders to 'reach down' the command chain, demand instant information and interfere with the conduct of military operations. Even if reach down is not exercised, certainly daily (if not hourly) contact between the levels of command is becoming the norm. As a result, a senior commander's time is consumed with press conferences, target boards, video conference links and so on. Consequently, a major challenge for commanders in the digital information/RMA era is to manage their time effectively so that sufficient free time is allowed for military thought to develop the

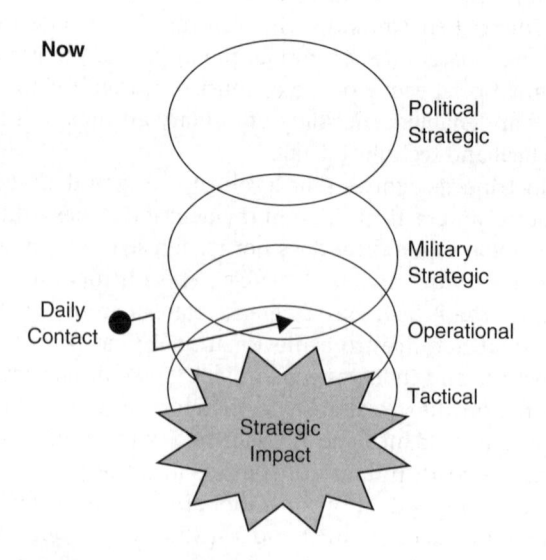

Figure 12.2 Tactical act, strategic impact

'operational idea' upon which the campaign plan is built. Again, this is nothing new. Montgomery empowered his chief of staff (Freddie de Guingand) during the Second World War in order to gain time to think and sleep. But the risk in the 'near perfect information world' is that commanders become slaves to mechanistic processes designed to feed the insatiable demands for information and neglect their operational art. Another pressure on commanders is the demand from the media for immediate information from commanders if a tactical act or action results in casualties or collateral damage on any scale. For example, during the Gulf War, the media were aware a coalition precision-guided munition had gone astray and had missed its intended target before the aircraft had landed. Hard-pressed commanders were being asked questions before they had the information. In Kosovo, the confused situation surrounding the alleged bombing of a refugee convoy in early April 1999 by NATO aircraft demonstrated the pressure and spill-over that tactical actions can have on the conduct of the operational and strategic levels.

Current and future trends affecting command

If the spectrum of conflict offers new challenges to military commanders, what of the dimensions and types of conflict? Again, during the Cold War, the graduated response through formal command states from 'military vigilance' to nuclear war was understood and practised; indeed, it was honed to peaks of military perfection. Now, the range of potential tasks is bewildering and labels remain in lag. This is not new. Just as the boundaries between peace and war have become blurred, so have the boundaries between the types or categories of conflict. Conflict, armed conflict and war have always defied simple categorisation. As Anthony Eden remarked during the Suez Crisis: 'We are not in a state of war, we are in armed conflict.'[39] What may have been described as insurgency in the postcolonial era or limited conflict in the Cold War may now be characterised as terrorism, organised crime or 'thuggery'. Individual conflict may spread across national, ethnic or factional boundaries.

As with the spectrum of conflict (see Figure 12.3), a generic model is useful if only to emphasise the complexity of the contemporary strategic environment. In response to conflict in all its guises, military force may be employed to deter conflict. The deterrence mission reached orchestrated heights during the Cold War. Nevertheless, it should not be discounted as a Cold War label, since deterrence aims to persuade an opponent from resorting to a particular course of action. The implicit

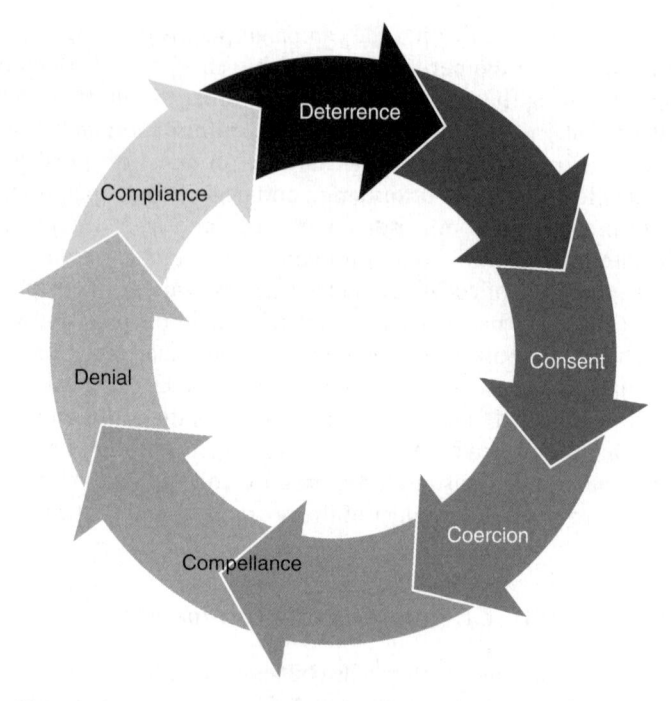

Figure 12.3 Military roles around the spectrum of conflict

threat in deterrence must be credible and backed by resolute political will, policy, demonstrated military capability and a willingness to escalate. Thus, deterrence remains a challenging mission for commanders, particularly when faced with enemies who are not clearly identified and who show scant regard for international norms of behaviour. Similarly, forces may deploy with consent to demonstrate resolve and poise or patrol near or in a zone of crisis to show the will of the international community and hope to defuse a crisis.

If such an option does not work, military force can be employed to coerce an opponent. Coercion is oft quoted but rarely understood.[40] During the Cold War, coercion theory became the home for social scientists such as Bernard Brodie and tended to merge into deterrence theory.[41] Coercive activity is regularly undertaken by forces deployed for other roles and missions. Coercion requires a clear understanding of the behaviour of target groups, an unambiguous signal of intent and may depend on a blend of physical and psychological factors. The risk is obvious. Pre-emptive coercive action can precipitate escalation in a conflict or lead an opponent to underestimate the risk to him, invoking a cry of disproportionate response. Coercion should, therefore, only be initiated as a deliberate policy consistent with an overall strategy or campaign plan.

In war or armed conflict, military activity may involve the use of force to destroy an opponent's military capability and supporting infrastructure to bring about defeat. The execution of such a plan may require more time than originally anticipated. A variety of causes may be at work, including friction. For example, the air operation during the 1991 Gulf War took nine days longer than expected because of unseasonal bad weather. And bad weather continued to dog air operations over Kosovo and Serbia in 1999. Indeed, the bombing offensive against Germany during the Second World War took considerably longer than envisaged to achieve an effect because of a range of factors, including raised expectations of bombing accuracy, inflated tactical level claims of the effects achieved and the failure to identify key target sets. Modern technology assists to reduce many of these historic limitations on destructive, attrition strategies, but will not eliminate them. A successful commander will not succeed efficiently or quickly by simple adherence to target lists.

Another successful type of operation is to deny or disrupt access to military forces, equipment or critical infrastructure. This denial may not be physical or destructive, it depends on the effect sought. For example, a critical bridge or choke point could be blocked rather than destroyed. Indeed, it may be counterproductive in campaign planning terms to destroy a target. For example, military engineers deployed to Bosnia in the NATO Implementation Force in 1996 had to rebuild bridges damaged or destroyed during Operation Deliberate Force in order to carry out other military operations.

Therefore, in both the spectrum of conflict and the types of response, complexity appears to be the theme. Complexity offers enormous challenges for commanders; technology will help, aid and assist but not solve many of these challenges. Dealing with complexity is not new. As we have seen, Clausewitz recognised both the reality of complexity requiring the 'genius' of a commander and the oft-quoted 'friction of war', in all its guises. So to summarise, as far as can be predicted (and this itself is a dangerous game), the current trends (not yet all fulfilled) affecting the planning, conduct and command of operations appear to include the following:

- the desire to apply technology, rather than men on the battlefield, will continue
- new technologies (or further developments in existing ones) have created a steady rise in the range, accuracy and lethality of weapon systems

- the mobility of platforms carrying those systems has been improved, leading to enhanced ground and air manoeuvre on and above the battlefield
- battlespace is expanding, which in turn will lead to a 'volumetric increase in the information' that is relevant to a commander
- expanding battlespace will increase the demand for timely and accurate information, and lead to compressed decision–action cycles in order to maintain the tempo of operations across a widely dispersed force
- however, achieving decisive synchronisation of operations in time, space and effect will remain ever complex
- alliance, coalition and multinational operations are now the norm; the inherent friction of working together must be overcome (this is a military as much as any political imperative)
- whilst command will remain predominately a human activity, much of control and communications activity can be automated

Taking these trends together, there will be a need to disperse units and formations whilst at the same time maintaining a common understanding of the battle across the force. This will require decentralisation of command whilst maintaining unity of effort; both in turn being dependent on high-capacity communications and information systems (CIS). Thus on land we are likely to see continuing attempts to develop an automated 'common battlefield picture', providing the equivalent of recognised air and maritime pictures, the technology for which is already mature. That said, uncertainty and ambiguity will not be banished from the battlefield in any environment as the volume of information being collected across a dispersed battlefield 'may potentially degrade the coherence of battlefield perception'.[42] In other words, internal friction and the fog of war will continue to affect the quality of decision making by a commander and the subsequent dissemination of orders arising from his decisions. This basic reality of conflict applies as much to the conduct of peace support operations.

The improved information flows promised by digitisation may not necessarily enhance the quality of decision making. As Colin Gray has argued persuasively, 'to know many things is not necessarily to know what those things mean'.[43] Whilst Gray demonstrates that judgement is at the top of a hierarchy that begins with data, it can also be argued that this model of converting data into information, information into knowledge, knowledge into wisdom and wisdom into judgement applies at all levels. Yet the weight of responsibility hangs heaviest at the top of the chain of command, where the penalties for error are often graver than those at the bottom of the chain. Therefore, the greater the degree of centralisation, the more we must ensure that the commander 'at the top' is not only blessed with timely and accurate information, but also with the quality of judgement to use that information effectively. This is no easy matter, with implications for the selection and training of senior commanders. Further, much hard-won battle experience in war indicates that the more fluid a tactical situation becomes, the greater the need for *decentralisation*. How to maintain the tempo of quality decision making at the appropriate levels of command is one of the greatest challenges of digitisation and, by implication, of the RMA. Also, it remains to be seen whether a decentralised command philosophy such as Mission Command can be retained in the RMA era. We suspect it should.

Centralised versus decentralised command

The argument for a 'top down' (or 'reach down') approach to command is gaining momentum. The early proponents of manoeuvre warfare (such as Lind[44]) argued for a bottom-up, recce-pull, approach to seizing the initiative. Since the Gulf War, however, the application of command, control, communications, computers and intelligence (C4I) supported by space systems have given credence to the view that analysts and photo interpreters far from the front may have a far better view of the battlefield than the forward troops. Take, for example, this conclusion after Desert Storm:

> Weapons and tactics have expanded the battlefield well beyond the range of human eyes, ears and of the electronic sensors owned by battalions, brigades and regiments. Maneuver warfare absolutely depends on accurate and timely intelligence about entities and events that are no longer easily or quickly sensed from the front lines: events at the full depth of the theater of operations and often beyond the reach of sensors under the direct control of combat commanders.[45]

Whilst this view appears to challenge the recce-pull paradigm of manoeuvre warfare, it hides a lot of practical difficulties. It presupposes that the necessary raw data or processed information (intelligence) from afar reaches the combat commander at formation headquarters, let alone the fighting man. What is the use of a mass of intelligence at the top of the chain of command when it is needed forward? Will its relevance for a particular local commander be seen at the top, or will the mass of detail be just more background noise? Will new systems tempt the higher operational commander to intervene on the battlefield when something looks very interesting but may prove just to be a trivial tactical side-show? Are we going to see new generations of Marshal Bazaines redirecting the guns and losing the battle almost won, but this time by remote as opposed to personal battlefield control?[46] And intelligence dates very quickly. Imagery is resource hungry and difficult to pass down the chain of command unless system capabilities expand enormously.

Demand will always expand to meet, and then exceed, capacity in a form of cyber-Parkinson's Law. Expectations of near 'perfect situational awareness' raised on peacetime exercises can rarely be satisfied on operations because of the friction involved: too many people are always chasing too much data on too few links. Bean-counting style intelligence tells us little about the attitudes and perceptions of the opposition, or of their real fighting power. This is why human-based intelligence (HUMINT) should never be ignored if it is available; after all, it is more likely to tell us about the psyche and will of an opponent – his moral as much as his physical condition – which helps us to determine whether he will stand and fight.

That said, we would argue that the case for centralised command is either decision- or resource-driven, or a combination of the two. The former is based on the need to speed critical decision making, but, as Leonhard admits, this must rest on higher commanders possessing more timely, relevant and accurate intelligence than their subordinates. The latter case is based on the need to concentrate force, particularly combat support, including air. An examination of the British Army's practice in the Second World War – particularly from the battles of Alam Halfa and El Alamein onwards – confirms this. For example, a typical Second World War 'lessons learned' document states: 'The principles of concentration of effort and centralisation of control in the hands of the highest authority who is in a position effectively to exercise this control apply to all arms, but in particular to the employment of artillery.'[47]

This approach, well suited to Montgomery's tidy, and largely attritional, battles, developed into an enduring artillery technique, now manifested in the principle of 'centralised command, decentralised control'. This well-founded practice in relation to relatively scarce combat support assets was developed during the Second World War in American, British and Soviet army doctrine.[48] It still has considerable relevance for the control of the resources required to conduct the 'deep battle', in the sense of the concentration of long-range fires as opposed to 'deep operations' that can be executed by a manoeuvre formation.

The case for decentralised command is based traditionally on the view that forward commanders have a better feel for the battle, and should be given as much freedom as possible in the planning and execution of their own plans, with a minimum of interference by the higher commander. However, the case for decentralisation (and this where we depart from Robert Leonhard) is also based on the fallibility of technology. A centralised system of command is fine when it is running smoothly in a benign environment, but what happens when it breaks down? A decentralised system of command, for all its dysfunctions, is harder to train for but gives a greater chance of initiative and success in most situations, although not all. The more fluid the situation, the lower the decision level should be set. But Mission Command also has a principle of unity of effort to give focus to subordinates' actions; meanwhile the superior commander cannot abrogate his responsibility for the actions of the whole force so a control means is also necessary. Mission Command also rests on trust and mutual understanding and timely decision making; it is thus a complete 'package' of which decentralisation is but one part. To summarise, the case for a decentralised system of command is based on the following:

- a realisation that friction is an enduring facet of warfare that will thwart attempts to overcentralise
- an understanding that the technology required for centralisation is not infallible; command systems highly reliant on current or future RMA technologies are vulnerable to attack
- a belief that a decentralised ethos engenders and supports local commanders' initiative, which will breed success
- a view that it is applicable and robust in all types of conflict
- an acknowledgement that it places a high demand on individual and collective training

Interoperability

In the meantime, for European nations such as Britain, France and Germany it will remain necessary at the very least to keep a close track on developments in the RMA and command, particularly if we wish to maintain interoperability with United States forces on alliance or coalition operations. This requirement has been acknowledged in Britain as follows:

> Leaving aside the academic debate on whether or not a revolution is underway, it is clear that exploiting these technologies will lead to significant improvements in military capability. They will inevitably be led by the US. If Britain and other Allies can successfully tap into these developments, the result will be more effective coalition operations. Conversely, there is potential for multinational operations to become more difficult if compatible capabilities are not preserved. This could lead to political as well as military problems. Our priority must therefore be to ensure that we maintain the ability to make a high quality contribution to multinational operations and to operate closely with US forces throughout the spectrum of potential operations. To do this we may need to be selective about the technologies we develop nationally or on a European basis, and be prepared to use US technologies in other areas in order to continue to make a leading contribution to multinational operations.[49]

Thus the problem has been recognised officially, but difficult choices and associated investment decisions will need to be made as to which technologies are essential, where we should buy into existing US programmes and where we should develop European ones. But this should not necessarily be a one-way street. After all, Europe can surely claim on the co-operation and goodwill of the United States as it is also in her military interests to maintain the best possible interoperability with her allies. For all concerned who accept that an RMA is under way, it will make good political, military and economic sense to agree on a *multinational* joint vision and to develop co-operative ventures as far as possible. Yet commonality of understanding and practice may become impeded by differences in terminology. Debate over the 'levels' of conflict or war illustrates some of the complexities involved in discussing the impact of the RMA.

Avoiding the doctrine trap

Although rapid advances in communications and technology can help commanders to exercise command and control over major operations, technology and the RMA does not, by itself, remove or reduce the need for commanders to develop operational art. Of course, as this pamphlet makes clear, the exercise of high command can embrace many styles and many forms. The machines, computers and communicators of the information age can enable, empower and assist, but they are unlikely to be a substitute for study of military history, campaigns and operational art; the exercise of command remains a human function. Fads and fashions in military doctrine come and go, but military judgement, intuition, insight and moral courage remain as important to 'RMA commanders' as they were to the Greeks and Romans. Yet there has also been an enduring quest to distil general principles of command and war in the pursuit of military excellence and victory.

The nature of command and leadership has been a source of debate throughout history. Theories abound on the links between the two and with management. Whilst military traditionalists often reject 'management' as an out-of-place business term, there is nonetheless much to manage in peace and war, from machines to men. Current British Army doctrine, for example, contends that command consists of three elements; leadership, decision making and control. But there has never been any doubt of the importance of leadership as a war-winning factor at all levels. Inspirational leadership can raise morale and sustaining morale has often proved decisive in the outcome of military operations, regardless of the medium or technology to hand. Of course, doctrine is important to shape military thought and guide campaign planning, but rarely does military doctrine – largely, but certainly not exclusively, written in the light of previous experience – conform to the strategies, plans and actions of the next, probably unforeseen, enemy. Indeed, as Sir Michael Howard remarked:

> I am tempted to declare that whatever doctrine the Armed Forces are working on, they have got it wrong. I am also tempted to declare that it does not matter that they have got it wrong. What does matter is their capacity to get it right quickly when the moment arrives. It is the task of military science in an age of peace to prevent the doctrine being too badly wrong.[50]

So it is much harder to write doctrine for the future than to record lessons from the past, and often this is fudged. We therefore hope that Michael Howard's warning is heeded by present and future generations of doctrine and concepts writers, whether working on the RMA or not, for large traps abound in the doctrine field.

Conclusions

In conclusion, we suggest that four main points may be highlighted:

1 First, advanced information-based technology promises much but it has not always 'delivered' on time and to cost. For every advance in technology, a counter can be developed, provided the necessary expertise, time and resources are available. Further, if we channel too much of our finite procurement resources into an RMA-based 'Western Way of Warfare' we may neglect, by default, to develop effective counters to our opponents' strategies who might employ different ways and means to attack us. Thus the dangers of asymmetric warfare should not be underestimated.
2 Second, after the end of the Cold War, and with the Gulf War and recent conflicts in Africa and the Former Republic of Yugoslavia in mind, we are also entitled to ask, 'Has warfare so fundamentally changed?' If war remains based on a complex interaction of political, economic, social and cultural factors, there is surely much more than technology at work. Rather than just an RMA, perhaps we are facing a more general 'Revolution in Strategic Affairs' as proposed by Lawrence Freedman.[51] We need to look beyond technology in order to understand how warfare may develop.
3 Third, and very broadly speaking, the European view of the RMA is largely a sceptical one, but not necessarily hostile, and neither should it be. Political and industrial pressures, as much as any military ones, will force Western Europe to seek to maintain 'military connectivity' with the United States; but it would be naive not to expect some political premium to be demanded for the technological access required.
4 Fourth, the act of command remains primarily a human activity. Of course, technology and RMA systems assist commanders in their exercise of command, but they do not offer a substitute for it. As we face a bewildering and uncertain future, with military operations likely around the spectrum of conflict, so we need a spectrum of response. The levels of conflict, and types and dimensions of war remain relevant, but only insofar as they are used as a guide and adapted to each operational environment or circumstance. There is no substitute for study and analysis in an attempt to understand the 'whys' and 'whats' of command, but to understand the 'hows' still requires an acceptance that command remains more of an art than a science. Doctrine for command should reflect this.[52]

Finally, if Europe is to adopt a pragmatic programme of 'high aims but limited resources' with regard to the United States and the RMA, then developing a common understanding of the nature and conduct of future war is vitally important. This applies equally to describing the spectrum and levels of conflict. If we are to share in the command of armed forces at the highest level, either in coalition or alliance operations, we must clearly understand and demonstrate proficiency at the business and mechanics of our trade. Yet there is much more to study than just the process itself. The *product* in terms of achieving the strategic ends, often with limited means, will require imaginative ways. This puts a premium on creative and flexible mission command, and on enhancing confidence, mutual trust and understanding amongst our friends and allies. Further, our prospective opponents should develop a healthy respect for, and understanding of, our strategic competence and will, as much as for our military hardware and associated technical and tactical skills. Yet above all, perhaps, sharing ideals will be as important as sharing doctrines and technologies. Thus the wider and more informed the mutual discussion and debate, the greater will be our understanding of the exercise of command in this, or any past or future, RMA. So as we aim for the end of the rainbow, whilst we know that we shall never reach it, the journey is nonetheless worthwhile.

Notes

1 Quoted by Earl H. Tilford, Jr, *The Revolution in Military Affairs: Prospects and Cautions*, (Carlisle, Pa: 1995).
2 Mary C. FitzGerald, 'The Dilemma in Moscow's Defensive Force Posture', in Willard C. Frank, Jr, and Philip S. Gillette (eds), *Soviet Military Doctrine from Lenin to Gorbachev, 1915–1991* (Westport, CT: 1992) pp.348–9.
3 See Alvin and Heidi Toffler, *War and Anti-War* (London: 1993) ch. 6, 'Third Wave War', pp.64–80.
4 See, for example, John Terraine, *White Heat: The New Warfare 1914–1918* (London: 1982) and Jonathan Bailey, *The First World War and the Birth of Modern Warfare* (Camberley: Strategic and Combat Studies Institute Occasional Paper Number 22, 1996).
5 The Strategic Defence Review, *Modern Forces for the Modern World*, Supporting Essay Three, 'The Impact of Technology' (London: 1998).
6 Colin S. Gray, 'A Contested Vision: The RMA Debate Today', paper prepared for the conference on 'Revolution in Military Affairs? Challenges to Governments in the Information Age', the Royal Institute of International Affairs, Chatham House, London, 21–22 May 1997.
7 Steven Metz, 'The Revolution in Military Affairs: Orthodoxy and Beyond', in Earl H. Tilford (ed.), *World View: The 1997 Strategic Assessment* (Carlisle, Pa: Strategic Studies Institute, US Army War College, February 1997) p.24.

8   Jon L. Boyes and Stephen J. Andriole (ed.), *Principles of Command and Control* (Washington, DC: 1987) p.412.
9   Alan D. Campen (ed.), *The First Information War* (Fairfax, VA: 1992) p.xi.
10 Ibid., p.x.
11 See, for example, John Keegan, *The Mask of Command* (London: 1987) pp.210–12 on the value of the telegraph to General Ulysses Grant; for a more detailed study of the impact of telegraphy on Union and Confederate command, see Edward Hagerman, *The American Civil War and the Origins of Modern Warfare* (Bloomington and Indianapolis: 1988) pp.40–3 and 103–5.
12 The fate of von Kluck's army is described in Hew Strachan, *European Armies and the Conduct of War* (London: 1983) p.133.
13 An optimistic view of the efficacy of air power in transforming theatre warfare is given a recent United States Air Force sponsored RAND study: David A. Ochmanek et al., *To Find and not to Yield* (Santa Monica, CA: 1998).
14 Thomas A. Keaney and Eliot A. Cohen, *Revolution in Warfare? Air Power in the Persian Gulf* (Annapolis, MD: 1995) p.321.
15 See D. French, *The British Way in War 1668–2000* (London: 1990).
16 The 'New World Order' speech by President Bush in 1991 and other influential books such as F. Fukuyama's *The End of History and the Last Man* (Harmondsworth: Penguin, 1993) made sweeping and what proved to be overly-optimistic statements on future peace rather than future conflict.
17 B. Boutros-Ghali, *An Agenda for Peace* (New York: 1992) p.2.
18 This term is employed to describe the use of forces in peacekeeping operations when the consent of the warring factions has been lost. It refers to incidents involving US forces in Somalia in 1993. For an account of these operations, see A. Parsons, *Cold War, Hot Peace* (London: Michael Joseph, 1995) pp.198–208.
19 *Wider Peacekeeping* (London: 1995).
20 As the situation in Bosnia worsened in 1994 and 1995, the traditional approaches to inter-positional peacekeeping became impossible to maintain. In the summer of 1995, NATO, in parallel with the major Croatian ground offensives (Operation Storm) launched Operation Deliberate Force to coerce the Serbs to negotiate. It was the combination of ground operations, diplomatic pressure and NATO bombing – rather than air power alone – that helped to set the necessary conditions for the Dayton peace agreement of November 1995. There are many accounts; for a good overview, see C. Bellamy, *Knights in White Armour* (London: 1996).
21 There is a hierarchy of US joint and single service doctrine in the 3-07 series. Most are available on the Internet.
22 See UK Joint Warfare Publication 3-50, *Peace Support Operations* (1998).
23 Legal opinion is divided over the right to humanitarian intervention. For an excellent short reader on the legal backdrop to post-Cold War armed conflict see C. Greenwood, *Command and the Laws of Armed Conflict*, Strategic and Combat Studies Institute Paper Number 4 (Camberley: 1993).
24 See Sir Michael Rose, *Fighting for Peace: Bosnia 1994* (London: 1998) for a description of the challenges facing senior commanders in complex peacekeeping missions.
25 *Shorter OED* (Oxford: 1985) p.705.
26 See *The Blue Helmets*, 4th edn (New York: 1997) p.5.

27 Cm. 3999, *The Strategic Defence Review* (London: 1998) p.14.
28 See P. Paret (ed.), *Makers of Modern Strategy* (Princeton, NJ: 1986), for an overview of the development of strategic thought. Although strategists reflect their contemporary environment, many enduring principles remain.
29 See P. Paret and Michael Howard (trans.) *On War* (Princeton, NJ: 1976) p.111.
30 Military commentators on the RMA in the USA in particular offer the notion of perfect information; information dominance has become one of the core capabilities of the US strategic doctrine *Joint Vision 2010*. See, for example, *1998 Strategic Assessment* (Washington, DC: 1998) for details.
31 Keegan, *The Mask of Command*.
32 Paul Addison and Angus Calder (eds), *Time to Kill: The Soldier's Experience of War in the West 1939–1945* (London: 1997).
33 Martin van Creveld, *On Future War* (London: 1991) pp.109–10.
34 Barry D. Watts, *Clausewitzian Friction and Future War*, McNair Paper 52 (Washington, DC: Institute for National Strategic Studies, National Defense University, October 1996) pp.27–33.
35 A. A. Svechin, *Strategiia [Strategy]* (Moscow: 1926).
36 Influence of individual thinkers often depends on access to their work in certain nations at certain times. For example, in nineteenth-century US and European military thinking Jomini was more influential than Clausewitz, yet Clausewitz has had greater and more lasting impact in shaping twentieth-century strategic thinking.
37 See Alex Danchev, *Alchemist of War, A Life of Basil Liddell Hart* (London: 1998) and B. Holden Reid, *J.F.C. Fuller, Military Thinker* (London: 1990) for examples of recent works on British twentieth-century military thinkers.
38 Nations have divergent doctrines for the component command model. The United Kingdom recognises the five listed, whereas the USA and NATO do not recognise logistics as a separate component command.
39 See R. Jackson, *Suez, The Forgotten Invasion* (Shrewsbury: 1996) p.32.
40 See A. Lambert, 'Coercion and Air Power', in S. Peach (ed.), *Perspectives on Air Power* (London: The Stationery Office, 1998).
41 See B. Brodie, *Strategy in the Missile Age* (Princeton, NJ: 1959).
42 See Douglas A. Magregor, *Breaking the Phalanx: A New Design for Landpower in the 21st Century* (Westport, CT: 1997) pp.50–1.
43 Colin S. Gray, *The American Revolution in Military Affairs: An Interim Assessment* (Camberley: Strategic and Combat Studies Institute Occasional Paper Number 28, 1997).
44 William S. Lind, *Maneuver Warfare* (Boulder, CO: Westview Press, 1985).
45 Campen, *First Information War*, p.52.
46 See ADP-2, *Command*, pp.2–21 to 2–22: 'The unfortunate Marshal of France Bazaine, for example, who tended personally to the siting of individual gun batteries rather than committing his reserves during the battle of Gravelotte-St Privat during the Franco-Prussian War, was neither the first nor the last commander to become thoroughly distracted and so lose a battle.' For a full account, see Michael Howard, *The Franco-Prussian War 1870–71* (London: 1981) p.173.
47 *Notes From Theatres of War*, No. 14: *Western Desert and Cyrenaica August/December 1942* (London: The War Office, June 1943) p.23.

48 For details of the trend towards centralisation, see J.B.A. Bailey, *Field Artillery and Firepower* (Oxford: The Military Press, 1989) pp.182–6 and 210–71.
49 The Strategic Defence Review, *Modern Forces for the Modern World*, p.2.
50 Michael Howard, 'Military Science in an Age of Peace', *RUSI Journal*, Vol. 118, No. 4 (December 1973) p.3.
51 Lawrence Freedman, *The Revolution in Strategic Affairs* (Oxford: 1998).
52 For a recent and very valuable contribution to the debate, see Jim Storr, 'A Command Philosophy for the Information Age: the Continuing Relevance of Mission Command' in (ed.), David Potts, *The Big Issue: Command and Combat in the Information Age*, Occasional Paper Number 45 (Shrivenham: Strategic and Combat Studies Institute, March 2002) pp.41–8. The British Army's doctrine for Mission Command will be updated in Army Doctrine Publication *Land Operations* (2003, forthcoming). In the meantime it was incorporated into Joint Warfare Publication 0–01 *British Defence Doctrine* (Second Edition, October 2001), pp.3–7.

Index

Aandalsnes, capture of (1940) 66, 67, 68
ACE Rapid Reaction Corps (ARRC) *see* Allied Command Europe Rapid Reaction Corps
Admiralty
  Dardanelles campaign (1915) 39–40
  Norway campaign (1940) 61, 65
Agenda for Peace, An (Boutros-Ghali) 155, 185
air forces *see* Luftwaffe; Royal Air Force
Air Ministry
  Directorate of Bombing Operations 132, 133
  and Norway campaign (1940) 65, 68
air power
  in First World War 114
  in Burma campaign 84, 91–2
  and Revolution in Military Affairs 183–4
  and weather 195
Alanbrooke, Field Marshal Viscount 8
  air-army co-operation 118
  relations with Alexander 17
Alexander, Field-Marshal Sir Harold (later Earl) 74, 75
Allen, Louis 93
Allied Command Europe Rapid Reaction Corps 139, 144
Allied Forces South East Asia (ALFSEA) HQ 79, 83, 84
Allied Military Committee 59
American Civil War 179, 182
amphibious operations
  First World War 36
  Gallipoli 42, 46
  inter-war period 54
Anderson, Duncan 88, 98
Annan, Kofi 152, 153, 159, 163
Applebaum, A. 158

Arakan campaigns 91
  First (1942) 74, 83, 93
  Second (1942–43) 75, 84, 85, 100
Arbuthnot, Rear-Admiral Sir Robert 31
Arcadian, HMS 51
Armstrong rifle 27
Army, Australian, in First World War 21
Army, British
  British Expeditionary Force (1914–18) 8, 16–17, 20, 22
  British Expeditionary Force (1940) 114, 118
  command structure in First World War 15, 19, 22
  command structure in Second World War 8, 198–9
  doctrine 21
  in First World War 15–24 *passim*
  at Gallipoli 43, 47–50
  multi-national operations 10, 21
  relations with RAF in France (1940) 5–6, 113, 114, 116, 118–21
  relations with RAF in Norway (1940) 67–8
  formations (First World War)
    2nd Army 11
    29th Division 43
  formations (Second World War); 14th Army 80, 81, 86, 88, 96, 101; 11th Army Group 79, 80; 21st Army Group 11; Burcorps (Burma Corps) 80, 83, 94, 98; V Corps 61; XV Corps 91, 93; 19th Division 103; 146 Brigade 65, 66; 148 Brigade 65, 66, 67; 1st Essex 77, 78; Special Air Service 85
Army, Canadian, in First World War 21

Index

Army, French
  command structure in Second World War 7
  mutinies of 1917 220
Army, German
  command structure in Second World War 8
  communications in First World War 182
  fighting methods (1940) 117
  formations
    Mountain Corps 64–5
Army, Indian
  14th Indian Division 93–4, 95
  17th Indian Division 106
  Gurkhas 102
Army, Iraqi, command structure in Gulf War 7
Army, Japanese, morale in Second World War 99–100
Army, Norwegian, defence of Lundeghoda line 67
Army, United States
  command structure in Gulf War 9
  command structure in Second World War 8–9
  command structure in Vietnam 7, 9
  multinational operations in First World War 21
Army Cooperation Command *see* Royal Air Force
Army Defence Doctrine 2 1, 9
Army Doctrine Publication: Operations 91, 101, 106
Arras (battle, 1917) 20
Article V operations 140, 143, 144
Asquith, Herbert 16
  relations with military 17–18
asymmetric warfare 202
Ataturk, Kemal 51
attrition
  British Army since Second World War 88
  Royal Navy in First World War 32
Auchinleck, General Sir Claude (later Field-Marshal) 74, 98, 118
Auftragstaktik see command, decentralised

Avonmouth, Operation (1940) 61, 63

Backhouse, Admiral (later Admiral of the Fleet) Sir Roger 45
Balaklava (battle) 7
Baldwin, Air Marshal Sir John 81, 84, 91
Barratt, Air Marshal Sir Arthur 118–19
Bartholomew, General Sir William 119
Battle of the Atlantic 130, 131
Bayly, Admiral Sir Lewis 26
Beatty, Admiral of the Fleet Sir David (later Earl) 4, 26
  accelerated promotion of 28
  choice of subordinates 30–1
  command style 27, 28, 45
  as naval thinker 29
  personality 10
  promotion of doctrine 31–2, 33
Befehlstaktik 10, 11, 36, 81
Bellamy, Christopher 9–10
Beresford, Lord Charles 41
Berney-Ficklin, Brigadier (later Major-General) Horatio 69
Birdwood, Lieutenant-General Sir William 36, 38
Blitzkrieg 178, 183
Bomber Offensive (Harris) 134
Bosnia (United Nations intervention) 143, 144, 148, 151, 161, 168, 195
Boutros-Ghali, Boutros 153, 154, 155, 164, 184
Bowhill, Air Chief Marshal Sir Frederick 129
Boyd, Colonel John 3
Boyd, Cycle *see* OODA loop
Boyle, Captain William 28
Brahimi, Lakhdar 159
  Brahimi Report 159–71 *passim*
Braithwaite, General Sir Walter 37, 47, 52
Brett James, Anthony 81
British Defence Doctrine 1
British Expeditionary Force *see* army, British
British Military Doctrine (BMD) 91, 93, 97, 99, 103

Brock, Admiral Sir Osmond 30
Brodie, Bernard 194
Brooke, Field Marshal Sir Alan *see* Alanbrooke, Field Marshal Viscount
Bulair (landing, 1915) 46
Burma campaign 74–86, 88–109 *passim*
  air power 84, 91–2
  logistics and supply 84, 92, 107
  maritime operations 91
Burney, Admiral Sir Cecil 30
Butler, J.R.M. 60, 65

'Calais plot' 18
Callwell, Major-General Sir Charles 36, 39
Calvert, Brigadier Michael 78, 88, 91, 92, 98
Cambridge, Duke of 16
Capital, Operation 81, 95, 100, 105–6
  see also Extended Capital, Operation
Carden, Admiral Sir Sackville 38, 43
Chatfield, Captain Ernle (later Baron) 28
Chamberlain, Neville 63, 64
Chiefs of Staff 60, 61, 63
Chindit operations 78, 82, 84, 92
Christison, Lieutenant-General Sir Philip 82
Churchill, Winston
  as First Sea Lord 16
  Battle of the Atlantic 130
  command relationships 8, 60
  Dardanelles campaign 39, 41
  Gallipoli campaign 38, 51
  Norwegian campaign 62–3, 64, 68
  on politics and war 2
  promotion of Beatty 28
  on Royal Navy in First World war 31
  on tanks 32
  and War Council 40
Clausewitz, Karl von 45, 128, 177, 191
  and concept of friction 59, 189–90
  and complexity 195
  and qualities of great commanders 126
coalition operations *see* multinational operations
Coastal Command *see* Royal Air Force
Cobb, Brigadier (later Major-General) Edwyn 82
coercion theory 194
Cohen, Eliot A. 184
combined operations *see* joint operations
command
  'battle command doctrine' 9
  defined 1–3, 108, 126
  importance of doctrine 201, 202
  in joint operations 43–4
  and levels of war 191–3
  manoeuvrist command 35–6
  in multinational operations 139–46 *passim*
  in peace support operations 187
  naval command 44–5
  see also 'mission command'
command, centralised 197–9
command, decentralised 10, 103, 197–9
Auftragstaktik 10, 11, 36, 50
command, high
  defined 2, 3, 177
  personality as a factor in 7, 10
  qualities required for 75
  role of doctrine 11
command and control (C2) 3
  British Army in First World War 23–4
  by communications and doctrine (C2CD) 33
  multinational operations 6, 20, 141, 148
  peace support operations 7
  impact of Revolution in Military Affairs 181–2
  Royal Air Force in Second World War 113
  Royal Navy in First World War 27, 31, 33, 46–7

command, control and
    communications (C3)
  impact of Revolution in Military
      Affairs 182
  Royal Navy in First World War
      31–2
command, control, communications,
    computers and intelligence (C4I)
    197
Committee of Imperial Defence 15
communications
  British Army in First World War 22
  at Gallipoli 49, 51
  German Army in First World
      War 182
  inter-war developments 182–3
  in Norway (1940) 68
  Royal Navy in First World War 31
  Second World War 183
  see also radios; telephones, field
Congo, Democratic Republic (DRC)
    (peace support operations) 147,
    160
Corbett, Sir Julian 36, 52, 53
Cowan, Major-General T.D.
    'Punch' 77
Cowan, Admiral Sir Walter 26, 30
Cunningham, Admiral of the Fleet Sir
    Andrew (later Viscount) 26

Daladier, Edouard 62
Dardanelles campaign
  failures of strategic cordination
      38–42 passim
  see also Gallipoli campaign
Dardanelles Committee 18
Dardanelles Commission 40
de Robeck, Vice-Admiral (later
    Admiral of the fleet) Sir John 36,
    37, 52, 53
  command style 46
de Guingand, Major-General Sir
    'Freddie' 193
Defeat into Victory (Slim) 5, 81, 84,
    85, 89, 91, 108
Democratic Republic of the Congo
    (DRC) see Congo, Democratic
    Republic
Derry, T.E. 65

Desert Storm, Operation 4
  see also Gulf War
Dietl, General Eduard 64
Dill, General (later Field Marshal) Sir
    John 2, 116, 119
'directive command' see command,
    decentralised
Dixon, Norman 26, 99
Donbaik (battle, 1943) 93
Douglas, Air Marshal Sir Sholto 120,
    121
Dreadnought, HMS 28
Dunkirk (battle, 1940) 116

East Timor (peace support operations)
    147
Eden, Sir Anthony 193
Eisenhower, General Dwight D. 20
Euryalus HMS 46, 51
Evan-Thomas, Admiral Sir Hugh 30
Evans, Geoffrey 104, 107
Executive Committee on Peace and
    Security see United Nations
Extended Capital, Operation 81, 86,
    93, 95, 100, 105–6
  see also Capital, Operation;
      Meiktila-Mandalay operation

Face of Battle, The (Keegan) 189
Festing, Lieutenant-Colonel (later
    Field Marshal) F.W. 117, 118,
    119
Field Service Regulations (FSR) 21, 40
First World War 4, 15–24 passim, 179
  air power 114
  'Easterners and Westerners' 16–17
  multinational operations 20–1
  see also Gallipoli; Jutland
Fisher, Admiral of the Fleet Sir John
    (later Baron) 26
  Dardanelles campaign 39, 41, 42
  Gallipoli campaign 38, 51
  on Jellicoe 44
  'Syndicate of Discontent' 28
Foch, General (later Marshal)
    Ferdinand 20
Force Protection 141
France
  Norwegian campaign 62

Index

France (campaign, 1940)   113
Franks, Lt. Gen. Frederick M.   9
Freedman, Lawrence   202
French, Field Marshal Sir John
   15–16, 19
   relations with Kitchener   17
   and coalition warfare   20
Freyberg, Lieutenant-Commander
   B.C. (later Lieutenant-General
   Lord)   46
friction in military operations
   189–90
Fuller, Major-General J.F.C.   108

Gallabat (battle, 1940)   77, 78
Gallipoli campaign   2, 4–5
   Army command in   47–9
   communications   49–50
   command structure   7, 11, 49, 50
   evacuation of Y beach   48, 50
   as manoeuvre warfare   34, 35–6
   lack of strategic clarity   37
   logistics failures   49
   naval command in   46–47
   see also Dardanelles Campaign;
      Suvla Bay landings
Giffard, General Sir George   74, 79
Global Positioning System (GPS)
   177, 181
Gort, General the Viscount   116–17
Gratis Military Officers (GMOs)   *see*
   United Nations
Gray, Colin S.   196
Greenslade, Brigadier Cyrus,   118
Guinness, Walter   *see* Moyne, Lord
Gulf War (1991)   7, 9, 21, 178, 182,
   183
   see also Desert Storm, Operation
Guderian, Colonel-General Heinz
   182
Gurkhas   *see* Army, Indian

Haig, General Sir Douglas (later Field
   Marshal Earl)   3
   and coalition warfare   20
   command of BEF   17, 23
   and dominion forces   21
   relations with Lloyd George   18
Halifax, Lord   64

Hamilton, General Sir Ian
   command at Gallipoli   42–4,
      47–52
   on Kitchener   39
   'mission command' style   10
   on importance of sea power   34
   strategy at Gallipoli   35
Handel, Michael   1
Hankey, Maurice   19, 40
Harris, Air Marshal Sir Arthur   3, 6,
   126–36 *passim*
   air power theory   127
   as a commander   126–7
   foreign and Dominion personnel,
      134
   insubordination of   135
   personality of   10, 133–4
   reputation of   126
   strategic judgement of   131
Haug, Major-General Hvinden   67
Heath, Admiral Sir Herbert   31
Heath, Lieutenant-General Sir Lewis
   75
Helles (battle, 1915)   43
Hickey, Michael   98
High Wood (battle, 1916)   22
'Historical School' (of naval thought)
   28, 29, 30, 33
History of the Second World War
   (Liddell Hart)   108
Hitler, Adolf   8
Hogg, Captain D.W.B.T.   117
Horne, General Sir Henry   22
Hotblack, Major-General Frederick   69
Hough, Richard   30
Howard, Sir Michael   3, 201
Hundred Days campaign (1918)   24
Hunter-Weston, Lieutenant-General
   Sir Aylmer   36, 43, 47, 48, 51
Hutton, Lieutenant-General Sir T.J.
   75, 78

Imphal (battle, 1944),   75, 84, 85, 92,
   96, 97,106
Implacable, HMS   47
information warfare   180, 190
Inskip, Sir Thomas   129
Integrated Mission Task Forces
   (IMTFs)   *see* United Nations

interoperability 199–200
Inter-Service Planning Staff 54, 61
Inter-Service Signals Board 61
Iraq
  'no-fly zone' operations 187
Iron Duke, HMS 27
Irrawaddy (crossing, 1942) 92
Irwin, Lieutenant-General Noel 74, 83, 93, 94, 100
Ismay, General Sir H.L. (later Lord) 'Pug' 65

Jackson, General Sir Mike 2
Jellicoe, Admiral Sir John (later Earl) 4
  as a 'regulator' 26, 27
  as a commander 44
  choice of subordinates 30–1
  personality of 10, 29, 30
Jerram, admiral sir Martyn 30
Jervis, Admiral Sir John (later Earl St. Vincent) 29–30
joint operations 4, 9
  First World War 36–7
  Gallipoli 42, 43, 51–4
Joint Services Command and Staff College 73
Joint Vision 2010 181
Jomini, Antoine-Henri 65, 191
Jutland (battle, 1916) 4, 27, 31, 32, 33
  decentralised command 10
  Burney's failure at 30

Katamura, Lieutenant-General Shihachi, 100
Keaney, Thomas A. 184
Keating, Colin 167
Keegan, John 1
Kelly, Howard 26
Keyes, Admiral of the Fleet Sir (later Baron) Roger
  Command style 45
  and Gallipoli 37, 38, 40, 46, 48, 50, 52, 53
  on Kitchener 41
Kimura, Lietenant-General Hyotaro 90, 95, 100, 105–6, 108
Kirke Committee 17
Kitchner, Field Marshal Lord 15–16, 19

Dardanelles campaign 39, 41, 42
Gallipoli campaign 37, 38, 47, 51
relations with Sir John French 17
strategic thinking 35
and War Council 40
Koe, Lieutenant Colonel (later Brigadier-General) Lancelot 48
Kohima (battle, 1944) 75, 85, 92, 97
Kosovo (NATO operations, 1999) 144, 148, 170, 187, 193
Kosovo Force (KFOR) 149
Krithia, Third Battle (1915), 35

Lawson, Joel S. 3
Leaders and Intelligence (Handel), 1
leadership 1
  defined 3
  and command 201
Leese, Lieutenant-General Sir Oliver 74, 79, 80, 82, 83, 84
Leonhard, Robert R. 198, 199
levels of conflict 191–3
Lewin, Ronald 97, 105
Liddell Hart, Sir B.H. 108
Lind, William 197
Little Big Horn (battle, 1876) 7
Lloyd, Major-General Wilfred 94, 100
Lloyd George, David 16
  and dominion forces 21
  relations with military 17–18
Lockyer, captain Highes 47
Loos (battle, 1915) 20
Ludlow-Hewitt, Air chief Marshal Sir Edgar 128–9
Luftwaffe 117–18, 119
Lunt, James 98

MacArthur, General Douglas 75, 77, 80
Mackenzie, Compton E.M. 43
Mandalay *see* Meiktila-Mandalay operation
manoeuvre warfare 3, 4, 5, 197
  defined 89–90, 91, 93, 95, 96–7, 100, 101
  Burma campaign 82, 88–102 *passim*
  Gallipoli campaign 34, 35–6
  Royal Navy in First World War 32

Manual of Combined Military Operations (1913) 40
Mask of Command (Keegan) 1, 189
Massy, Lieutenant-General H.R.S. 61, 67
Mathews, Lieutenant Colonel Godfrey 48
Meiktila-Mandalay operation 84, 86, 88, 92, 95, 105
  see also Extended Capital, Operation
Messervy, General Sir Frank 82
Military Technical Revolution (MTR) 178
Ministry of Economic Warfare (MEW) 132–3
'mission command' 10, 11, 23, 50, 81–2, 103–4, 141, 142, 197, 199
MO7 *see* War Office
Monro, General sir Charles 38, 41, 53
Montgomery, Field Marshal Bernard 73–4, 80, 82, 88, 89, 193,
  command style 10–11, 82, 198
Morgan, Major-General Harold de R. 66, 67
Morris, Colonel A.R. 105
Mountbatten, Vice-Admiral Lord Louis 79, 83, 90, 102
Moyne, Lord 41
multinational operations 6, 20–1, 139–46 *passim*, 148–50
  interoperability 199–200
Myitkina (battle, 1944) 84

Napoleonic Wars 179
Narvik operations (1940) 62, 64, 66
NATO *see* North Atlantic Treaty Organisation
Naval Review (journal) 28
Nelson, Horatio 3, 44
Neuve Chapelle (battle, 1915) 20
Nivelle, General Robert 18
Newall, Marshal of the Royal Air Force Sir (later Baron) Cyril 129
North Atlantic Treaty Organisation 21, 139, 140, 144, 148–9
  see also Kosovo Force
Norway campaign (1940) 5, 59–69 *passim*

command structure 11, 54, 59–61, 66–9
communications 68
failure of Allied strategy 62–3, 69
Nye, Lieutenant-General Sir Archibald 89, 107

Ogarov, Marshal N.V. 178
Old, Brigadier-General W.D. 81, 84
Omaha Beach (battle) 8
On the Psychology of Military Incompetence (Dixon) 26
On War (Clausewitz) 188
OODA loop 3–4, 51
Organisation for Security and Co-operation in Europe 185
Overy, Richard 132

Paget, General B.C.H. 67
Palin, R.H. 148
Patton, General George S. 135
Paul, Operation (1940) 62
Peace support operations (PSOs) 6, 7, 9–10, 146–71 *passim*, 184–6
  see also United Nations
Percival, Lieutenant-General Arthur 75, 77, 78
Perrett, Bryan 101, 105
Pershing, General John J. 21
Pimlott, John 2
Plunkett, Admiral Sir Reginald 26, 29, 30
Plymouth, Operation 63
Politico-military relations 2, 6, 8, 9
  in First World War 15–16, 17
Portal, Marshal of the Royal Air Force Sir Charles 'Peter' (later Viscount) 133, 134, 135
Pownall, Lieutenant-General Sir Henry 79
Princess Royal, HMS 26

Queen Elizabeth, SS 41, 42, 48, 51, 53
Quinlan, General Sir Edward 74

R4, Operation (1940) 61, 64, 65
radio communications 8, 22, 182–3
  see also communications
Rangoon 82, 84, 90, 92

Rapidly Deployable Mission
  Headquarters see United Nations
Rees, Major-General T.W. 'Pete' 77
Revolution in Military Affairs (RMA)
  7, 11, 21, 177–203 passim
  air power in 183–4
  centralised and decentralised
    command 197–9
  defined 177
  impact of new communications
    technology 182–3
  levels of war 191–3
  peace-building 186–7
  post-Cold War conflict 184–5
  Soviet views of 178
'Revolution in Strategic Affairs' 202
Reynaud, Paul 60, 62, 64, 69
Richmond, Admiral Sir Herbert 30, 39
Robertson, General (later Field-
  Marshal) Sir William 2, 17, 18
Rodger, Nicholas 32
Rome, Colonel Claude 78
Royal Air Force
  area bombing 131–2
  creation of 114
  relations with Army in France
    (1940) 5–6, 113, 114, 116,
    118–21
  relations with Army in Norway
    (1940) 67–8
  Army Co-operation Command 6,
    129
  Bomber-Command 6, 128, 129,
    131–2, 133
  Coastal Command 6, 128, 129–30
  Fighter Command 129
  Operational Training Unit 128
  Third Tactical Air Force 81
Royal Marines 66
Royal Navy
  command performance at Gallipoli
    46–7
  in First World War 27
  fire support at Gallipoli 42, 47
  relations with Army at Gallipoli 43
  Norwegian Campaign 65
Ruge, General Otto 67, 69
Rules of the Game (Gordon) 26
Rupert, Prince 32

Rwanda, (UN mission) 166, 167, 170
  see also United Nations Assistance
    Mission for Rwanda

Sandhurst, Royal Military Academy
  75
Samuels, Martin 23
Scoones, General Sir Geoffry 82, 83
Scott, Major-General J. Bruce 77, 98
SFOR see Stabilisation Force in
  Bosnia and Herzogovina
SHAEF see Supreme Headquarters
  Allied Expeditionary Force
Sickleforce 66, 67, 69
Sierra Leone (peace support
  operations) 147, 148, 160
signals see communications
Slim, Lieutenant-General (later
  Field-Marshal Viscount) William
  as a commander 11, 75, 77, 79–86,
    97–9, 103–7
  as a manoeuvrist 5, 10, 82, 89,
    90–109 passim
  logistics 84
  organisation of his HQ 79–81,
    104–5
  physical robustness 75–6
  rapid promotion of 73
  relations with allies 101–2
  reputation of 74, 89
Somalia (UN intervention) 166, 167,
  168
Somme (battle, 1916) 8, 22–3
South East Asia Command (SEAC) 79
'spectrum of conflict' 184, 187–8
spring offensive (1918) 20
Stabilisation Force in Bosnia and
  Herzogovina (SFOR) 143
Standby Forces High Readiness
  Brigade (SHIRBRIG) see United
  Nations
Staff College (Camberley) 47, 73,
  77, 89
Stillwell, General Joseph 82, 83, 84,
  101–2
Strategic Defence Review 179–80, 188
Stratford Operation (1940) 61, 63, 65
Stopford, Lieutenant-General Sir
  Frederick 48–9, 51

Stopford, Lieutenant-General Sir Montagu 82, 103
Strachan, Hew 19
Stratton, Captain W.H. 117
Sturdee, Admiral Sir Frederick Doveton 30
Suez Crisis 193
Supreme Headquarters Allied Expeditionary Force 19
Supreme War Council 20, 59
Suvla Bay landings (1915) 48–9, 50, 51, 52, 53
Svechin, A.A. 191, 192
'Syndicate of Discontent' 28

telephones, field 22
Tetten (battle, 1940) 67
Thomas, Hugh Evan *see* Evan-Thomas, Admiral Sir Hugh
Thomas, I.N.A. 89–90, 93, 96, 103
Thursday, Operation 78
Tilford, Earl H. 179
Toffler, Alvin and Heidi 178
Time to Kill (Addison and Calder) 189
Trondheim, proposed British attack on 64, 65–6
Turkey, strategic importance in First World War 34
Tyrwhitt, Admiral Sir Reginald 26

United Nations 6, 21, 146–71 *passim*
  Advisory Committee on Administrative and Budgetary Questions (ACABQ) 166
  conflict prevention and peacebuilding 168–9, 185
  command problems of UN operations 146–50
  Department of Peacekeeping Operations (DKPO) 7, 146, 151–6, 161, 163, 165, 166
  Department of Political Affairs (DPA) 163, 166
  ECPS Information and Strategic Analysis Secretariat (EIASAS) 166–7
  Executive Committee on Peace and Security (ECPS) 163, 166, 169

  Gratis Military Officers (GMOs) 154–5, 165
  Integrated Mission Task Forces (IMTFs) 163
  mandate issues 150–2, 160, 185–6
  Non-Aligned Movement 154, 165
  Rapidly Deployable Mission Headquarters (RDMHQ) 154, 165
  reform of peacekeeping management 152–71 *passim*
  Security Council 146, 151–2, 160, 161, 162, 166, 167
  Special Representatives of the Secretary-General (SRSGs) 151–2, 164
  Standby Forces High Readiness Brigade (SHIRBRIG) 156–8, 164
United Nations Assistance Mission in Sierra Leone (UNAMSIL) 147, 148, 160, 162
  see also Sierra Leone (United Nations intervention)
United Nations Assistance Mission for Rwanda (UNAMIR) 162, 167
  see also Rwanda (United Nations mission)
United Nations Mission in Ethiopia and Eritrea (UNMEE) 157
United Nations Protection Force (UNPROFOR) 155, 161, 162
  see also Bosnia (United Nations intervention)
United Nations Standby Arrangement System (UNSAS) 157, 158, 163, 165, 168, 169

Vagts, Alfred 61
van Creveld, Martin 23, 189
Vian, Admiral of the Fleet Sir Philip 26
Vietnam War 7, 9

Walker, Johnny, 26
Walker, General Sir Mike 143
Wann, Group Captain A.H. 121
War Cabinet 18–19, 40
  Norwegian campaign 63, 64, 65

War Council   18, 38, 40
  in Second World War   60
War Office
  air power in 1940   114, 116, 117, 119
  Dardanelles campaign (1915)   39–40
  MO7 (branch)   117, 119
  Norwegian campaign (1940)   65
Warrender, Vice Admiral Sir George   30
Watts, Barry D.   190
Wavell, General Sir Archibald (later Field Marshal Earl)   74, 77, 93, 94
Wellington, Duke of   5
Wemyss, Admiral of the Fleet Sir Rosslyn (later Lord Wester)   38, 46, 51

Weserubung, Operation   64
Western European Union (WEU)   185
Whitehead torpedo   27
Wilfred, Operation (1940)   62, 64
Wilson, General Sir Henry   18
Wilson, McLandburgh   171
Wilson, Woodrow   21
Wingate, Brigadier (later Major-General) Orde   78, 82–3, 84
Woodall, Lieutenant-Colonel John   121

Ypres (battle, 1916)   20
Ypres (battle, 1917)   11